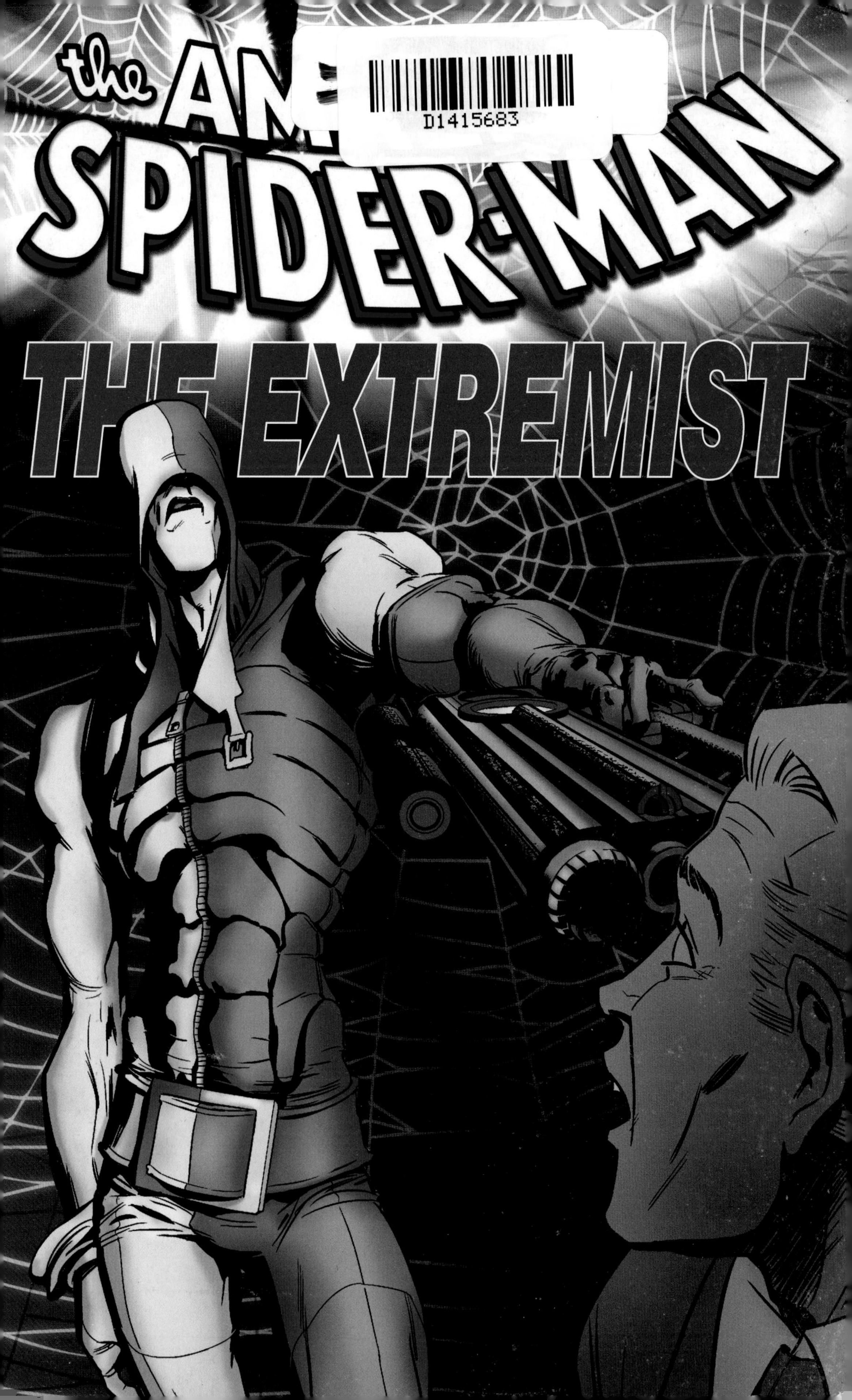
the AM
SPIDER-MAN
THE EXTREMIST

the AMAZING SPIDER-MAN
THE EXTREMIST

Writer: **FRED VAN LENTE**

Artists: **JAVIER RODRIGUEZ** (Issues #8-9), **PATRICK OLLIFFE** (Issue #9),
NICK DRAGOTTA (Issues #9-10) & **PEPE LARRAZ** (Issues #11-12)

Colorists: **MUNTSA VICENTE** (Issue #8) & **ANDRES MOSSA** (Issues #9 & #11-12)

Color Art Assistant (Issue #10): **BRAD SIMPSON**

Letterers: **VC'S JOE CARAMAGNA** (Issue #8) & **CLAYTON COWLES** (Issues #9-12)

Cover Artist: **JELENA DJURDJEVIC**

Editor: **TOM BRENNAN**

Supervising Editor: **STEPHEN WACKER**

Executive Editor: **TOM BREVOORT**

Collection Editor: **CORY LEVINE**

Editorial Assistants: **JAMES EMMETT** & **JOE HOCHSTEIN**

Assistant Editors: **MATT MASDEU, ALEX STARBUCK** & **NELSON RIBEIRO**

Editors, Special Projects: **JENNIFER GRÜNWALD** & **MARK D. BEAZLEY**

Senior Editor, Special Projects: **JEFF YOUNGQUIST**

Senior Vice President of Sales: **DAVID GABRIEL**

SVP of Brand Planning & Communications: **MICHAEL PASCIULLO**

Editor in Chief: **AXEL ALONSO**

Chief Creative Officer: **JOE QUESADA**

Publisher: **DAN BUCKLEY**

Executive Producer: **ALAN FINE**

SPIDER-MAN: THE EXTREMIST. Contains material originally published in magazine form as WEB OF SPIDER-MAN #8-12. First printing 2011. ISBN# 978-0-7851-5670-3. Published by MARVEL WORLDWIDE, INC., a subsidiary of MARVEL ENTERTAINMENT, LLC. OFFICE OF PUBLICATION: 135 West 50th Street, New York, NY 10020. Copyright © 2010 and 2011 Marvel Characters, Inc. All rights reserved. $15.99 per copy in the U.S. and $17.50 in Canada (GST #R127032852); Canadian Agreement #40668537. All characters featured in this issue and the distinctive names and likenesses thereof, and all related indicia are trademarks of Marvel Characters Inc. No similarity between any of the names, characters, persons, and/or institutions in this magazine with those of any living or dead person or institution is intended, and any such similarity which may exist is purely coincidental. **Printed in the U.S.A.** ALAN FINE, EVP - Office of the President, Marvel Worldwide, Inc. and EVP & CMO Marvel Characters B.V.; DAN BUCKLEY, Publisher & President - Print, Animation & Digital Divisions; JOE QUESADA, Chief Creative Officer; JIM SOKOLOWSKI, Chief Operating Officer; DAVID BOGART, SVP of Business Affairs & Talent Management; TOM BREVOORT, SVP of Publishing; C.B. CEBULSKI, SVP of Creator & Content Development; DAVID GABRIEL, SVP of Publishing Sales & Circulation; MICHAEL PASCIULLO, SVP of Brand Planning & Communications; JIM O'KEEFE, VP of Operations & Logistics; DAN CARR, Executive Director of Publishing Technology; JUSTIN F. GABRIE, Director of Publishing & Editorial Operations; SUSAN CRESPI, Editorial Operations Manager; ALEX MORALES, Publishing Operations Manager; STAN LEE, Chairman Emeritus. For information regarding advertising in Marvel Comics or on Marvel.com, please contact John Dokes, SVP Integrated Sales and Marketing, at jdokes@marvel.com. **Manufactured between 4/7/2011 and 4/26/2011** by QUAD/GRAPHICS, DUBUQUE, IA, USA.

10 9 8 7 6 5 4 3 2 1

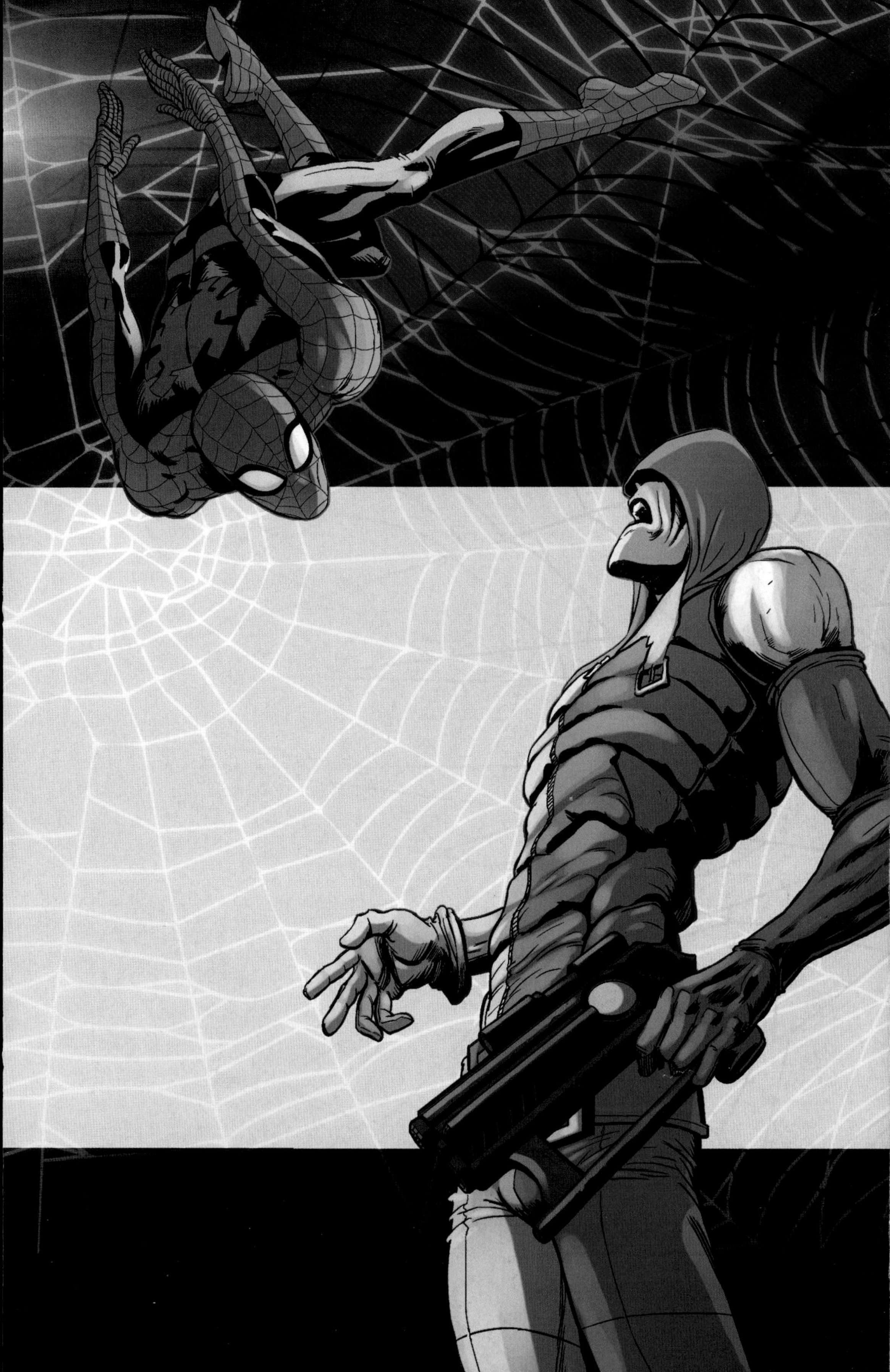

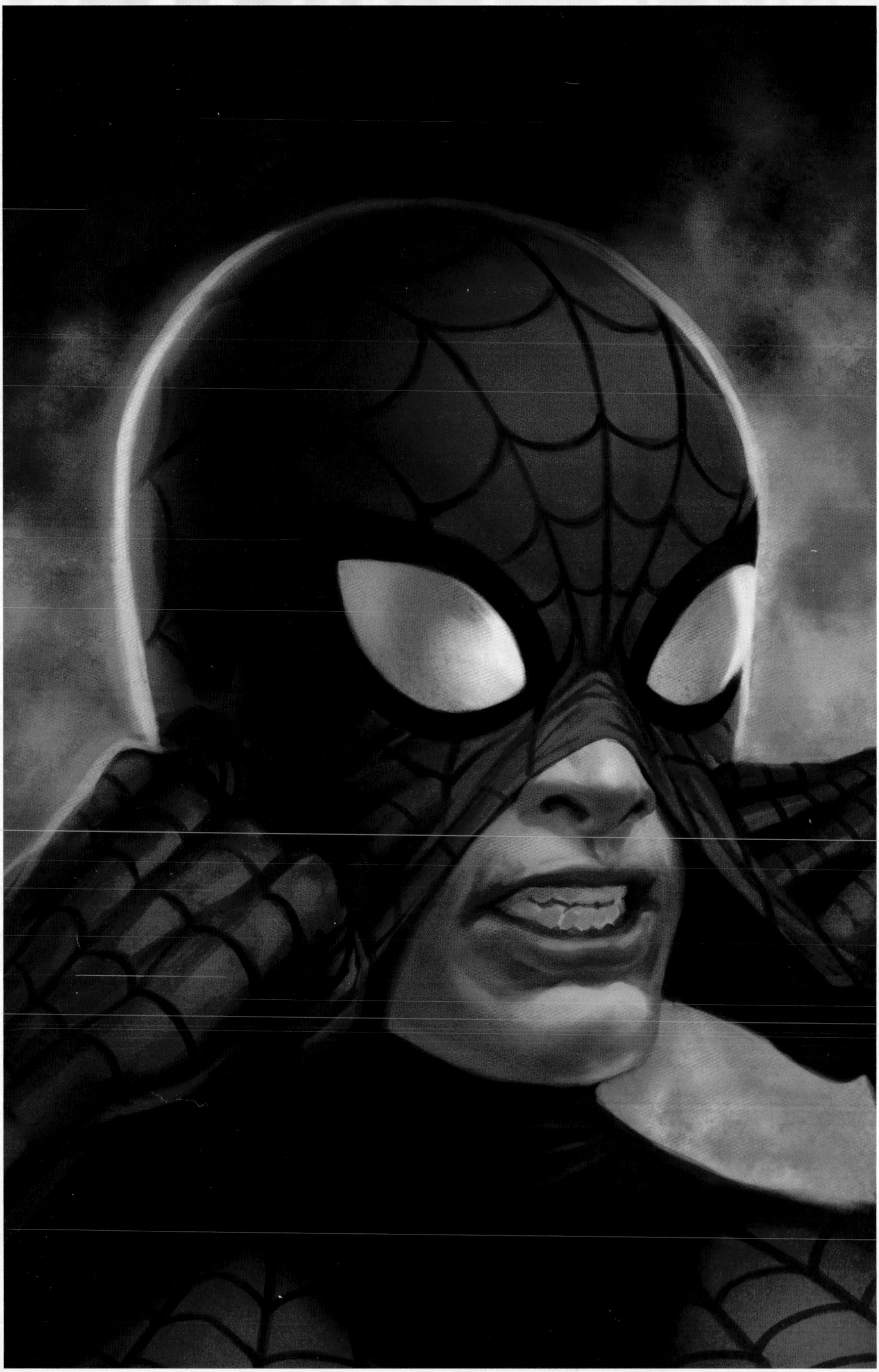

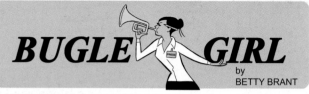

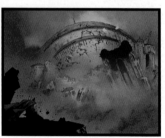

FALL OF THE GODS?
The realm of Asgard falls in Broxton as The Sentry, overwhelmed by madness, drove the ancient structure to the ground in the final…(more)

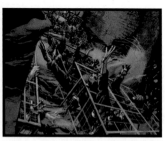

SOMETHING'S COOKING IN THE KITCHEN
After an intense firefight in Hell's Kitchen, dozens of H.A.M.M.E.R. agents have been confirmed missing… (more)

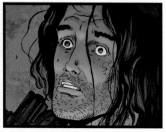

WHO WAS BEN REILLY?
Search of the City's archives find detailed accounts on a Ben Reilly -- but who is he? No one in the city seems to know! (more)

DAILY BUGLE
SPIDERMAN RETURNS!!

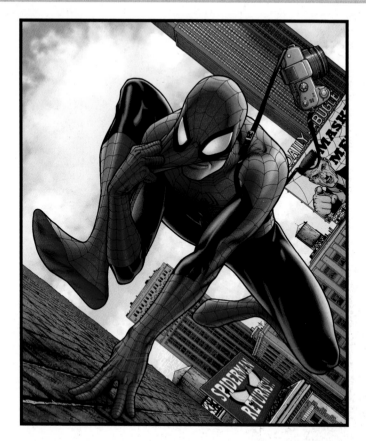

Peter Parker's life has only started to get more complicated recently. Granted, the ol' "Parker Luck" has always plagued him but, now, things seem to be getting worse than ever.

To the world at large, Peter is known by his alter ego, Spider-Man. In the past few weeks, though, Spidey's had to face down his toughest and deadliest foes. With opponents coming at him from every angle, Spider-Man's had to face a gauntlet of some of his fiercest opponents.

The worst, though, came when Peter's longtime boss, Mayor J. Jonah Jameson, fired him. After falsifying a photo to make the mayor look like a hero, Peter quickly became the most unemployable photographer in the city. For once, Peter Parker was more of a menace to the public than the web-slinging Spider-Man.

Deflated, weakened, and exhausted, Peter Parker is the most vulnerable he's been in a long, long time.

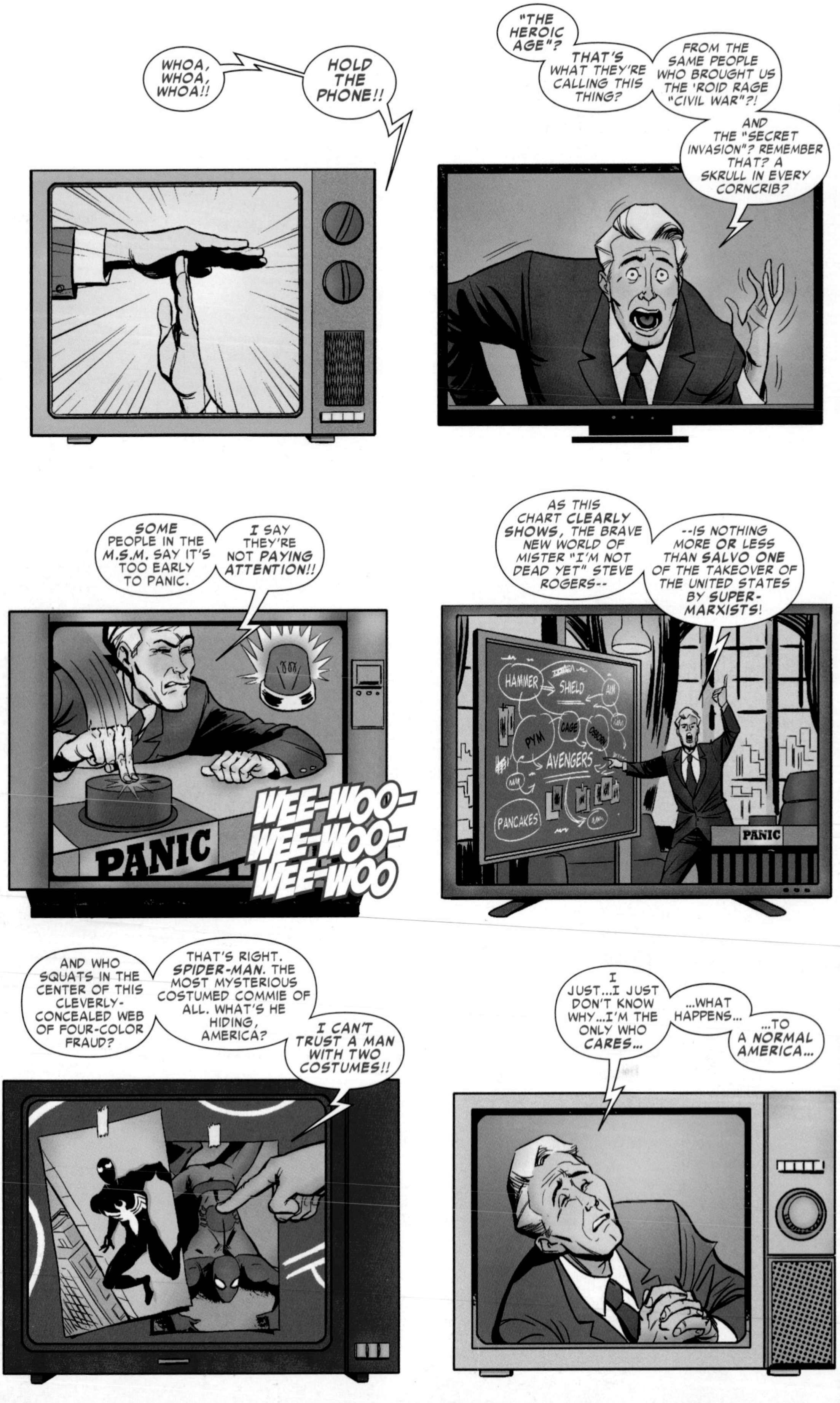
WHOA, WHOA, WHOA!!
HOLD THE PHONE!!
"THE HEROIC AGE"?
THAT'S WHAT THEY'RE CALLING THIS THING?
FROM THE SAME PEOPLE WHO BROUGHT US THE 'ROID RAGE "CIVIL WAR"?!
AND THE "SECRET INVASION"? REMEMBER THAT? A SKRULL IN EVERY CORNCRIB?
SOME PEOPLE IN THE M.S.M. SAY IT'S TOO EARLY TO PANIC.
I SAY THEY'RE NOT PAYING ATTENTION!!
PANIC
WEE-WOO-WEE-WOO-WEE-WOO
AS THIS CHART CLEARLY SHOWS, THE BRAVE NEW WORLD OF MISTER "I'M NOT DEAD YET" STEVE ROGERS--
--IS NOTHING MORE OR LESS THAN SALVO ONE OF THE TAKEOVER OF THE UNITED STATES BY SUPER-MARXISTS!
HAMMER
SHIELD
AIM
PYM
CAGE
OSBORN
AVENGERS
PANCAKES
PANIC
AND WHO SQUATS IN THE CENTER OF THIS CLEVERLY-CONCEALED WEB OF FOUR-COLOR FRAUD?
THAT'S RIGHT. SPIDER-MAN. THE MOST MYSTERIOUS COSTUMED COMMIE OF ALL. WHAT'S HE HIDING, AMERICA?
I CAN'T TRUST A MAN WITH TWO COSTUMES!!
I JUST...I JUST DON'T KNOW WHY...I'M THE ONLY WHO CARES...
...WHAT HAPPENS...
...TO A NORMAL AMERICA...

YOU'RE WATCHING THE MARK OF BRANDEN--THE VOICE FOR REAL AMERICA!

FFSSSSSSSSSSS!!!

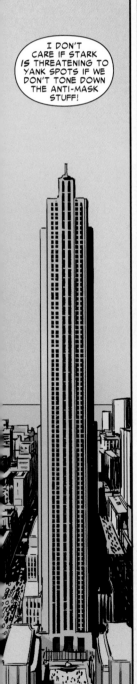

I DON'T CARE IF STARK *IS* THREATENING TO YANK SPOTS IF WE DON'T TONE DOWN THE ANTI-MASK STUFF!

WE'RE *DESTROYING* OUR TIME SLOT! I GOT ADVERTISERS WAITING IN ALLEYS *ON THEIR KNEES* TO TAKE HIS PLACE!

MARK BRANDEN.

YOU TELL MR. *VINCIBLE* HE CAN STICK A REPULSOR RAY UP HIS...

WH-WHO ARE YOU SUPPOSED TO BE?

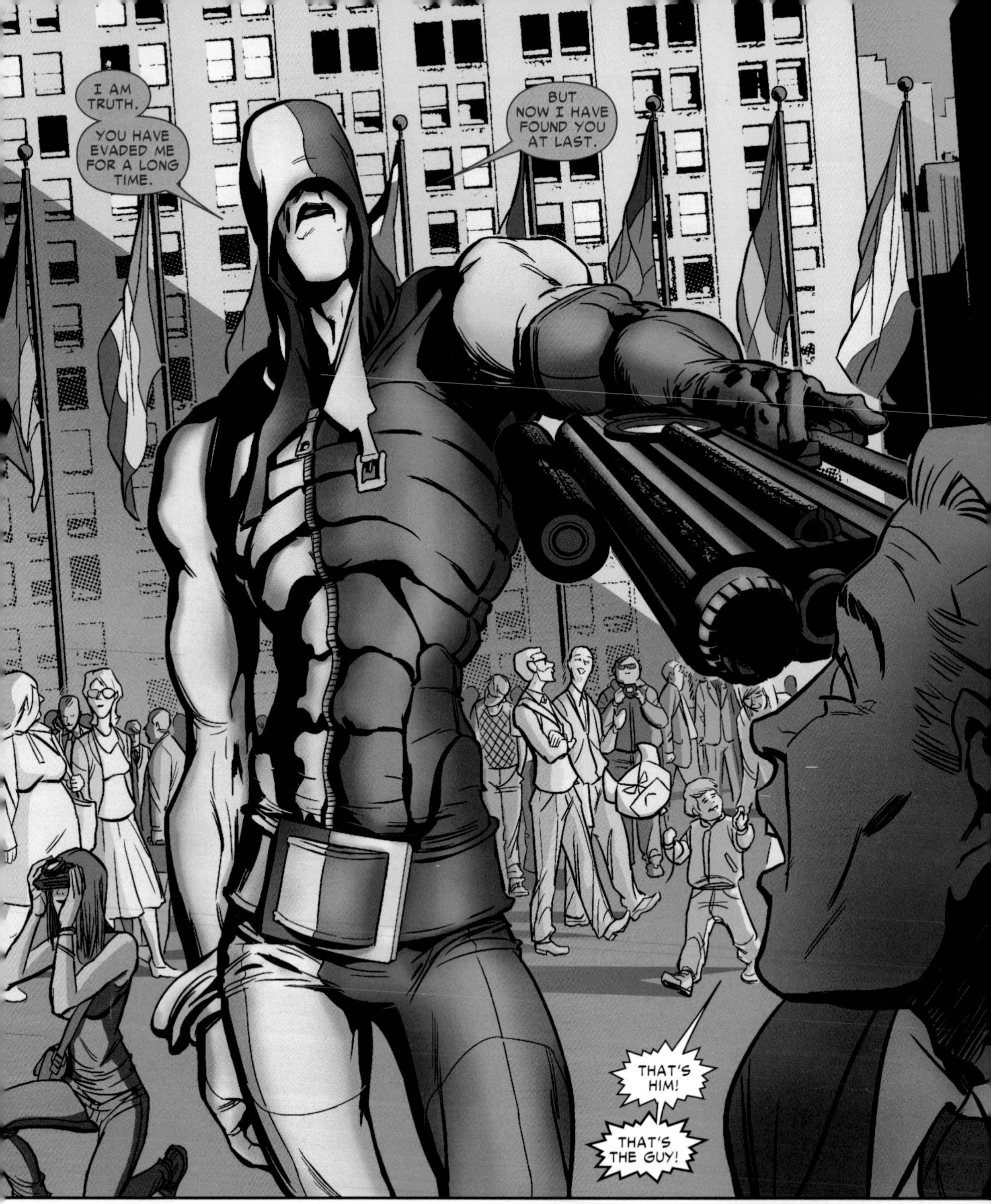
I AM TRUTH.
YOU HAVE EVADED ME FOR A LONG TIME.
BUT NOW I HAVE FOUND YOU AT LAST.
THAT'S HIM!
THAT'S THE GUY!

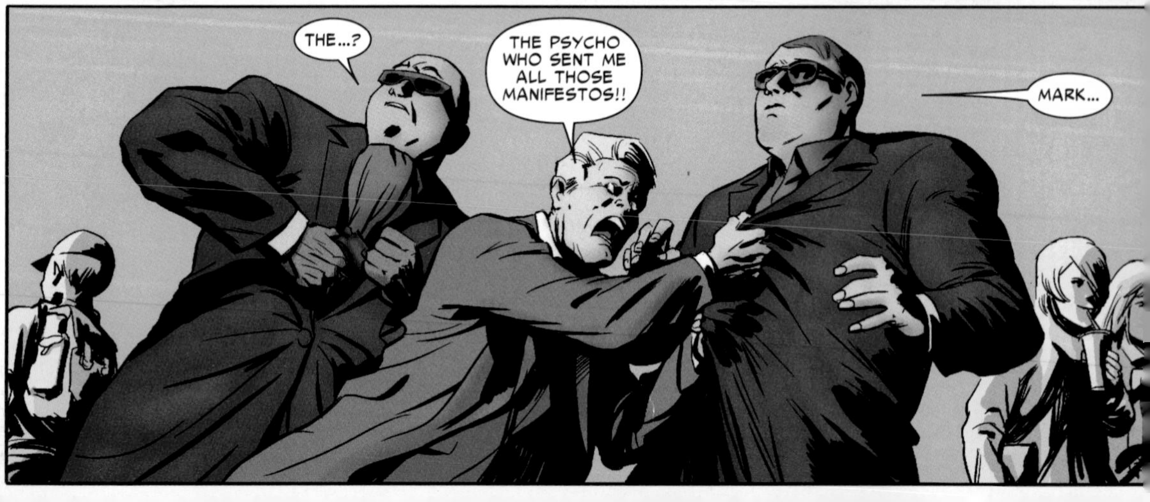
THE...?
THE PSYCHO WHO SENT ME ALL THOSE MANIFESTOS!!
MARK...

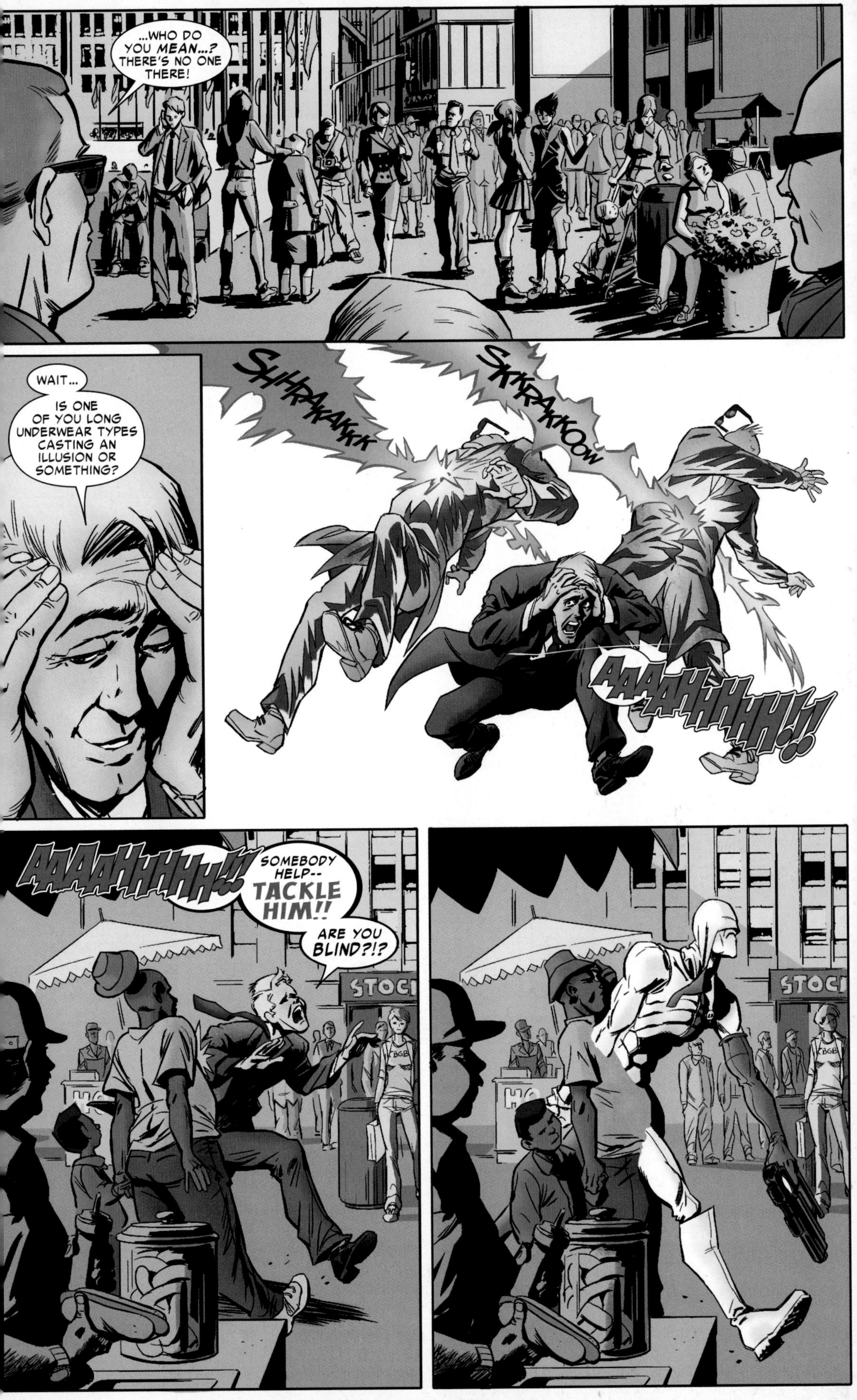
...WHO DO YOU MEAN...? THERE'S NO ONE THERE!
WAIT...
IS ONE OF YOU LONG UNDERWEAR TYPES CASTING AN ILLUSION OR SOMETHING?
SHHRAKAKKK
SKKRAKKOOW
AAAAHHHHH!!!
AAAAHHHHH!!!
SOMEBODY HELP-- TACKLE HIM!!
ARE YOU BLIND?!?
STOC
CBGB
CBGB
STOC

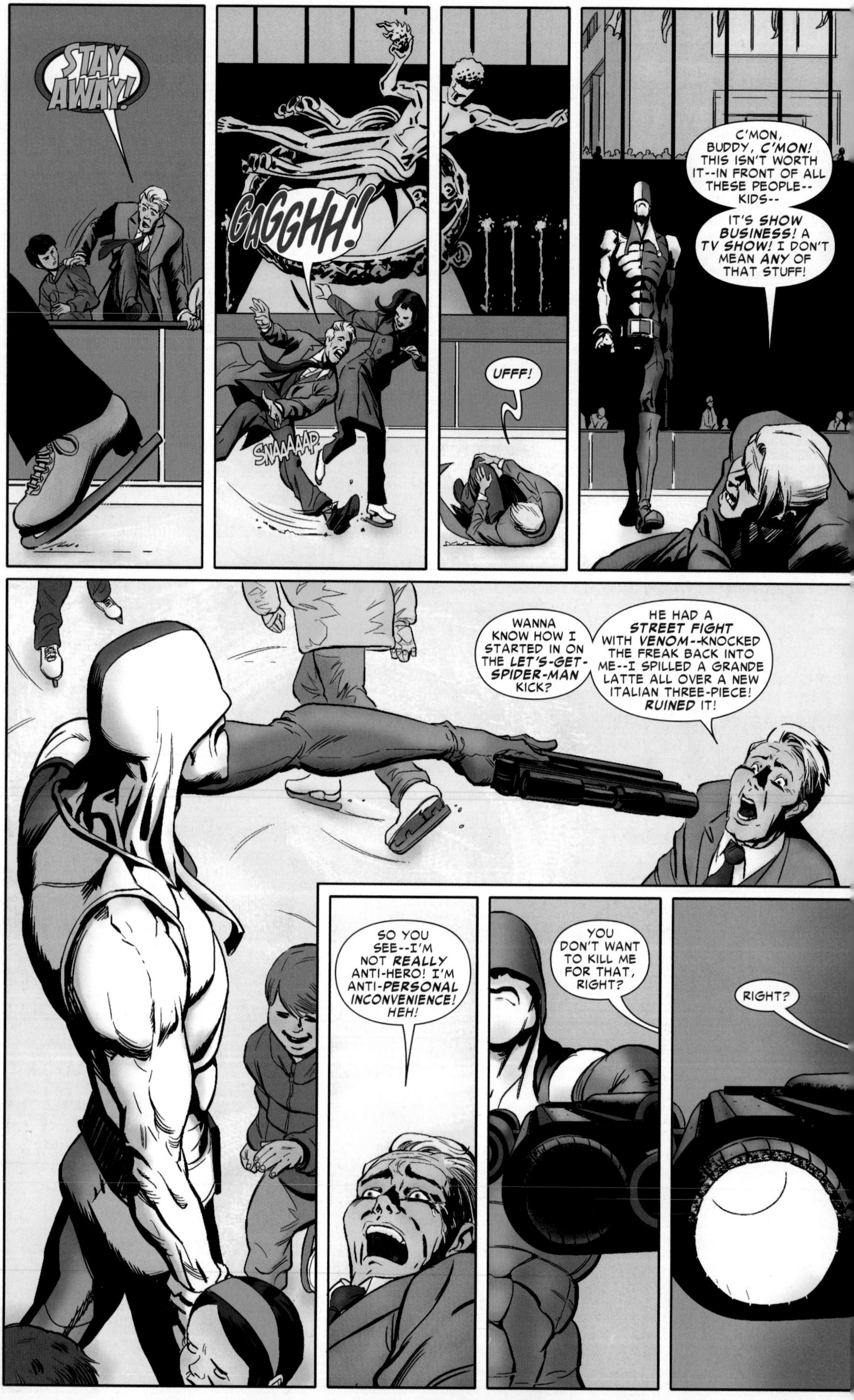
STAY AWAY!
GAGGHH!
SNAAAAAP
UFFF!
C'MON, BUDDY, C'MON! THIS ISN'T WORTH IT--IN FRONT OF ALL THESE PEOPLE--KIDS--
IT'S SHOW BUSINESS! A TV SHOW! I DON'T MEAN ANY OF THAT STUFF!
WANNA KNOW HOW I STARTED IN ON THE LET'S-GET-SPIDER-MAN KICK?
HE HAD A STREET FIGHT WITH VENOM--KNOCKED THE FREAK BACK INTO ME--I SPILLED A GRANDE LATTE ALL OVER A NEW ITALIAN THREE-PIECE! RUINED IT!
SO YOU SEE--I'M NOT REALLY ANTI-HERO! I'M ANTI-PERSONAL INCONVENIENCE! HEH!
YOU DON'T WANT TO KILL ME FOR THAT, RIGHT?
RIGHT?

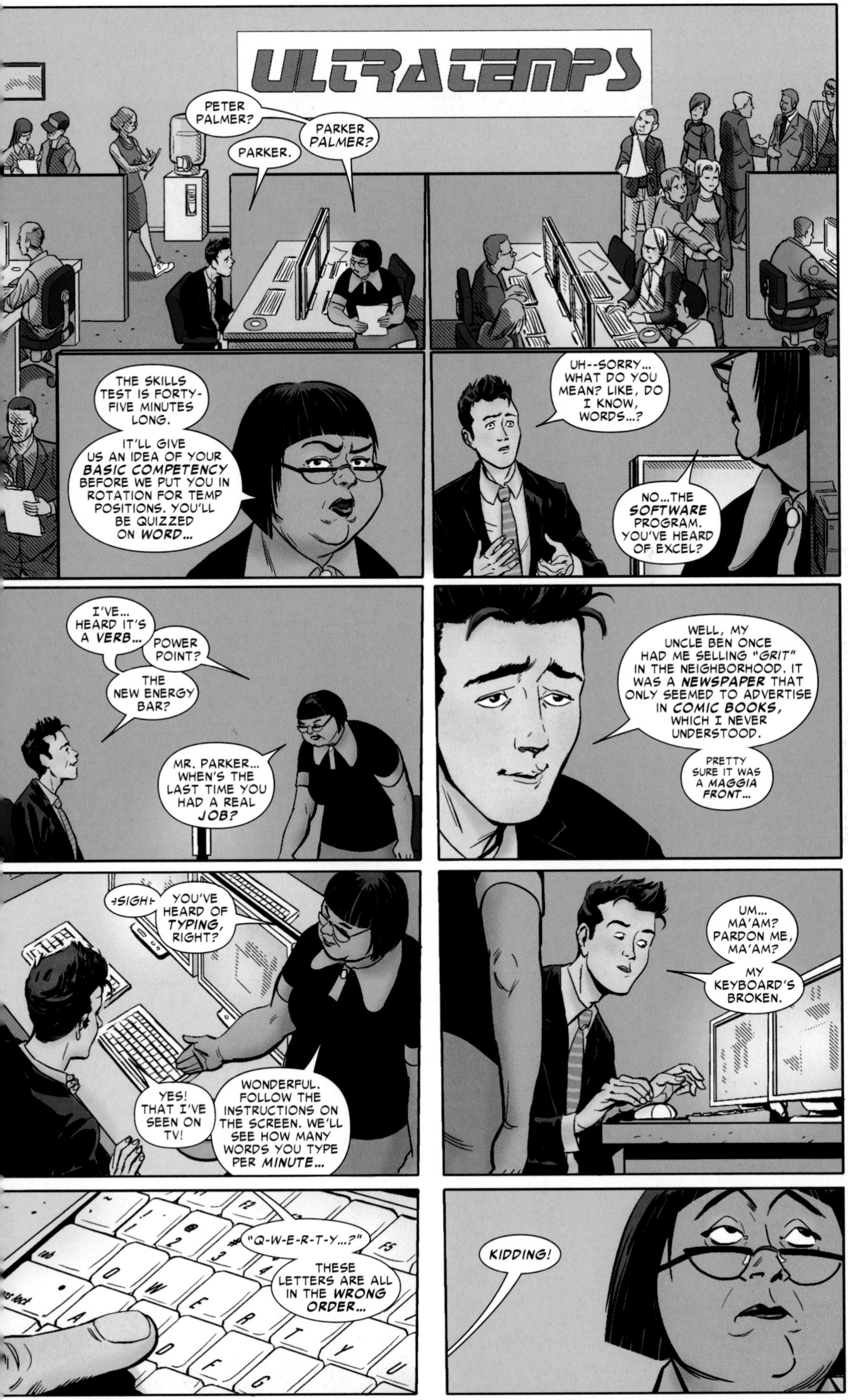

ULTRATEMPS
PETER PALMER?
PARKER.
PARKER PALMER?
THE SKILLS TEST IS FORTY-FIVE MINUTES LONG.
IT'LL GIVE US AN IDEA OF YOUR BASIC COMPETENCY BEFORE WE PUT YOU IN ROTATION FOR TEMP POSITIONS. YOU'LL BE QUIZZED ON WORD...
UH--SORRY... WHAT DO YOU MEAN? LIKE, DO I KNOW, WORDS...?
NO...THE SOFTWARE PROGRAM. YOU'VE HEARD OF EXCEL?
I'VE... HEARD IT'S A VERB...
POWER POINT?
THE NEW ENERGY BAR?
MR. PARKER... WHEN'S THE LAST TIME YOU HAD A REAL JOB?
WELL, MY UNCLE BEN ONCE HAD ME SELLING "GRIT" IN THE NEIGHBORHOOD. IT WAS A NEWSPAPER THAT ONLY SEEMED TO ADVERTISE IN COMIC BOOKS, WHICH I NEVER UNDERSTOOD.
PRETTY SURE IT WAS A MAGGIA FRONT...
-SIGH-
YOU'VE HEARD OF TYPING, RIGHT?
YES! THAT I'VE SEEN ON TV!
WONDERFUL. FOLLOW THE INSTRUCTIONS ON THE SCREEN. WE'LL SEE HOW MANY WORDS YOU TYPE PER MINUTE...
UM... MA'AM? PARDON ME, MA'AM?
MY KEYBOARD'S BROKEN.
"Q-W-E-R-T-Y...?"
THESE LETTERS ARE ALL IN THE WRONG ORDER...
KIDDING!

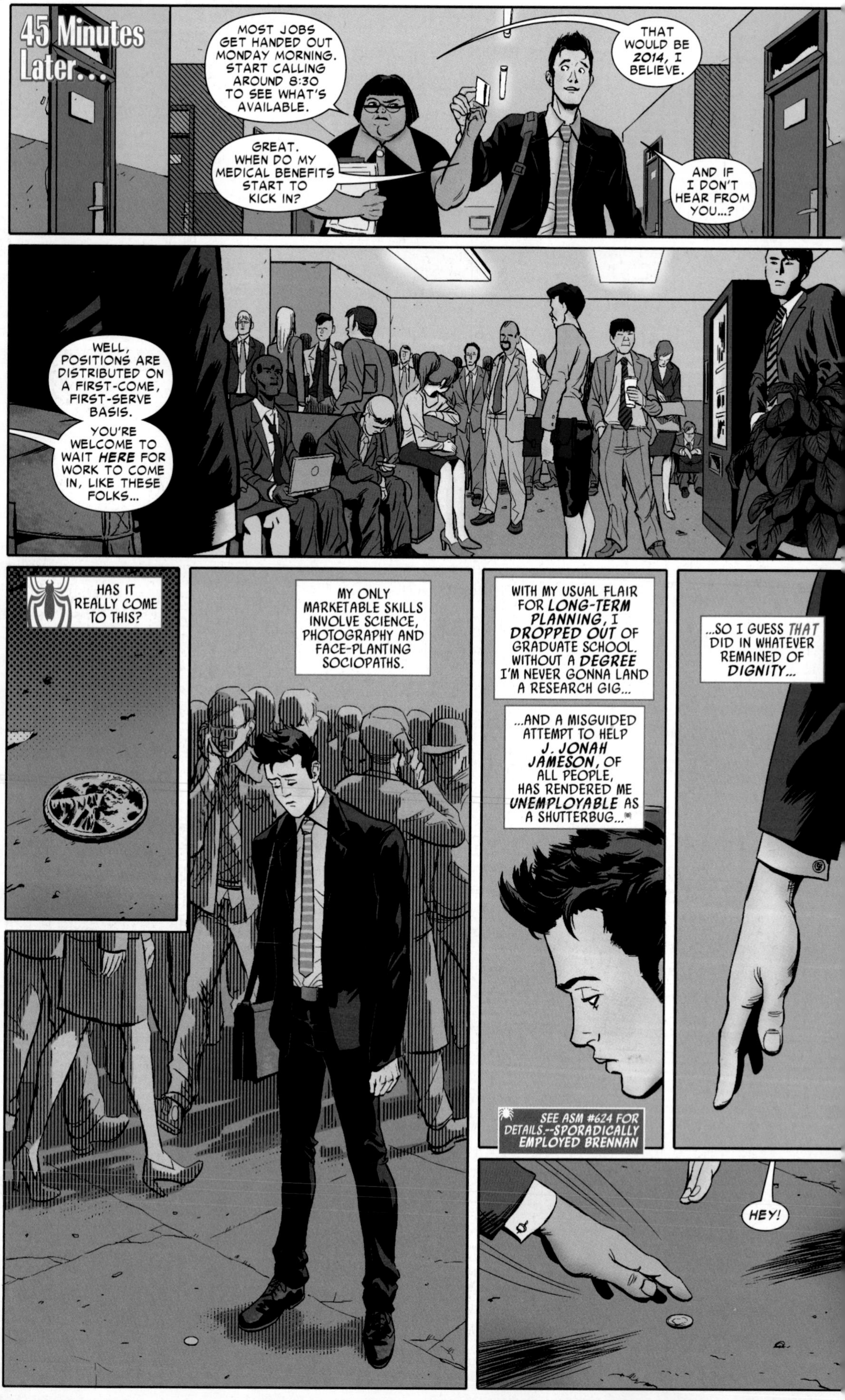
45 Minutes Later...
MOST JOBS GET HANDED OUT MONDAY MORNING. START CALLING AROUND 8:30 TO SEE WHAT'S AVAILABLE.
THAT WOULD BE 2014, I BELIEVE.
GREAT. WHEN DO MY MEDICAL BENEFITS START TO KICK IN?
AND IF I DON'T HEAR FROM YOU...?
WELL, POSITIONS ARE DISTRIBUTED ON A FIRST-COME, FIRST-SERVE BASIS.
YOU'RE WELCOME TO WAIT HERE FOR WORK TO COME IN, LIKE THESE FOLKS...
HAS IT REALLY COME TO THIS?
MY ONLY MARKETABLE SKILLS INVOLVE SCIENCE, PHOTOGRAPHY AND FACE-PLANTING SOCIOPATHS.
WITH MY USUAL FLAIR FOR LONG-TERM PLANNING, I DROPPED OUT OF GRADUATE SCHOOL. WITHOUT A DEGREE I'M NEVER GONNA LAND A RESEARCH GIG...
...AND A MISGUIDED ATTEMPT TO HELP J. JONAH JAMESON, OF ALL PEOPLE, HAS RENDERED ME UNEMPLOYABLE AS A SHUTTERBUG...*
* SEE ASM #624 FOR DETAILS.--SPORADICALLY EMPLOYED BRENNAN
...SO I GUESS THAT DID IN WHATEVER REMAINED OF DIGNITY...
HEY!

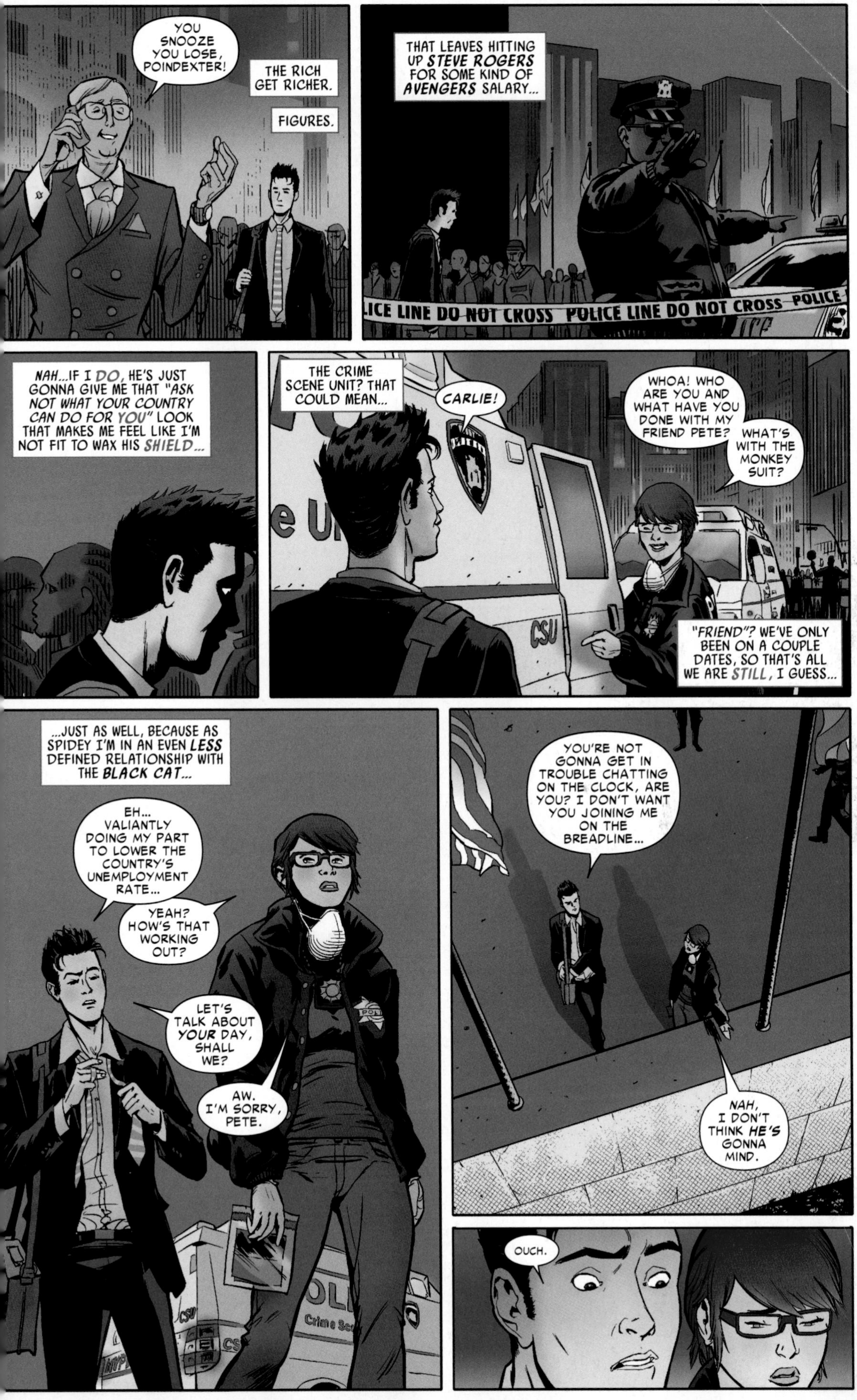

YOU SNOOZE YOU LOSE, POINDEXTER!
THE RICH GET RICHER.
FIGURES.
THAT LEAVES HITTING UP STEVE ROGERS FOR SOME KIND OF AVENGERS SALARY...
LICE LINE DO NOT CROSS POLICE LINE DO NOT CROSS POLICE
NAH...IF I DO, HE'S JUST GONNA GIVE ME THAT "ASK NOT WHAT YOUR COUNTRY CAN DO FOR YOU" LOOK THAT MAKES ME FEEL LIKE I'M NOT FIT TO WAX HIS SHIELD...
THE CRIME SCENE UNIT? THAT COULD MEAN...
CARLIE!
WHOA! WHO ARE YOU AND WHAT HAVE YOU DONE WITH MY FRIEND PETE?
WHAT'S WITH THE MONKEY SUIT?
CSU
"FRIEND"? WE'VE ONLY BEEN ON A COUPLE DATES, SO THAT'S ALL WE ARE STILL, I GUESS...
...JUST AS WELL, BECAUSE AS SPIDEY I'M IN AN EVEN LESS DEFINED RELATIONSHIP WITH THE BLACK CAT...
EH... VALIANTLY DOING MY PART TO LOWER THE COUNTRY'S UNEMPLOYMENT RATE...
YEAH? HOW'S THAT WORKING OUT?
LET'S TALK ABOUT YOUR DAY, SHALL WE?
AW. I'M SORRY, PETE.
YOU'RE NOT GONNA GET IN TROUBLE CHATTING ON THE CLOCK, ARE YOU? I DON'T WANT YOU JOINING ME ON THE BREADLINE...
NAH, I DON'T THINK HE'S GONNA MIND.
OUCH.

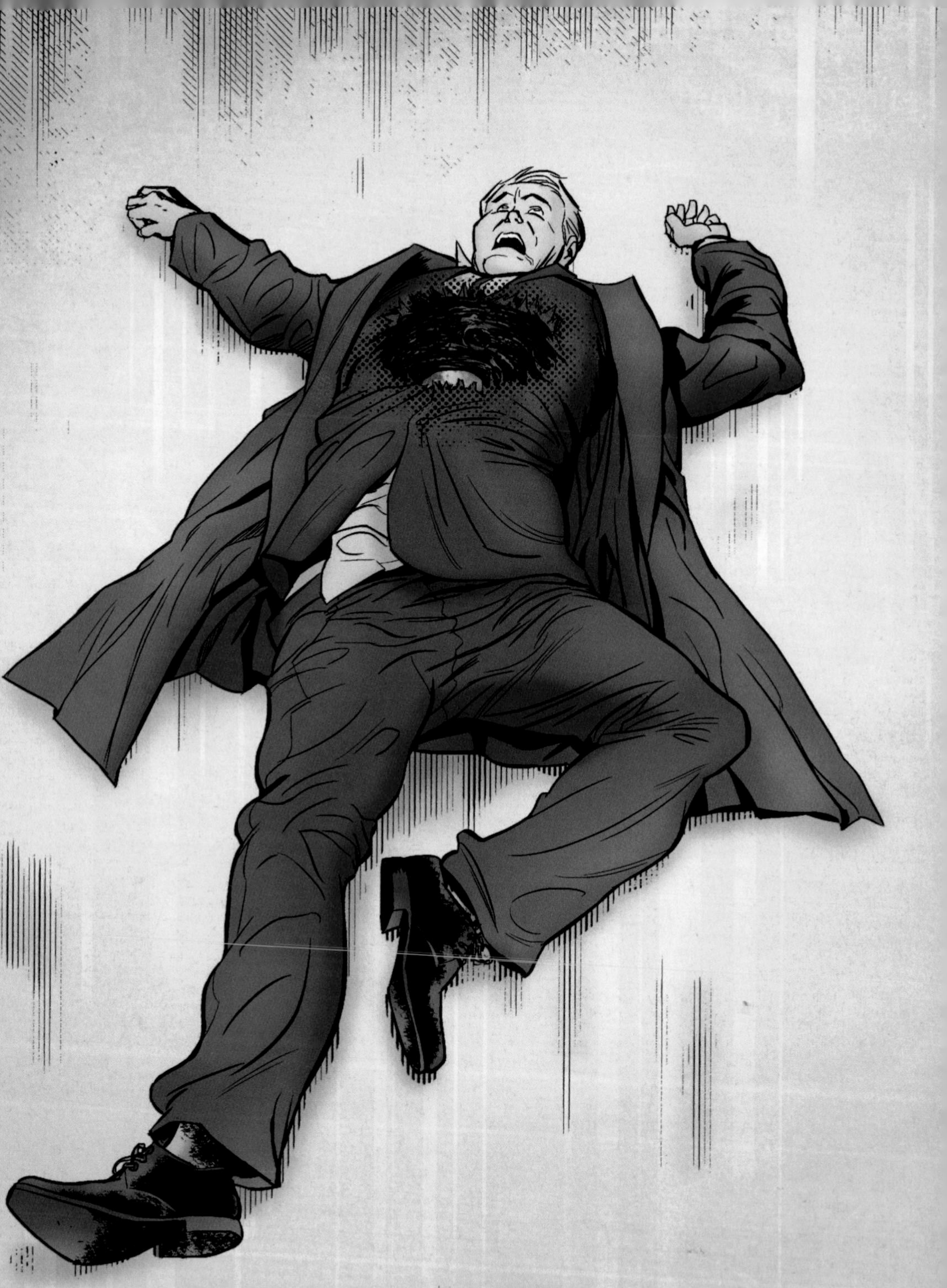

THE AMAZING SPIDER-MAN IN

THE EXTREMIST

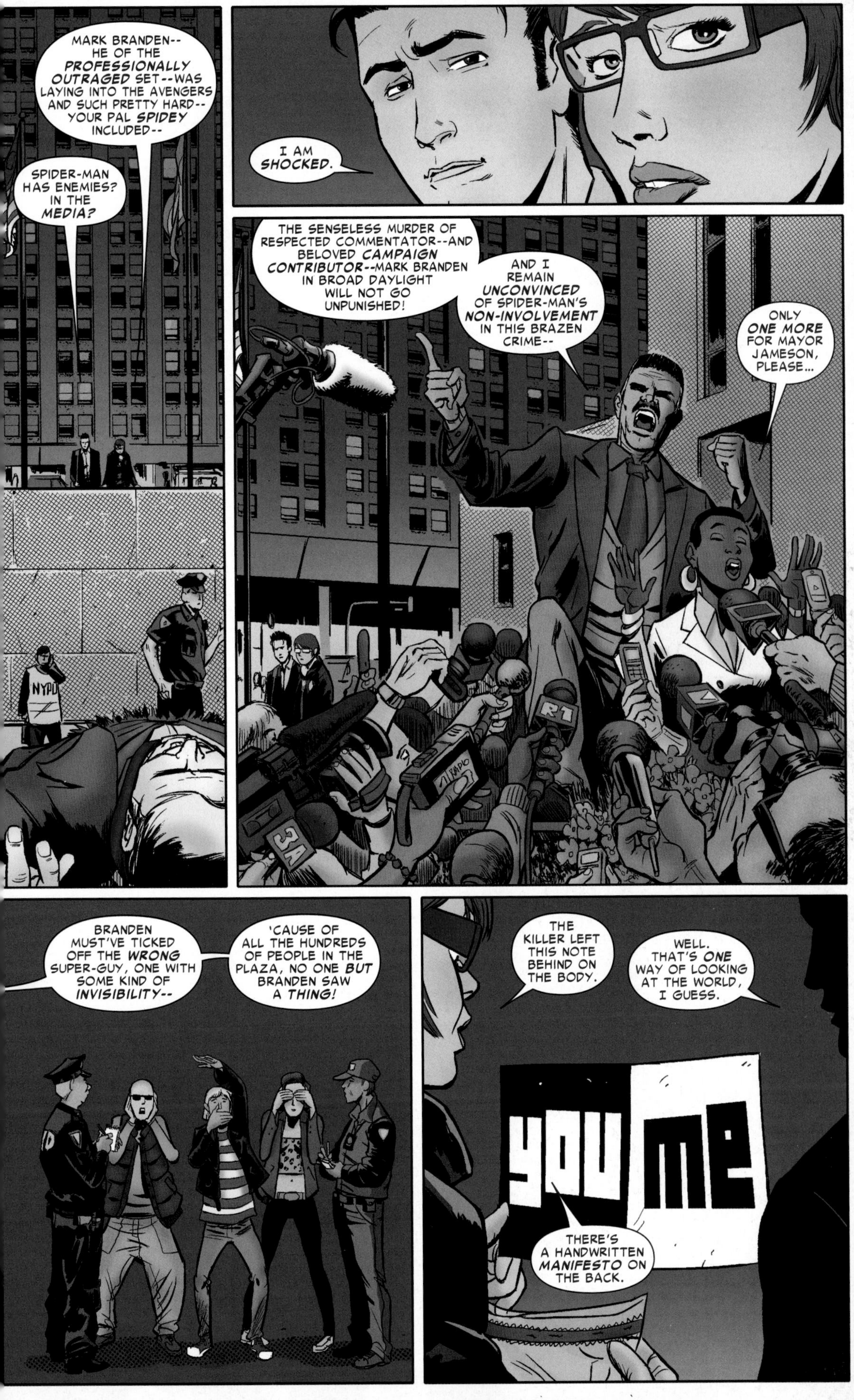
MARK BRANDEN-- HE OF THE PROFESSIONALLY OUTRAGED SET--WAS LAYING INTO THE AVENGERS AND SUCH PRETTY HARD-- YOUR PAL SPIDEY INCLUDED--
SPIDER-MAN HAS ENEMIES? IN THE MEDIA?
I AM SHOCKED.
THE SENSELESS MURDER OF RESPECTED COMMENTATOR--AND BELOVED CAMPAIGN CONTRIBUTOR--MARK BRANDEN IN BROAD DAYLIGHT WILL NOT GO UNPUNISHED!
AND I REMAIN UNCONVINCED OF SPIDER-MAN'S NON-INVOLVEMENT IN THIS BRAZEN CRIME--
ONLY ONE MORE FOR MAYOR JAMESON, PLEASE...
NYPD
BRANDEN MUST'VE TICKED OFF THE WRONG SUPER-GUY, ONE WITH SOME KIND OF INVISIBILITY--
'CAUSE OF ALL THE HUNDREDS OF PEOPLE IN THE PLAZA, NO ONE BUT BRANDEN SAW A THING!
THE KILLER LEFT THIS NOTE BEHIND ON THE BODY.
WELL. THAT'S ONE WAY OF LOOKING AT THE WORLD, I GUESS.
YOU
ME
THERE'S A HANDWRITTEN MANIFESTO ON THE BACK.

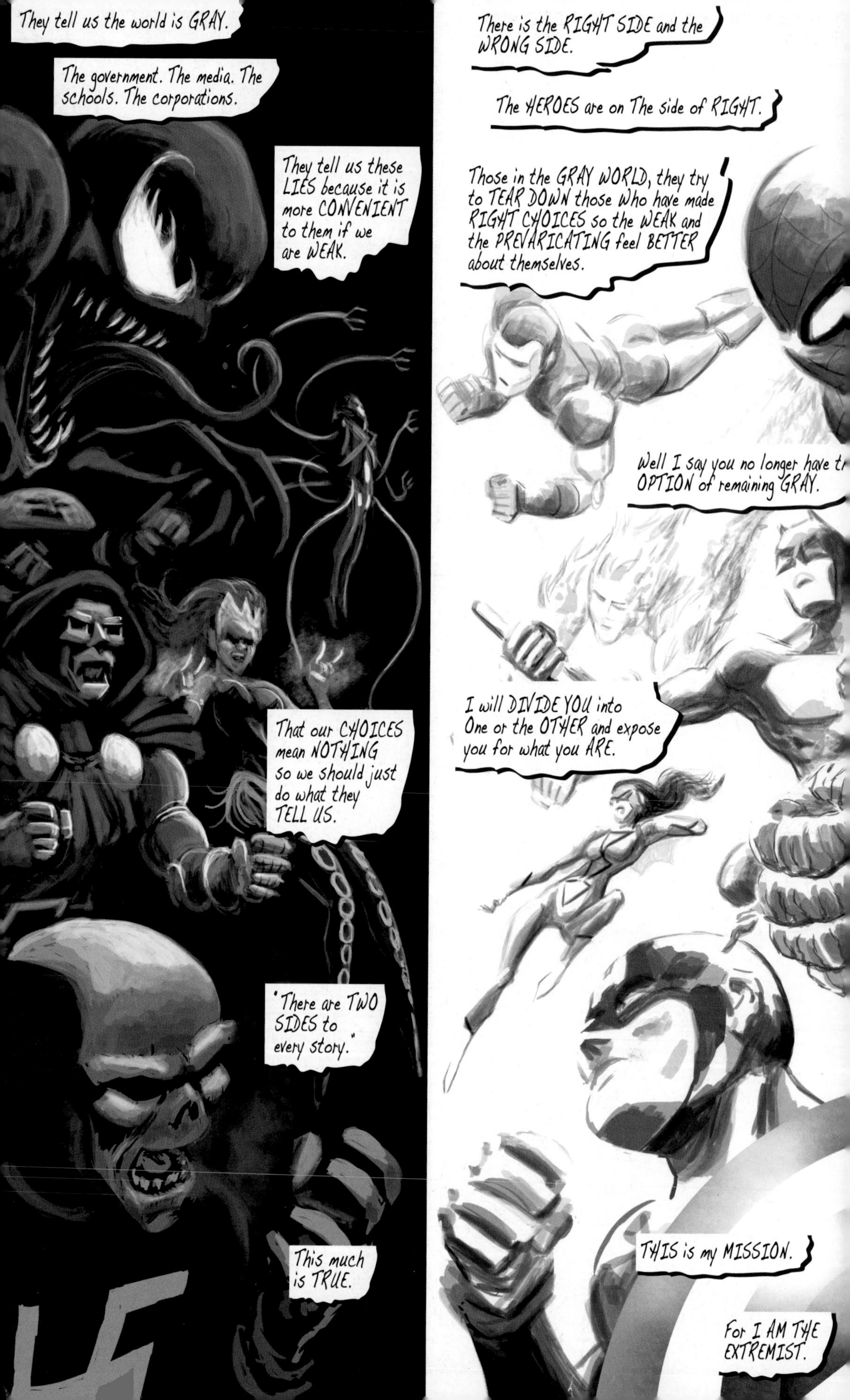
They tell us the world is GRAY.
The government. The media. The schools. The corporations.
They tell us these LIES because it is more CONVENIENT to them if we are WEAK.
That our CHOICES mean NOTHING so we should just do what they TELL US.
"There are TWO SIDES to every story."
This much is TRUE.
There is the RIGHT SIDE and the WRONG SIDE.
The HEROES are on The side of RIGHT.
Those in the GRAY WORLD, they try to TEAR DOWN those Who have made RIGHT CHOICES so the WEAK and the PREVARICATING feel BETTER about themselves.
Well I say you no longer have t
OPTION of remaining GRAY.
I will DIVIDE YOU into One or the OTHER and expose you for what you ARE.
THIS is my MISSION.
For I AM THE EXTREMIST.

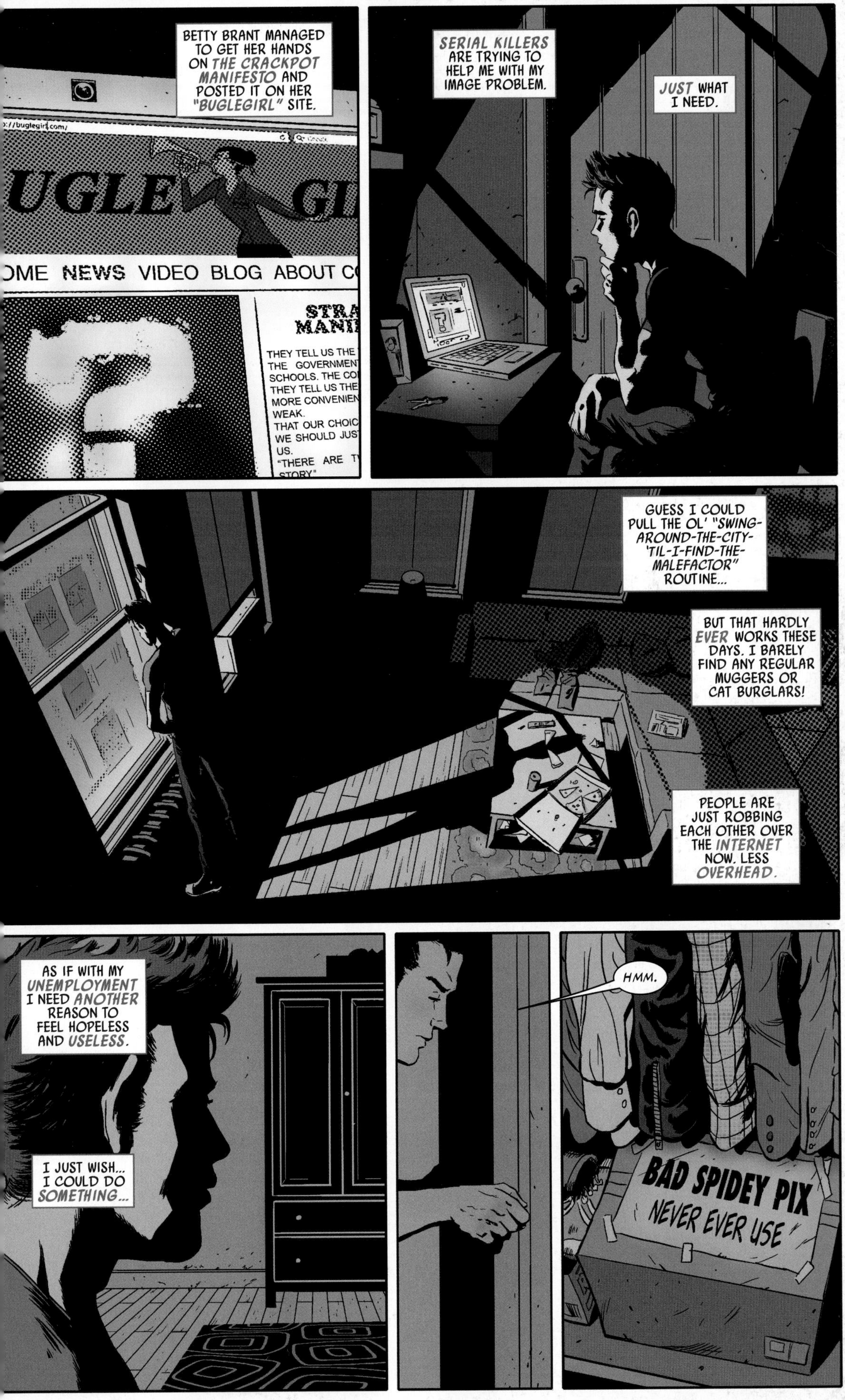

BETTY BRANT MANAGED TO GET HER HANDS ON THE CRACKPOT MANIFESTO AND POSTED IT ON HER "BUGLEGIRL" SITE.
://buglegirl.com/
UGLE GI
OME NEWS VIDEO BLOG ABOUT C
STRA
MANI
THEY TELL US THE
THE GOVERNMENT
SCHOOLS. THE CO
THEY TELL US THE
MORE CONVENIEN
WEAK.
THAT OUR CHOIC
WE SHOULD JUS
US.
"THERE ARE T
STORY"
SERIAL KILLERS ARE TRYING TO HELP ME WITH MY IMAGE PROBLEM.
JUST WHAT I NEED.
GUESS I COULD PULL THE OL' "SWING-AROUND-THE-CITY-'TIL-I-FIND-THE-MALEFACTOR" ROUTINE...
BUT THAT HARDLY EVER WORKS THESE DAYS. I BARELY FIND ANY REGULAR MUGGERS OR CAT BURGLARS!
PEOPLE ARE JUST ROBBING EACH OTHER OVER THE INTERNET NOW. LESS OVERHEAD.
AS IF WITH MY UNEMPLOYMENT I NEED ANOTHER REASON TO FEEL HOPELESS AND USELESS.
I JUST WISH... I COULD DO SOMETHING...
HMM.
BAD SPIDEY PIX
NEVER EVER USE

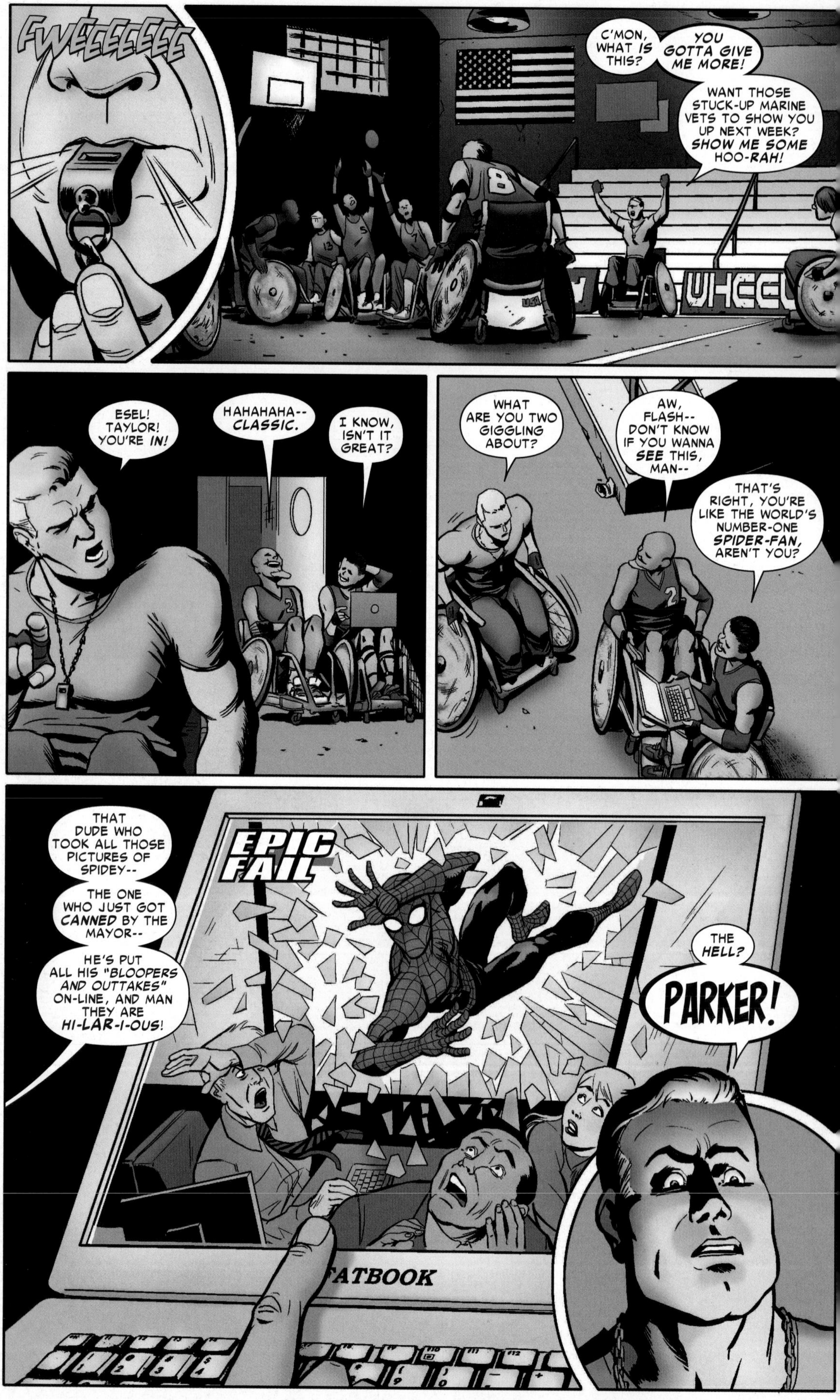
FWEEEEEEE
C'MON, WHAT IS THIS?
YOU GOTTA GIVE ME MORE!
WANT THOSE STUCK-UP MARINE VETS TO SHOW YOU UP NEXT WEEK? SHOW ME SOME HOO-RAH!
ESEL! TAYLOR! YOU'RE IN!
HAHAHAHA-- CLASSIC.
I KNOW, ISN'T IT GREAT?
WHAT ARE YOU TWO GIGGLING ABOUT?
AW, FLASH-- DON'T KNOW IF YOU WANNA SEE THIS, MAN--
THAT'S RIGHT, YOU'RE LIKE THE WORLD'S NUMBER-ONE SPIDER-FAN, AREN'T YOU?
THAT DUDE WHO TOOK ALL THOSE PICTURES OF SPIDEY--
THE ONE WHO JUST GOT CANNED BY THE MAYOR--
HE'S PUT ALL HIS "BLOOPERS AND OUTTAKES" ON-LINE, AND MAN THEY ARE HI-LAR-I-OUS!
EPIC FAIL
THE HELL?
PARKER!
FATBOOK

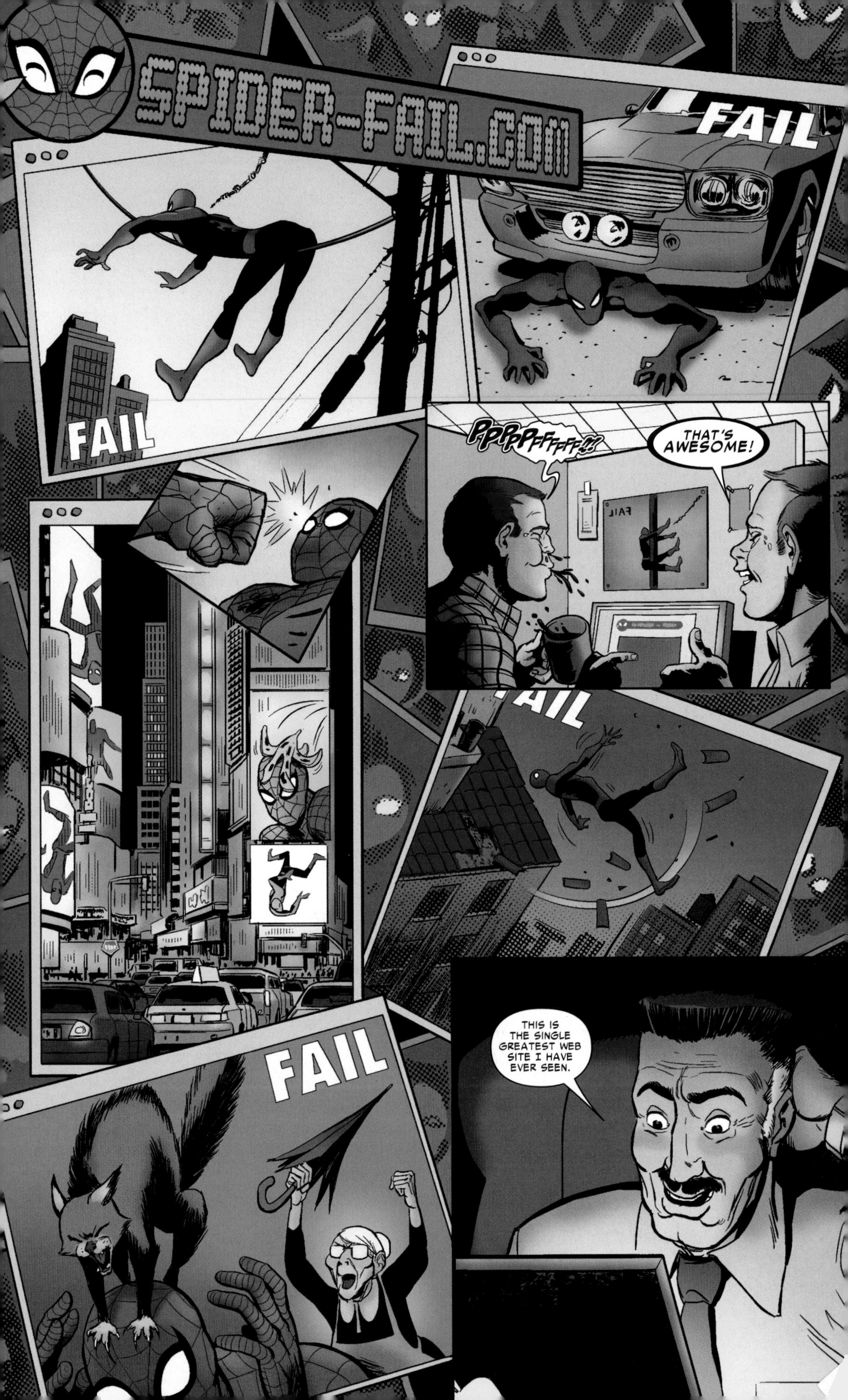

SPIDER-FAIL.COM
FAIL
FAIL
PPPPPFFFFFF!!
THAT'S AWESOME!
FAIL
FAIL
FAIL
THIS IS THE SINGLE GREATEST WEB SITE I HAVE EVER SEEN.

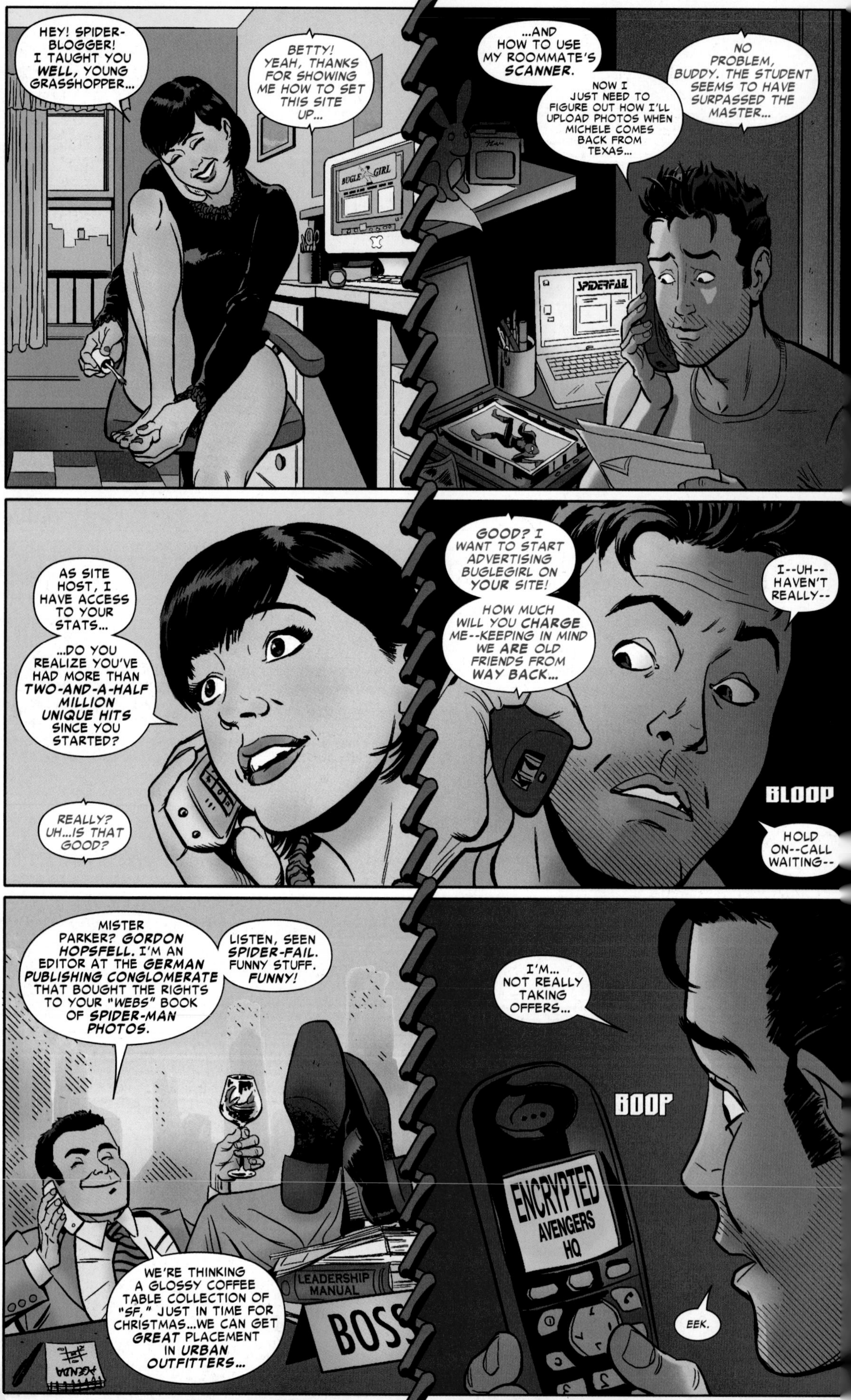
HEY! SPIDER-BLOGGER! I TAUGHT YOU WELL, YOUNG GRASSHOPPER...
BETTY! YEAH, THANKS FOR SHOWING ME HOW TO SET THIS SITE UP...
...AND HOW TO USE MY ROOMMATE'S SCANNER.
NOW I JUST NEED TO FIGURE OUT HOW I'LL UPLOAD PHOTOS WHEN MICHELE COMES BACK FROM TEXAS...
NO PROBLEM, BUDDY. THE STUDENT SEEMS TO HAVE SURPASSED THE MASTER...
BUGLE GIRL
SPIDERFAIL
AS SITE HOST, I HAVE ACCESS TO YOUR STATS...
...DO YOU REALIZE YOU'VE HAD MORE THAN TWO-AND-A-HALF MILLION UNIQUE HITS SINCE YOU STARTED?
REALLY? UH...IS THAT GOOD?
GOOD? I WANT TO START ADVERTISING BUGLEGIRL ON YOUR SITE!
HOW MUCH WILL YOU CHARGE ME--KEEPING IN MIND WE ARE OLD FRIENDS FROM WAY BACK...
I--UH--HAVEN'T REALLY--
BLOOP
HOLD ON--CALL WAITING--
MISTER PARKER? GORDON HOPSFELL. I'M AN EDITOR AT THE GERMAN PUBLISHING CONGLOMERATE THAT BOUGHT THE RIGHTS TO YOUR "WEBS" BOOK OF SPIDER-MAN PHOTOS.
LISTEN, SEEN SPIDER-FAIL. FUNNY STUFF. FUNNY!
WE'RE THINKING A GLOSSY COFFEE TABLE COLLECTION OF "SF," JUST IN TIME FOR CHRISTMAS...WE CAN GET GREAT PLACEMENT IN URBAN OUTFITTERS...
LEADERSHIP MANUAL
BOSS
I'M... NOT REALLY TAKING OFFERS...
BOOP
ENCRYPTED
AVENGERS HQ
EEK.

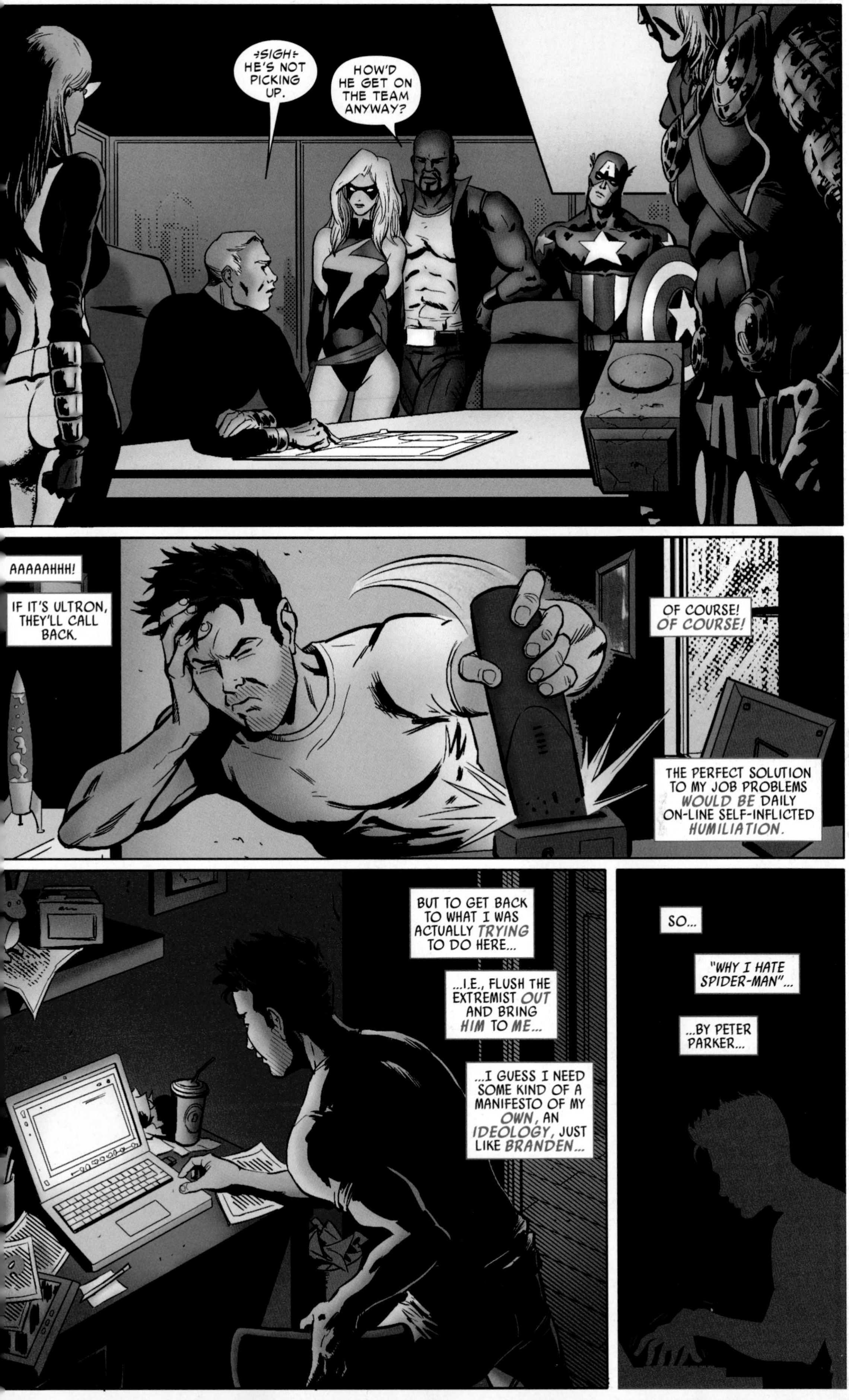

=SIGH= HE'S NOT PICKING UP.
HOW'D HE GET ON THE TEAM ANYWAY?
AAAAAHHH!
IF IT'S ULTRON, THEY'LL CALL BACK.
OF COURSE! OF COURSE!
THE PERFECT SOLUTION TO MY JOB PROBLEMS WOULD BE DAILY ON-LINE SELF-INFLICTED HUMILIATION.
BUT TO GET BACK TO WHAT I WAS ACTUALLY TRYING TO DO HERE...
...I.E., FLUSH THE EXTREMIST OUT AND BRING HIM TO ME...
...I GUESS I NEED SOME KIND OF A MANIFESTO OF MY OWN, AN IDEOLOGY, JUST LIKE BRANDEN...
SO...
"WHY I HATE SPIDER-MAN"...
...BY PETER PARKER...

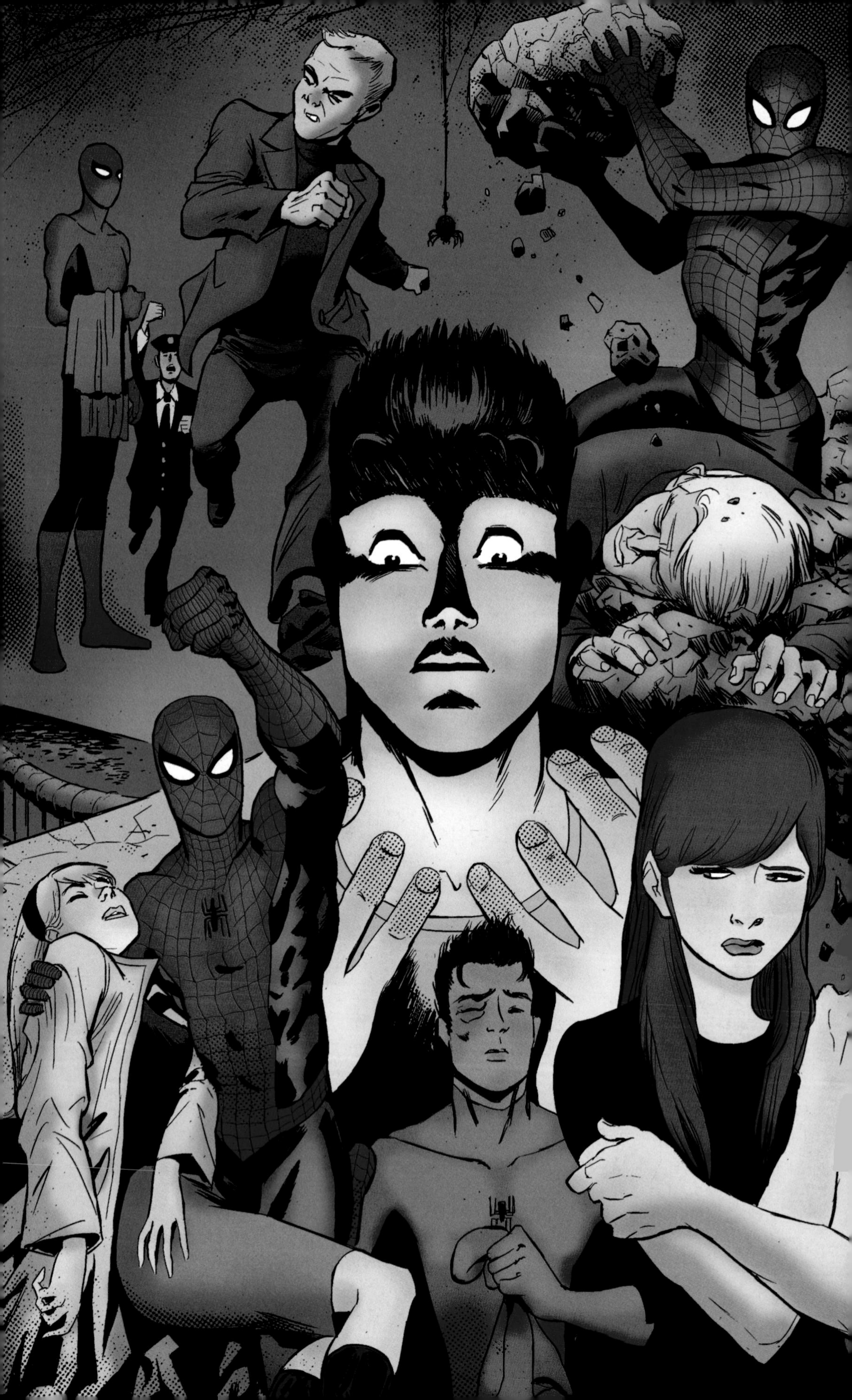

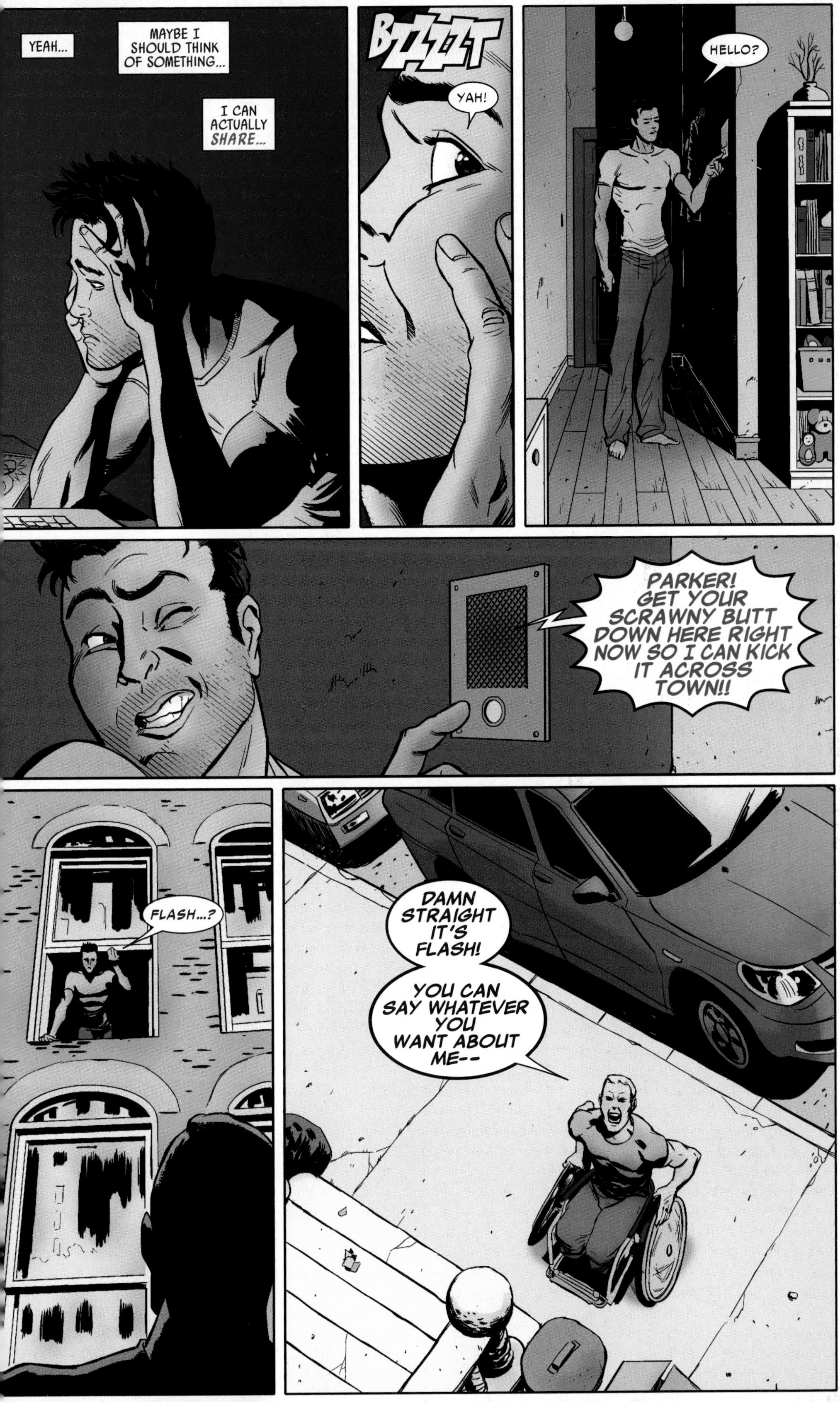
YEAH...
MAYBE I SHOULD THINK OF SOMETHING...
I CAN ACTUALLY SHARE...
BZZZT
YAH!
HELLO?
PARKER! GET YOUR SCRAWNY BUTT DOWN HERE RIGHT NOW SO I CAN KICK IT ACROSS TOWN!!
FLASH...?
DAMN STRAIGHT IT'S FLASH!
YOU CAN SAY WHATEVER YOU WANT ABOUT ME--

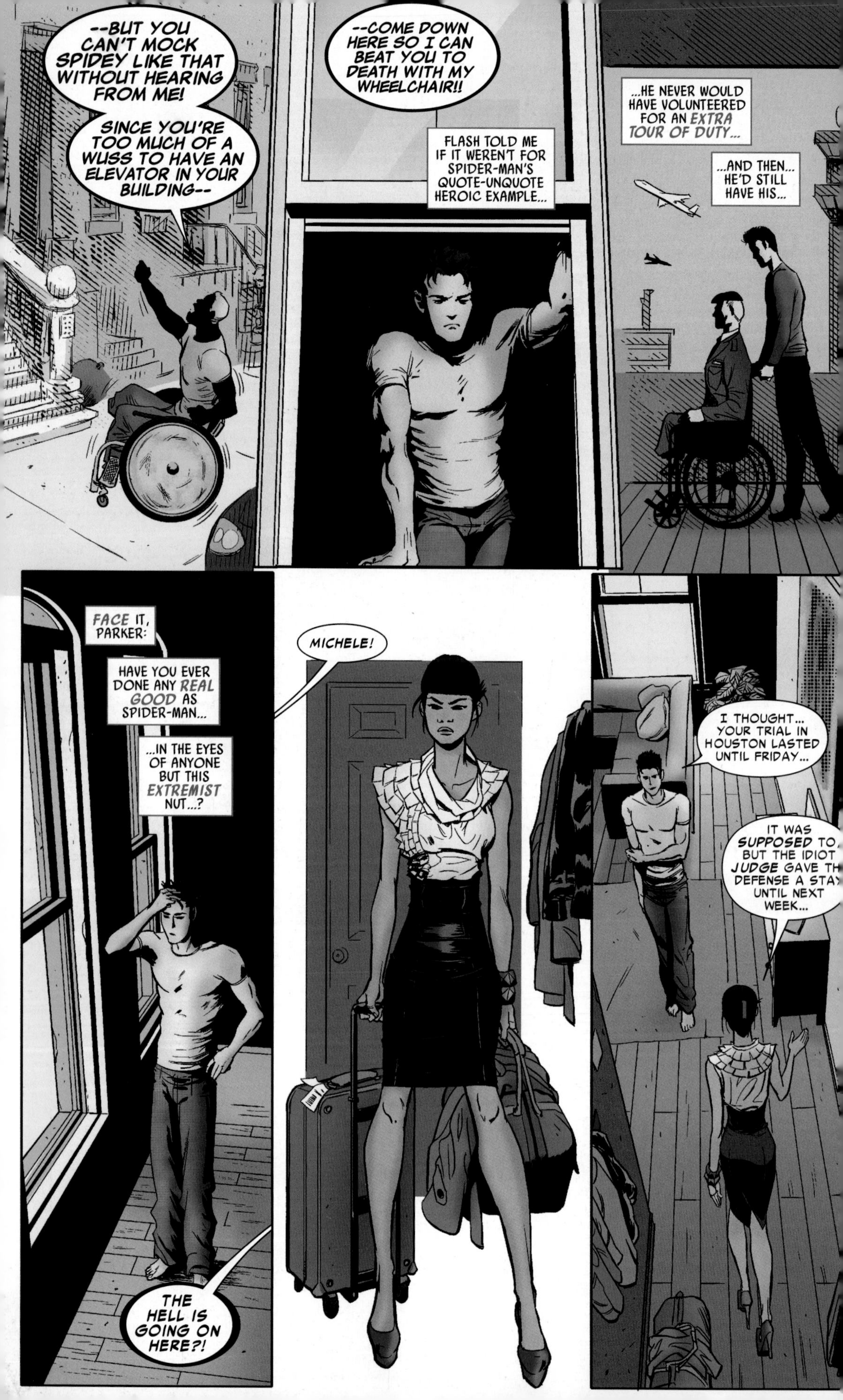
--BUT YOU CAN'T MOCK SPIDEY LIKE THAT WITHOUT HEARING FROM ME!
SINCE YOU'RE TOO MUCH OF A WUSS TO HAVE AN ELEVATOR IN YOUR BUILDING--
--COME DOWN HERE SO I CAN BEAT YOU TO DEATH WITH MY WHEELCHAIR!!
FLASH TOLD ME IF IT WEREN'T FOR SPIDER-MAN'S QUOTE-UNQUOTE HEROIC EXAMPLE...
...HE NEVER WOULD HAVE VOLUNTEERED FOR AN EXTRA TOUR OF DUTY...
...AND THEN... HE'D STILL HAVE HIS...
FACE IT, PARKER:
HAVE YOU EVER DONE ANY REAL GOOD AS SPIDER-MAN...
...IN THE EYES OF ANYONE BUT THIS EXTREMIST NUT...?
THE HELL IS GOING ON HERE?!
MICHELE!
I THOUGHT... YOUR TRIAL IN HOUSTON LASTED UNTIL FRIDAY...
IT WAS SUPPOSED TO, BUT THE IDIOT JUDGE GAVE TH DEFENSE A STAY UNTIL NEXT WEEK...

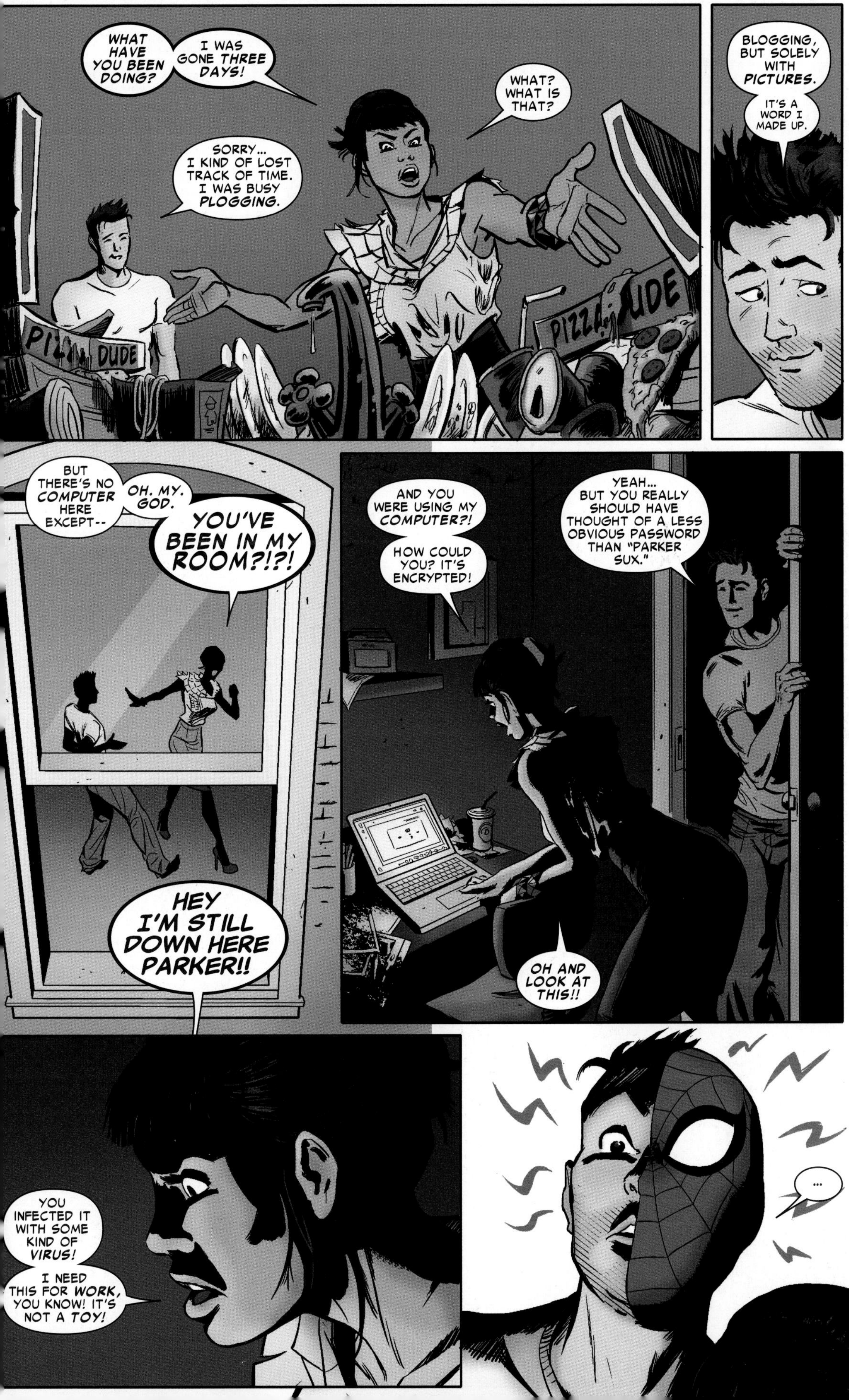
WHAT HAVE YOU BEEN DOING?
I WAS GONE THREE DAYS!
SORRY... I KIND OF LOST TRACK OF TIME. I WAS BUSY PLOGGING.
WHAT? WHAT IS THAT?
BLOGGING, BUT SOLELY WITH PICTURES.
IT'S A WORD I MADE UP.
BUT THERE'S NO COMPUTER HERE EXCEPT--
OH. MY. GOD.
YOU'VE BEEN IN MY ROOM?!?!
HEY I'M STILL DOWN HERE PARKER!!
AND YOU WERE USING MY COMPUTER?!
HOW COULD YOU? IT'S ENCRYPTED!
YEAH... BUT YOU REALLY SHOULD HAVE THOUGHT OF A LESS OBVIOUS PASSWORD THAN "PARKER SUX."
OH AND LOOK AT THIS!!
YOU INFECTED IT WITH SOME KIND OF VIRUS!
I NEED THIS FOR WORK, YOU KNOW! IT'S NOT A TOY!
...

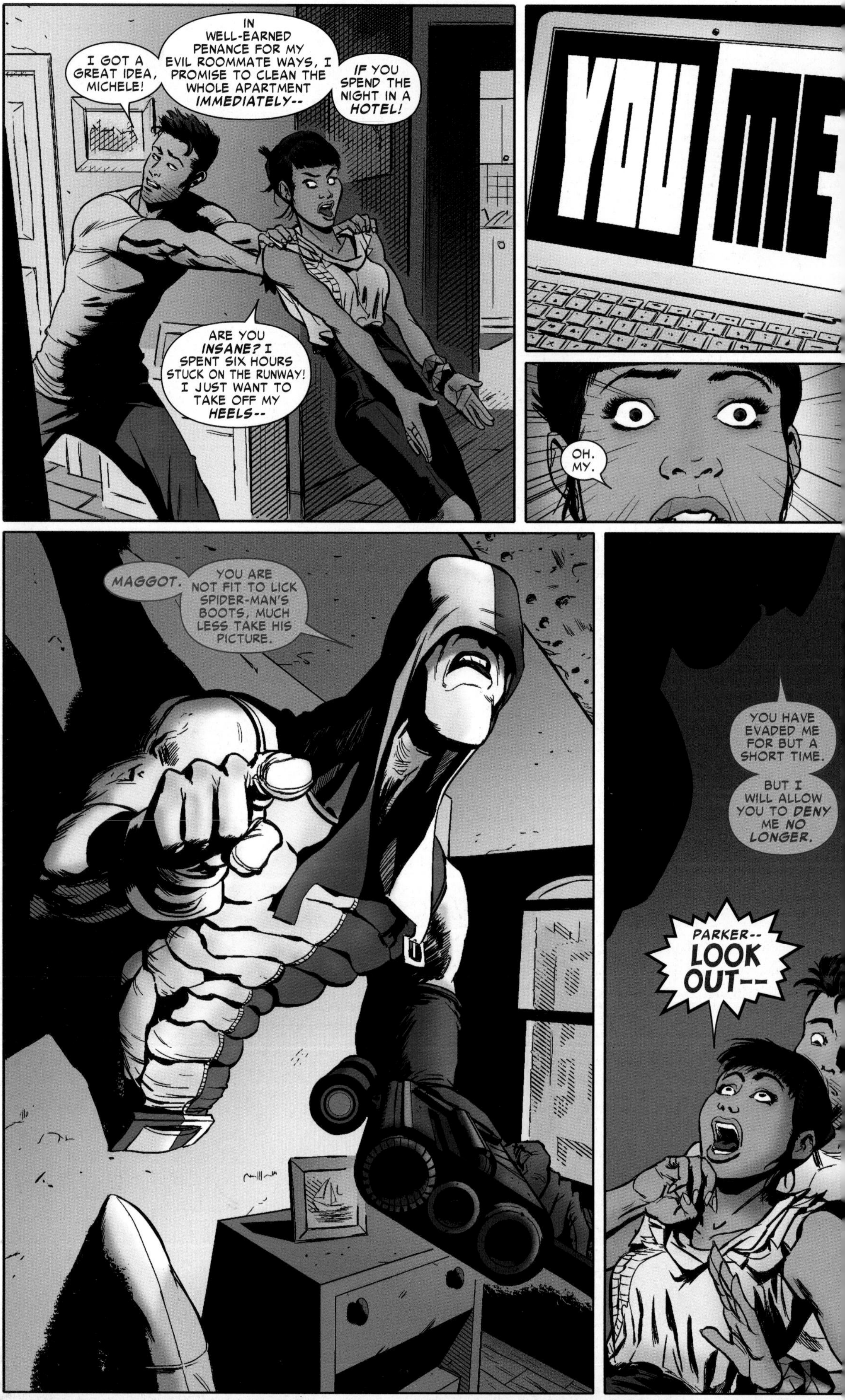
I GOT A GREAT IDEA, MICHELE!
IN WELL-EARNED PENANCE FOR MY EVIL ROOMMATE WAYS, I PROMISE TO CLEAN THE WHOLE APARTMENT IMMEDIATELY--
IF YOU SPEND THE NIGHT IN A HOTEL!
ARE YOU INSANE? I SPENT SIX HOURS STUCK ON THE RUNWAY! I JUST WANT TO TAKE OFF MY HEELS--
YOU
ME
OH. MY.
MAGGOT.
YOU ARE NOT FIT TO LICK SPIDER-MAN'S BOOTS, MUCH LESS TAKE HIS PICTURE.
YOU HAVE EVADED ME FOR BUT A SHORT TIME.
BUT I WILL ALLOW YOU TO DENY ME NO LONGER.
PARKER-- LOOK OUT--

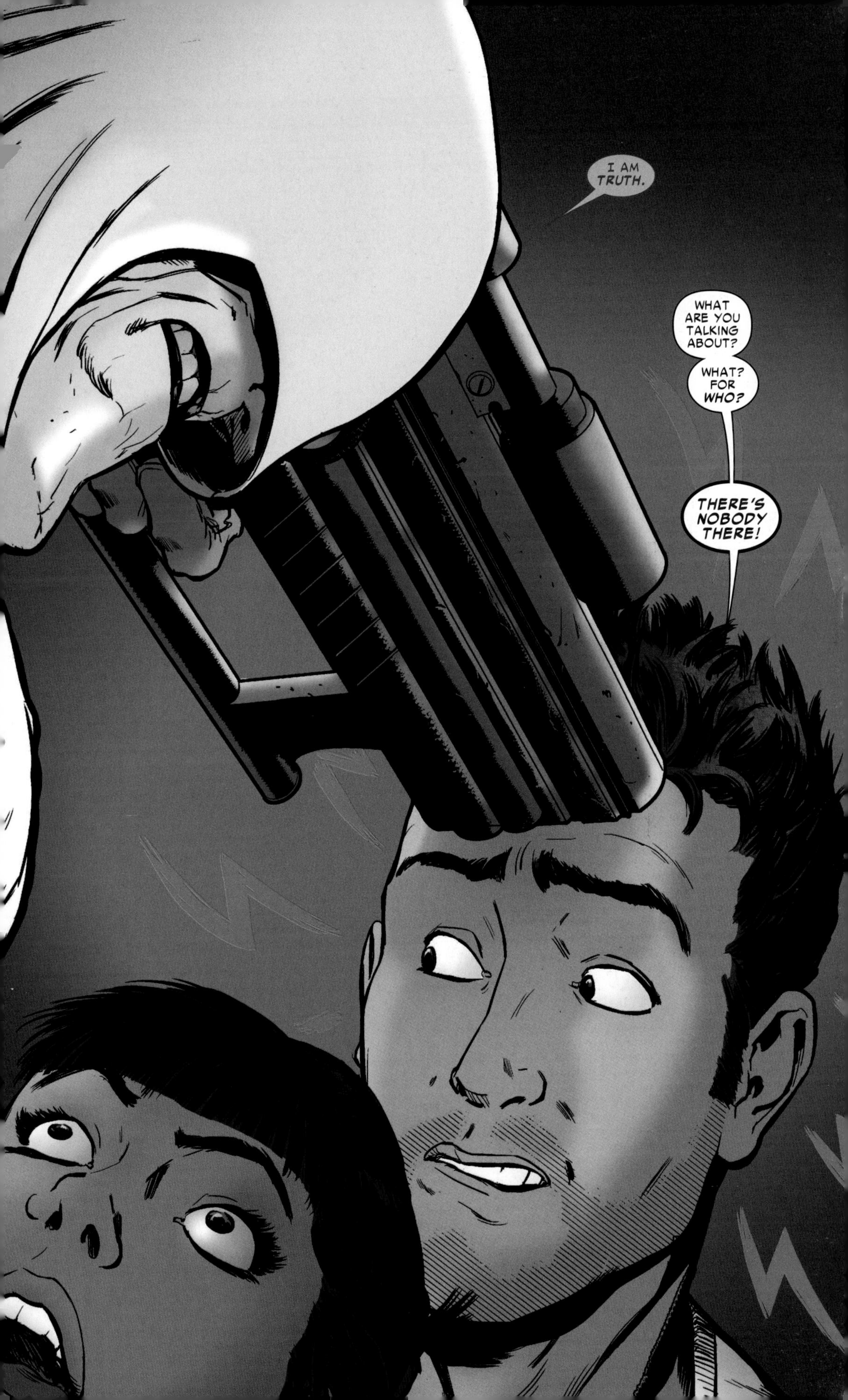
I AM TRUTH.
WHAT ARE YOU TALKING ABOUT?
WHAT? FOR WHO?
THERE'S NOBODY THERE!

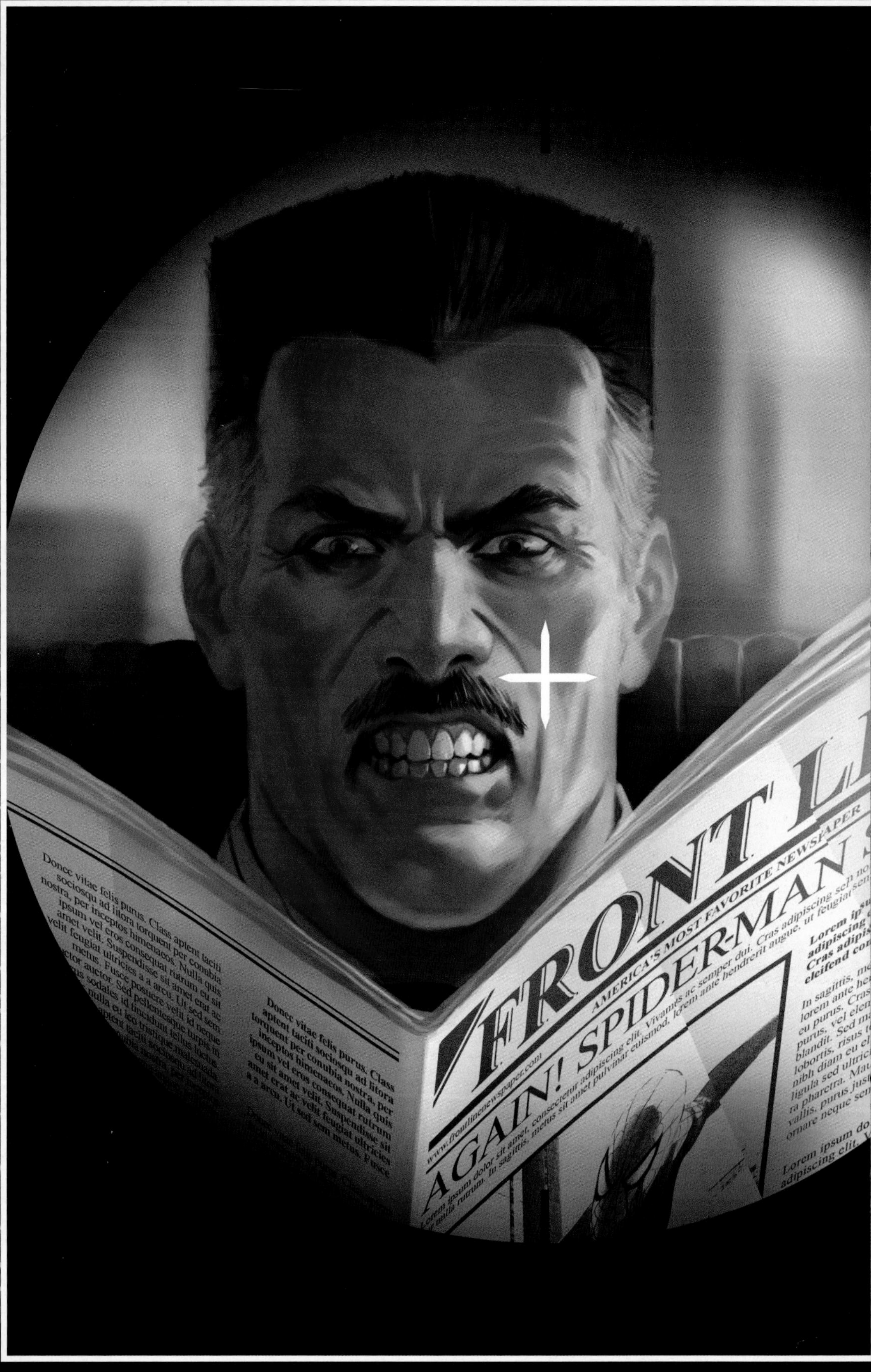
FRONT
AMERICA'S MOST FAVORITE NEWSPAPER
www.frontlinenewspaper.com
AGAIN! SPIDER-MAN

WEB OF SPIDER-MAN #9

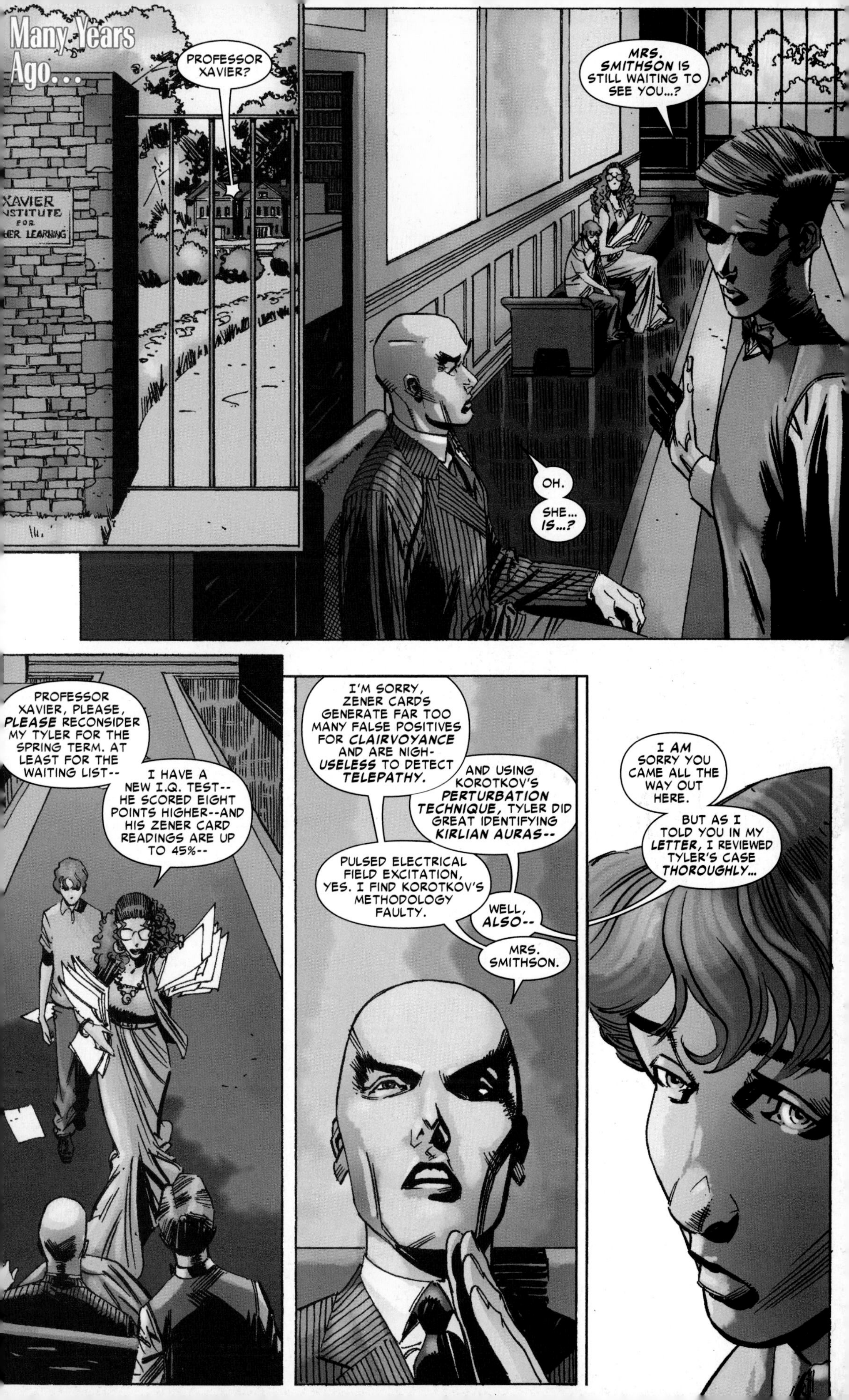
Many Years Ago...
XAVIER INSTITUTE FOR HER LEARNING
PROFESSOR XAVIER?
MRS. SMITHSON IS STILL WAITING TO SEE YOU...?
OH.
SHE... IS...?
PROFESSOR XAVIER, PLEASE, PLEASE RECONSIDER MY TYLER FOR THE SPRING TERM. AT LEAST FOR THE WAITING LIST--
I HAVE A NEW I.Q. TEST-- HE SCORED EIGHT POINTS HIGHER--AND HIS ZENER CARD READINGS ARE UP TO 45%--
I'M SORRY, ZENER CARDS GENERATE FAR TOO MANY FALSE POSITIVES FOR CLAIRVOYANCE AND ARE NIGH-USELESS TO DETECT TELEPATHY.
AND USING KOROTKOV'S PERTURBATION TECHNIQUE, TYLER DID GREAT IDENTIFYING KIRLIAN AURAS--
PULSED ELECTRICAL FIELD EXCITATION, YES. I FIND KOROTKOV'S METHODOLOGY FAULTY.
WELL, ALSO--
MRS. SMITHSON.
I AM SORRY YOU CAME ALL THE WAY OUT HERE.
BUT AS I TOLD YOU IN MY LETTER, I REVIEWED TYLER'S CASE THOROUGHLY...

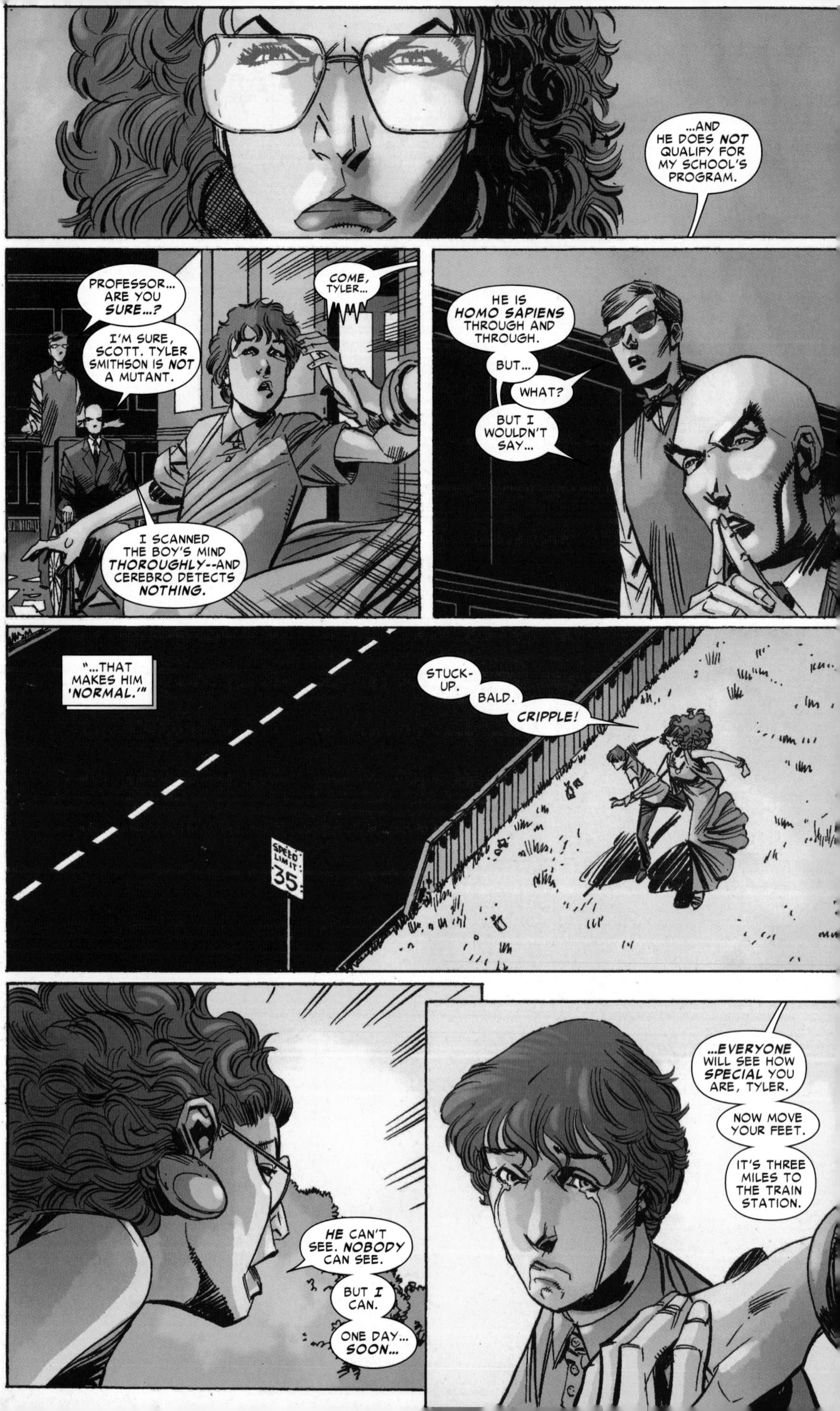
...AND HE DOES NOT QUALIFY FOR MY SCHOOL'S PROGRAM.
PROFESSOR... ARE YOU SURE...?
I'M SURE, SCOTT. TYLER SMITHSON IS NOT A MUTANT.
COME, TYLER...
I SCANNED THE BOY'S MIND THOROUGHLY--AND CEREBRO DETECTS NOTHING.
HE IS HOMO SAPIENS THROUGH AND THROUGH.
BUT...
WHAT?
BUT I WOULDN'T SAY...
"...THAT MAKES HIM 'NORMAL.'"
STUCK-UP.
BALD.
CRIPPLE!
SPEED LIMIT 35
HE CAN'T SEE. NOBODY CAN SEE.
BUT I CAN.
ONE DAY... SOON...
...EVERYONE WILL SEE HOW SPECIAL YOU ARE, TYLER.
NOW MOVE YOUR FEET.
IT'S THREE MILES TO THE TRAIN STATION.

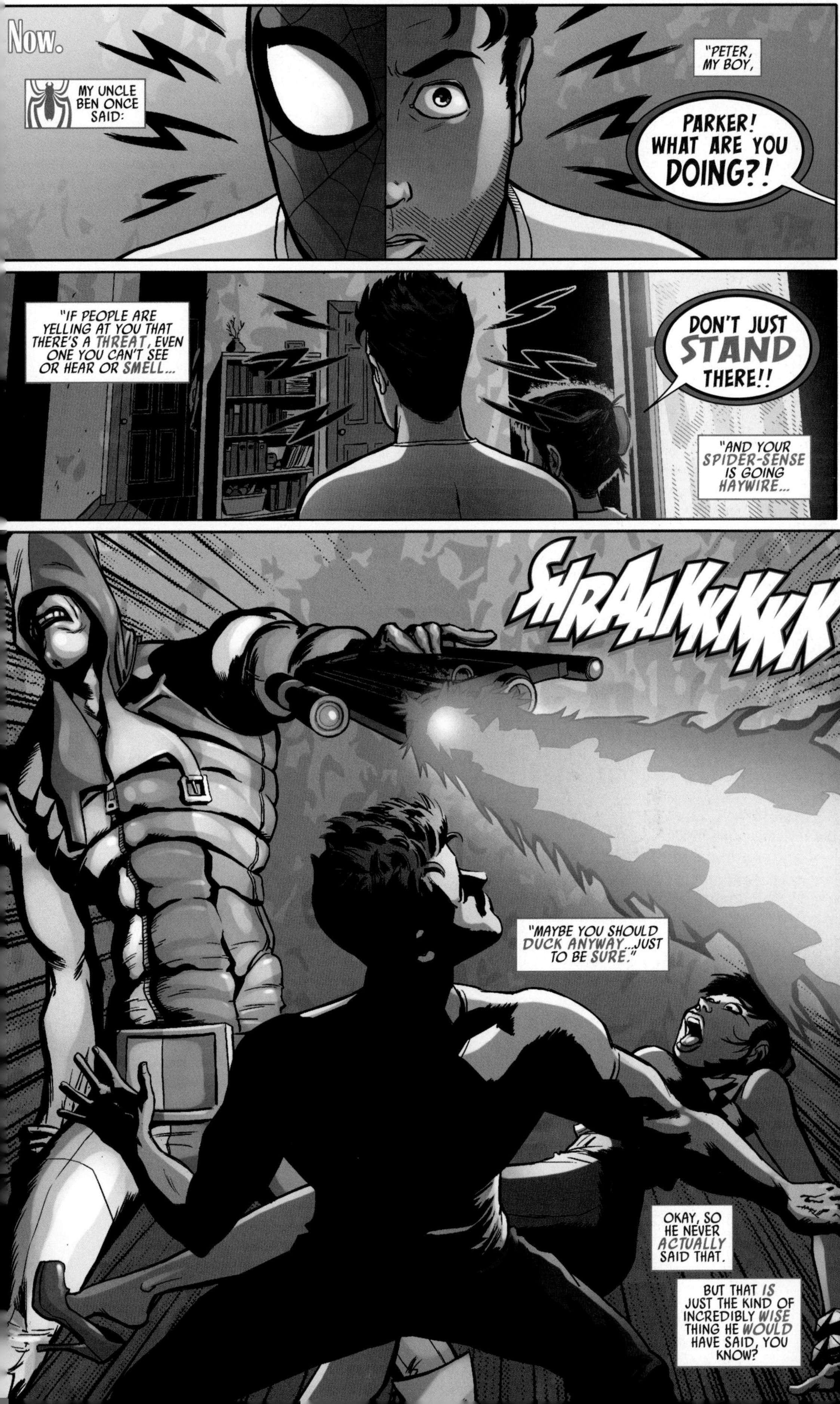

Now.
MY UNCLE BEN ONCE SAID:
"PETER, MY BOY,
PARKER! WHAT ARE YOU DOING?!
"IF PEOPLE ARE YELLING AT YOU THAT THERE'S A THREAT, EVEN ONE YOU CAN'T SEE OR HEAR OR SMELL...
DON'T JUST STAND THERE!!
"AND YOUR SPIDER-SENSE IS GOING HAYWIRE...
SHRAAKKKKK
"MAYBE YOU SHOULD DUCK ANYWAY...JUST TO BE SURE."
OKAY, SO HE NEVER ACTUALLY SAID THAT.
BUT THAT IS JUST THE KIND OF INCREDIBLY WISE THING HE WOULD HAVE SAID, YOU KNOW?

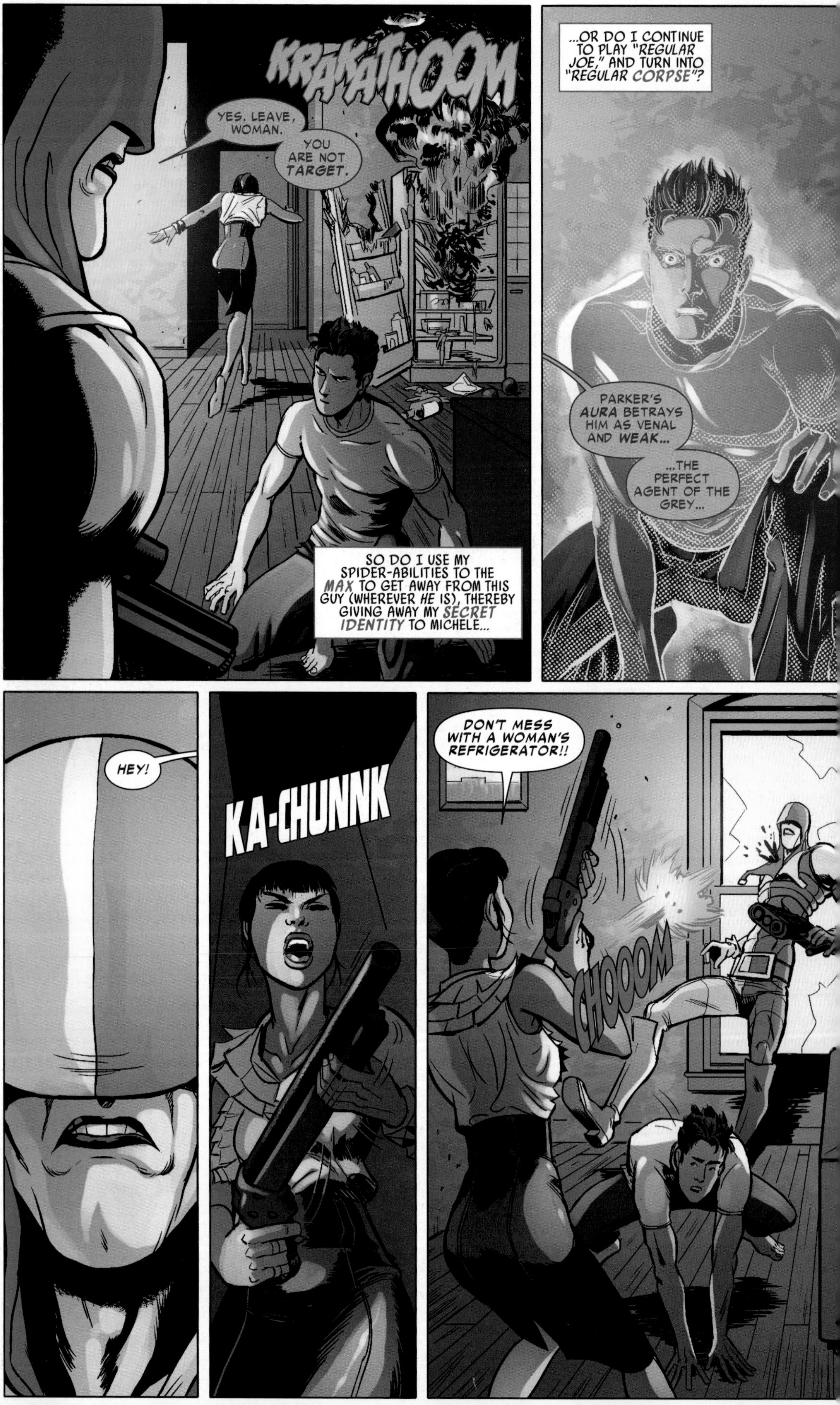
KRAKATHOOM
YES. LEAVE, WOMAN.
YOU ARE NOT TARGET.
SO DO I USE MY SPIDER-ABILITIES TO THE MAX TO GET AWAY FROM THIS GUY (WHEREVER HE IS), THEREBY GIVING AWAY MY SECRET IDENTITY TO MICHELE...
...OR DO I CONTINUE TO PLAY "REGULAR JOE," AND TURN INTO "REGULAR CORPSE"?
PARKER'S AURA BETRAYS HIM AS VENAL AND WEAK...
...THE PERFECT AGENT OF THE GREY...
HEY!
KA-CHUNNK
DON'T MESS WITH A WOMAN'S REFRIGERATOR!!
CHOOOM

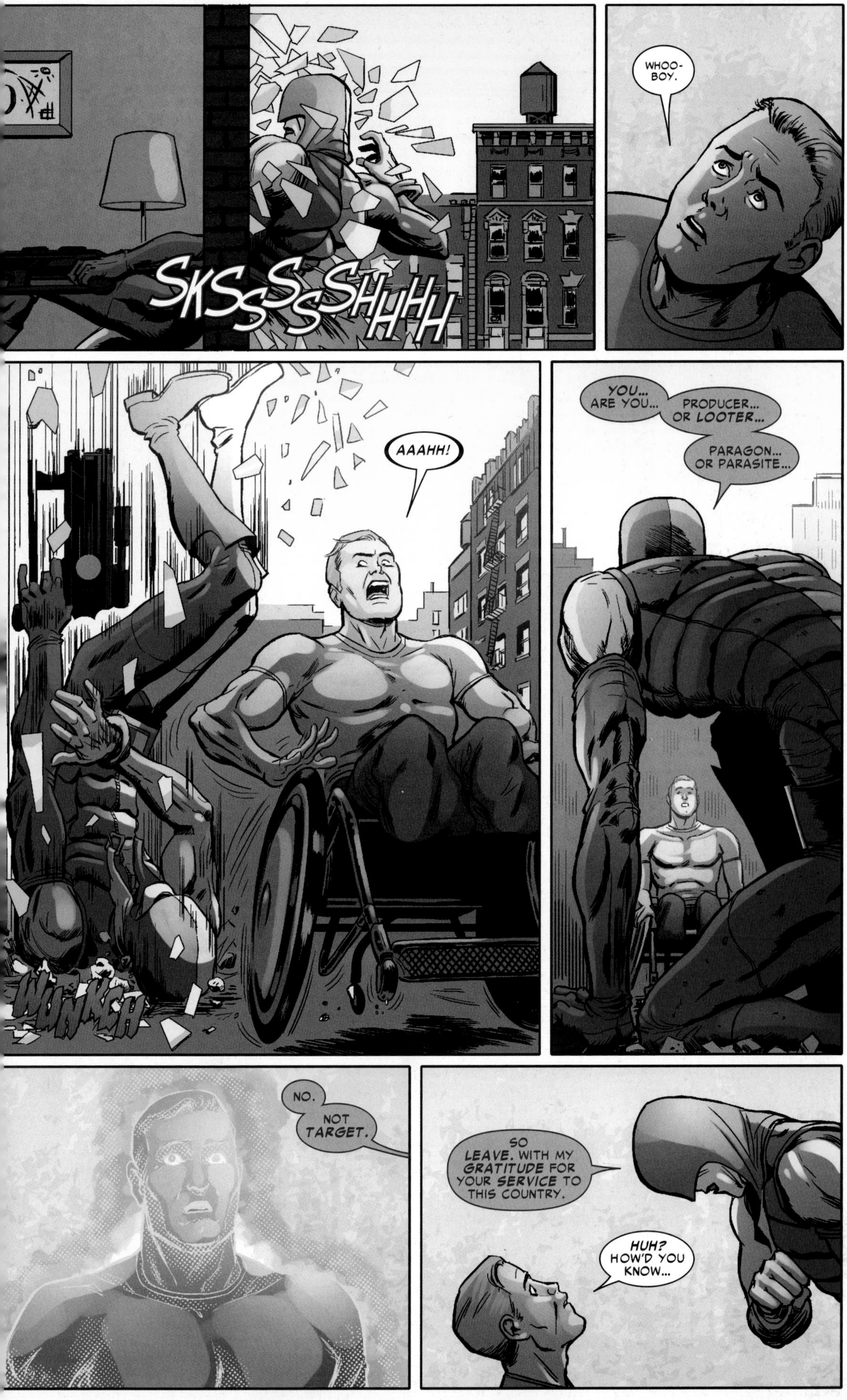
SKSSSSSHHHH
WHOO-BOY.
AAAHH!
WUNKCH
YOU... ARE YOU...
PRODUCER... OR LOOTER...
PARAGON... OR PARASITE...
NO.
NOT TARGET.
SO LEAVE. WITH MY GRATITUDE FOR YOUR SERVICE TO THIS COUNTRY.
HUH? HOW'D YOU KNOW...

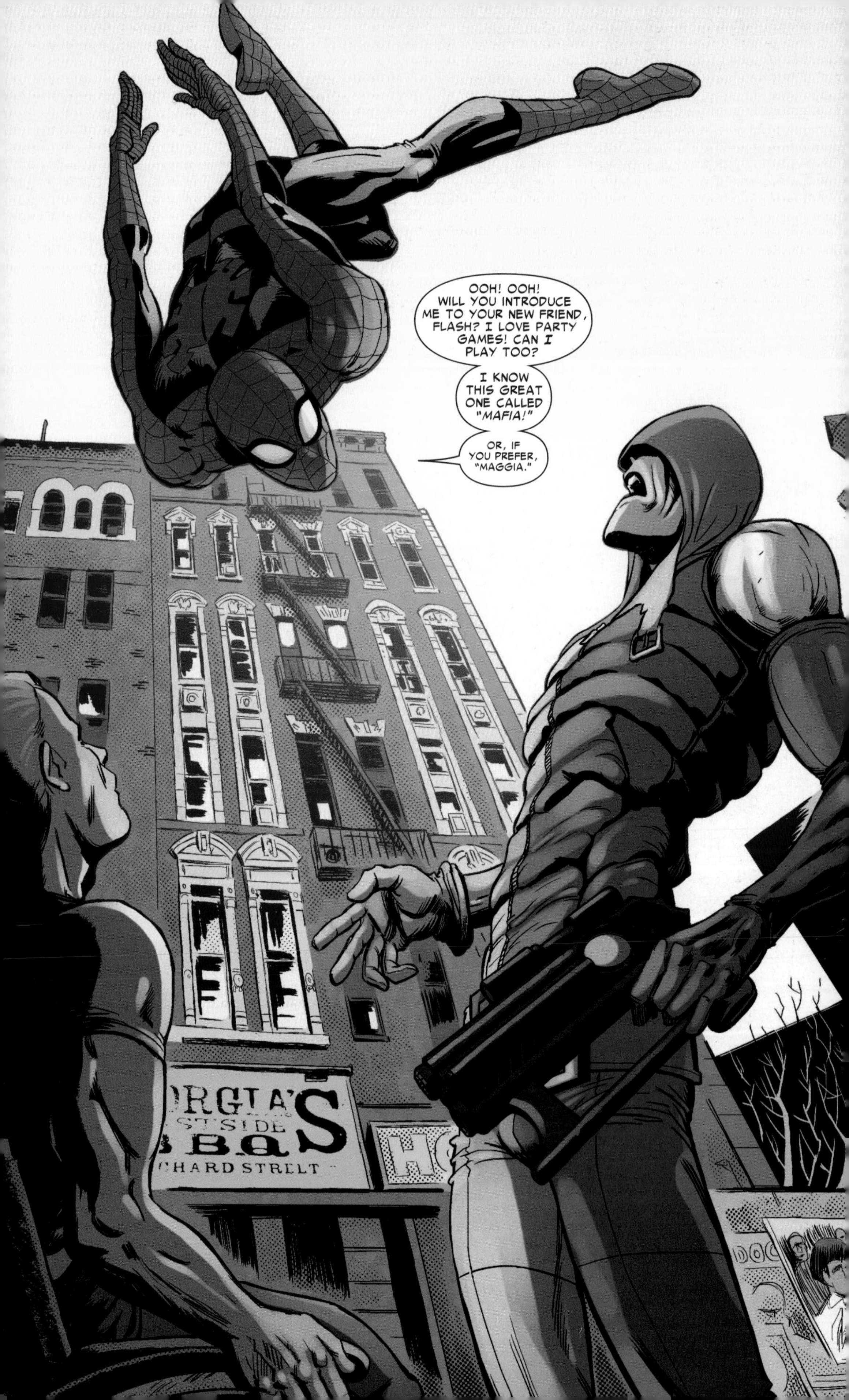
OOH! OOH! WILL YOU INTRODUCE ME TO YOUR NEW FRIEND, FLASH? I LOVE PARTY GAMES! CAN *I* PLAY TOO?
I KNOW THIS GREAT ONE CALLED *"MAFIA!"*
OR, IF YOU PREFER, "MAGGIA."
RGIA'S
ST SIDE
B.Q.
CHARD STRELT

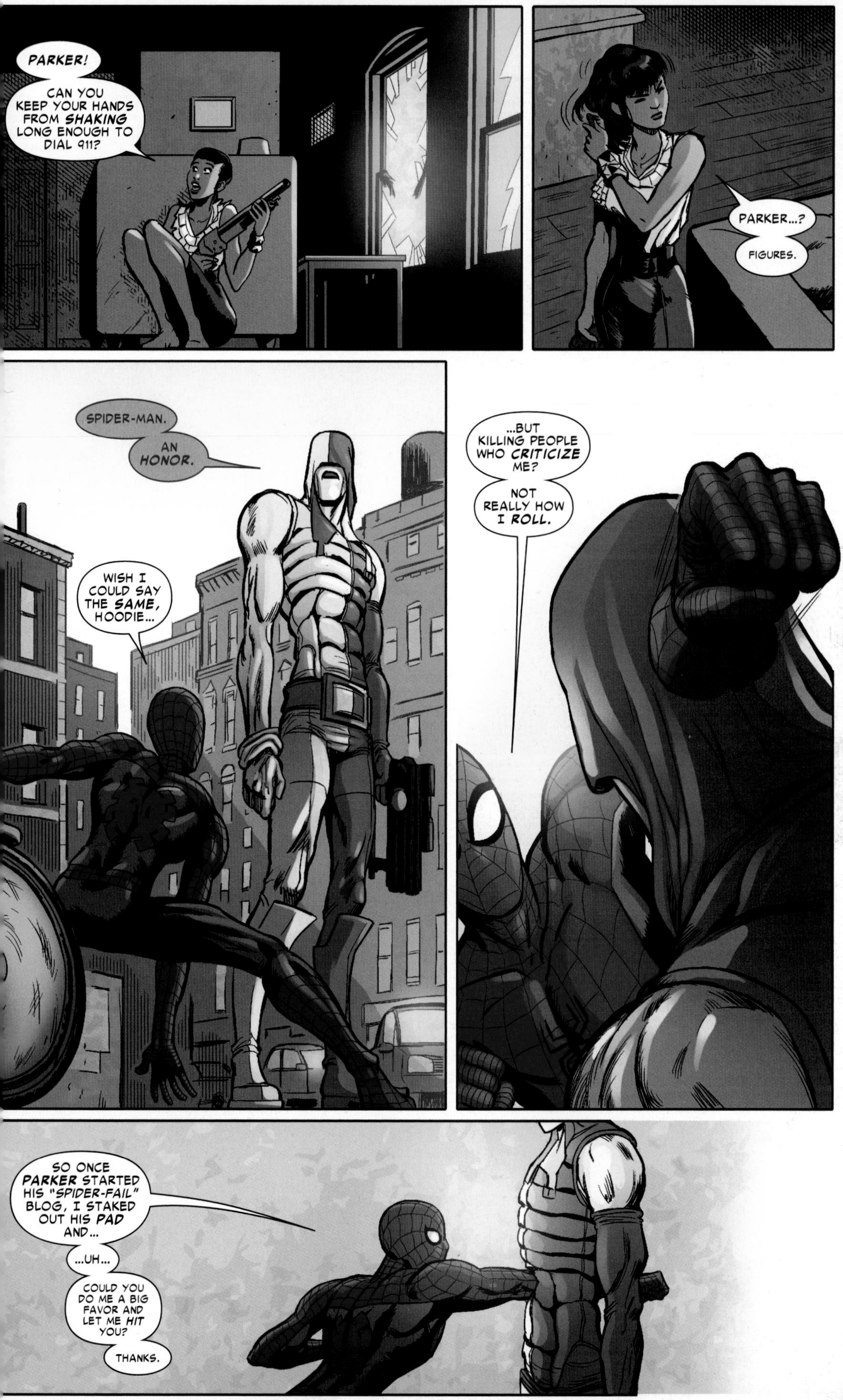
PARKER!
CAN YOU KEEP YOUR HANDS FROM SHAKING LONG ENOUGH TO DIAL 911?
PARKER...?
FIGURES.
SPIDER-MAN.
AN HONOR.
WISH I COULD SAY THE SAME, HOODIE...
...BUT KILLING PEOPLE WHO CRITICIZE ME?
NOT REALLY HOW I ROLL.
SO ONCE PARKER STARTED HIS "SPIDER-FAIL" BLOG, I STAKED OUT HIS PAD AND...
...UH...
COULD YOU DO ME A BIG FAVOR AND LET ME HIT YOU?
THANKS.

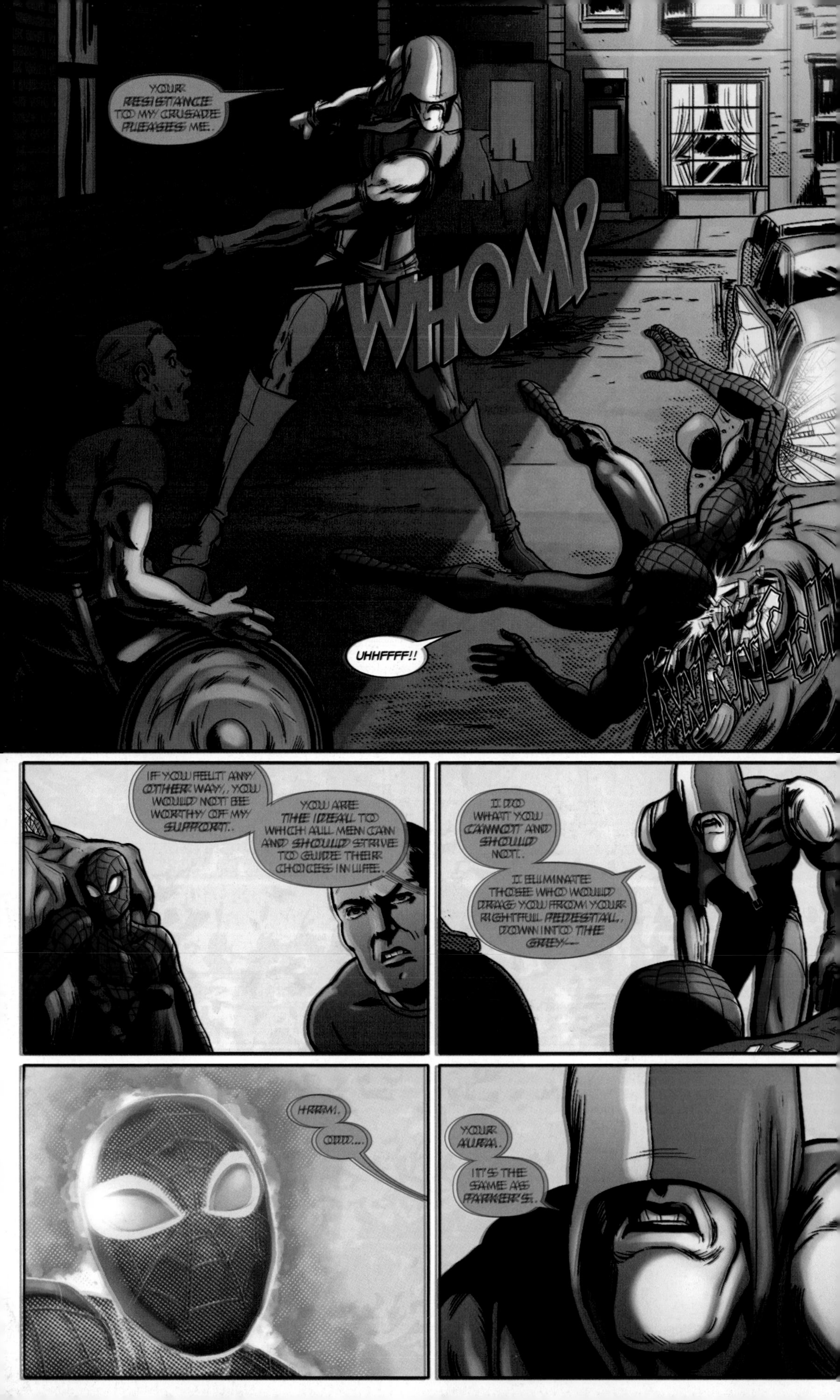
YOUR RESISTANCE TO MY CRUSADE PLEASES ME.
WHOMP
UHHFFFF!!
IF YOU FELT ANY OTHER WAY, YOU WOULD NOT BE WORTHY OF MY SUPPORT.
YOU ARE THE IDEAL TO WHICH ALL MEN CAN AND SHOULD STRIVE TO GUIDE THEIR CHOICES IN LIFE.
I DO WHAT YOU CANNOT AND SHOULD NOT.
I ELIMINATE THOSE WHO WOULD DRAG YOU FROM YOUR RIGHTFUL PEDESTAL, DOWN INTO THE GREY--
HRRM.
ODD...
YOUR AURA.
IT'S THE SAME AS PARKER'S.

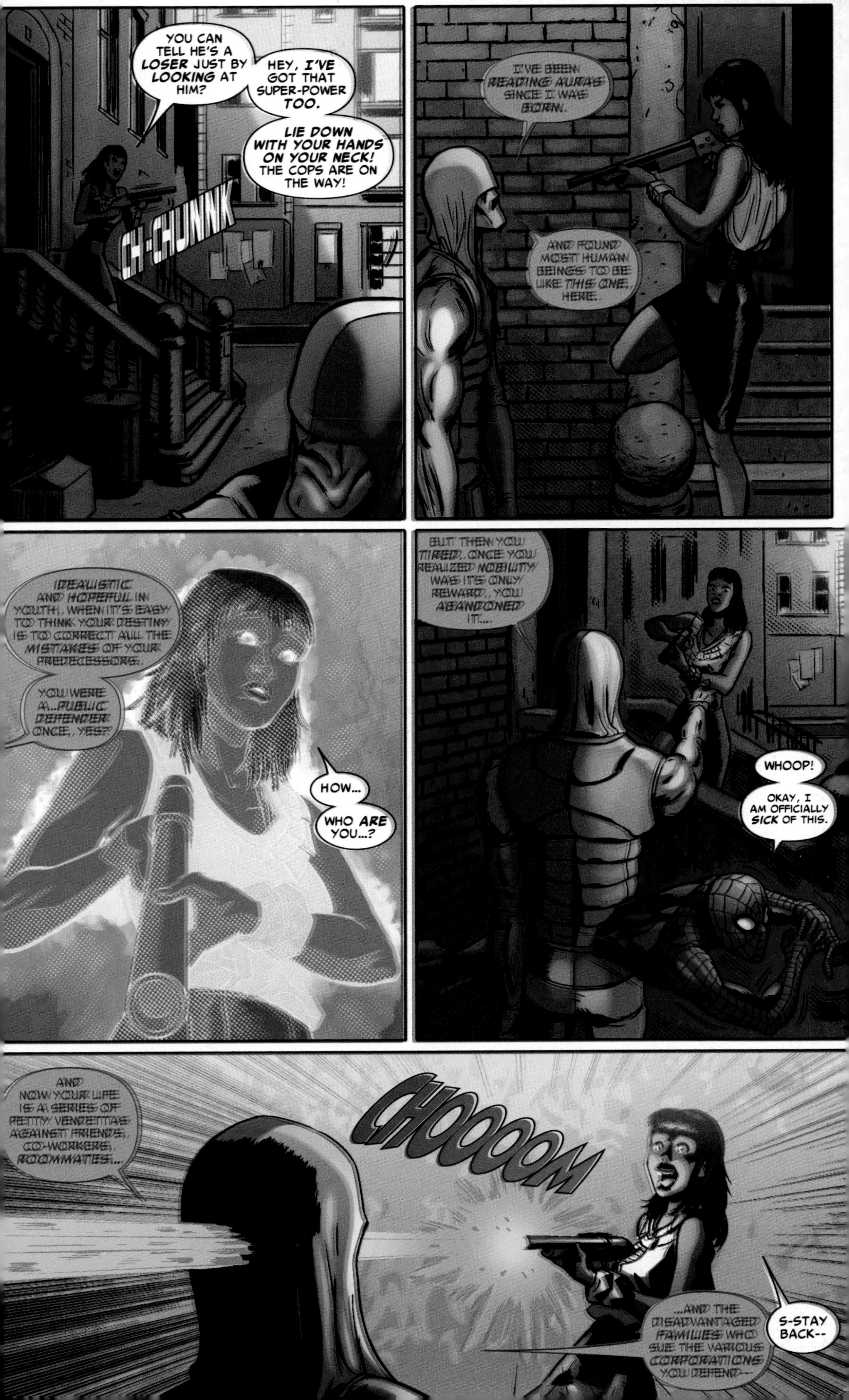

YOU CAN TELL HE'S A LOSER JUST BY LOOKING AT HIM?
HEY, I'VE GOT THAT SUPER-POWER TOO.
LIE DOWN WITH YOUR HANDS ON YOUR NECK! THE COPS ARE ON THE WAY!
CH-CHUNNK
I'VE BEEN READING AURAS SINCE I WAS BORN.
AND FOUND MOST HUMAN BEINGS TO BE LIKE THIS ONE, HERE.
IDEALISTIC AND HOPEFUL IN YOUTH, WHEN IT'S EASY TO THINK YOUR DESTINY IS TO CORRECT ALL THE MISTAKES OF YOUR PREDECESSORS.
YOU WERE A...PUBLIC DEFENDER ONCE, YES?
HOW...
WHO ARE YOU...?
BUT THEN YOU TIRED. ONCE YOU REALIZED NOBILITY WAS ITS ONLY REWARD, YOU ABANDONED IT...
WHOOP!
OKAY, I AM OFFICIALLY SICK OF THIS.
AND NOW YOUR LIFE IS A SERIES OF PETTY VENDETTAS AGAINST FRIENDS, CO-WORKERS, ROOMMATES...
CHOOOOM
...AND THE DISADVANTAGED FAMILIES WHO SUE THE VARIOUS CORPORATIONS YOU DEFEND--
S-STAY BACK--

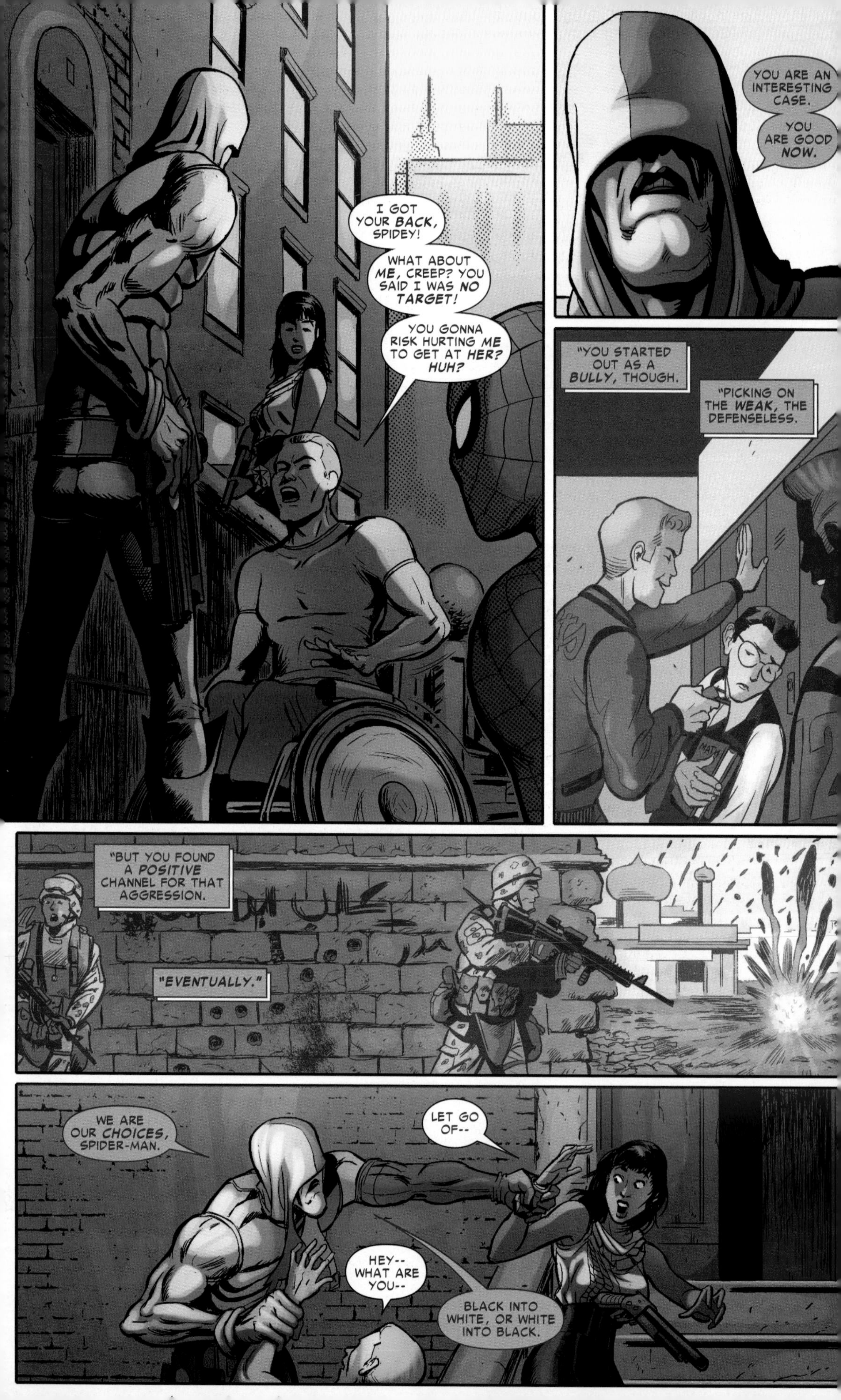

I GOT YOUR BACK, SPIDEY!
WHAT ABOUT ME, CREEP? YOU SAID I WAS NO TARGET!
YOU GONNA RISK HURTING ME TO GET AT HER? HUH?
YOU ARE AN INTERESTING CASE.
YOU ARE GOOD NOW.
"YOU STARTED OUT AS A BULLY, THOUGH.
"PICKING ON THE WEAK, THE DEFENSELESS.
MATH
"BUT YOU FOUND A POSITIVE CHANNEL FOR THAT AGGRESSION.
"EVENTUALLY."
WE ARE OUR CHOICES, SPIDER-MAN.
LET GO OF--
HEY-- WHAT ARE YOU--
BLACK INTO WHITE, OR WHITE INTO BLACK.

BUT NOT GREY.

NEVER GREY.

HEEELLLLLP!

HOW IS HE *DOING* THAT?!

WEEEOOOO WEEEOOOO WEEEOOOO

STOP! COME BACK HERE!

OR...

OR I'LL SAY "STOP" AGAIN!

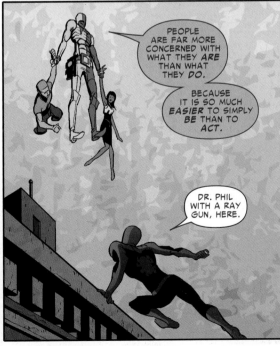

PEOPLE ARE FAR MORE CONCERNED WITH WHAT THEY *ARE* THAN WHAT THEY DO.

BECAUSE IT IS SO MUCH *EASIER* TO SIMPLY *BE* THAN TO *ACT.*

DR. PHIL WITH A RAY GUN, HERE.

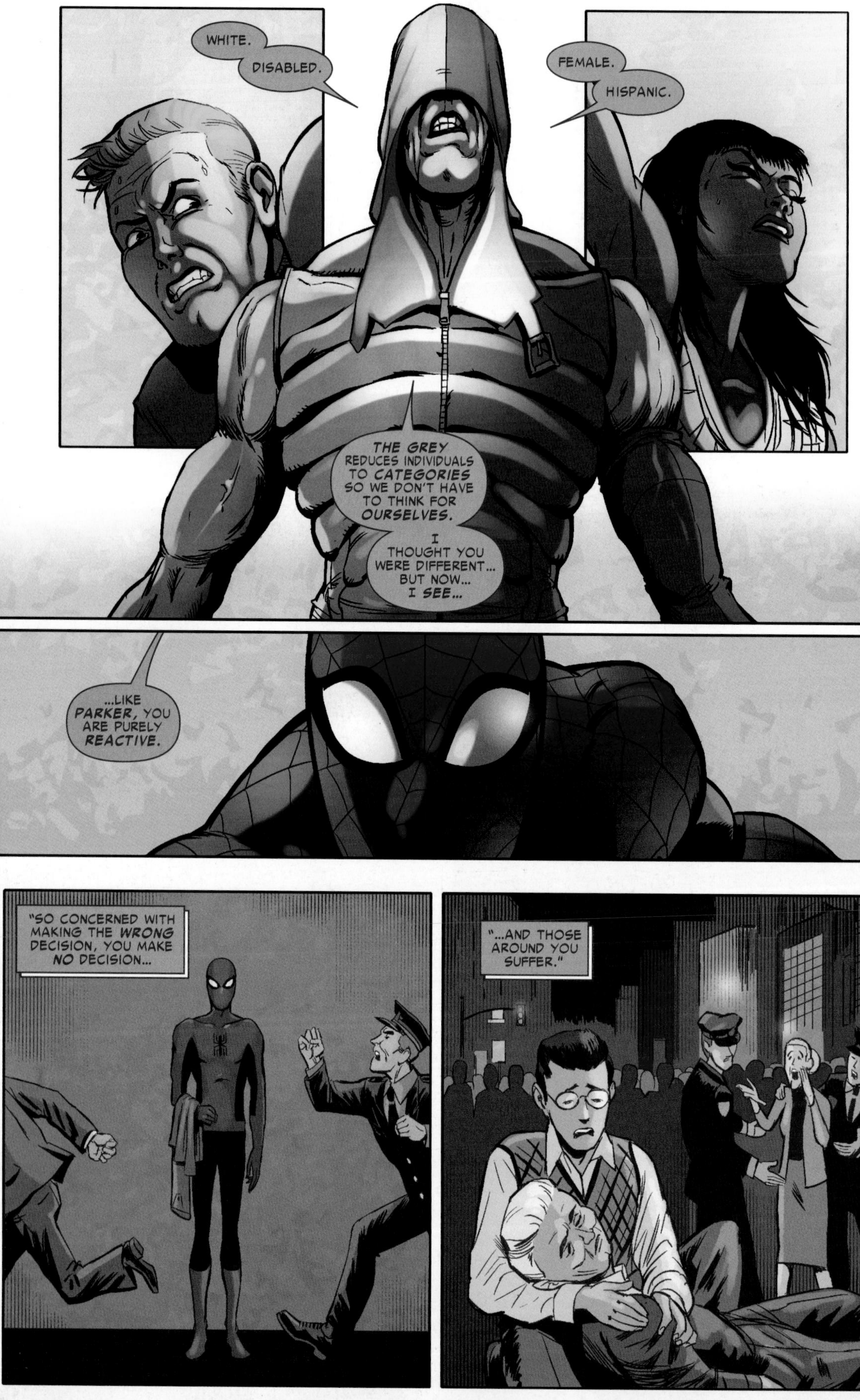

WHITE.
DISABLED.
FEMALE.
HISPANIC.
THE GREY REDUCES INDIVIDUALS TO CATEGORIES SO WE DON'T HAVE TO THINK FOR OURSELVES.
I THOUGHT YOU WERE DIFFERENT... BUT NOW... I SEE...
...LIKE PARKER, YOU ARE PURELY REACTIVE.
"SO CONCERNED WITH MAKING THE WRONG DECISION, YOU MAKE NO DECISION...
"...AND THOSE AROUND YOU SUFFER."

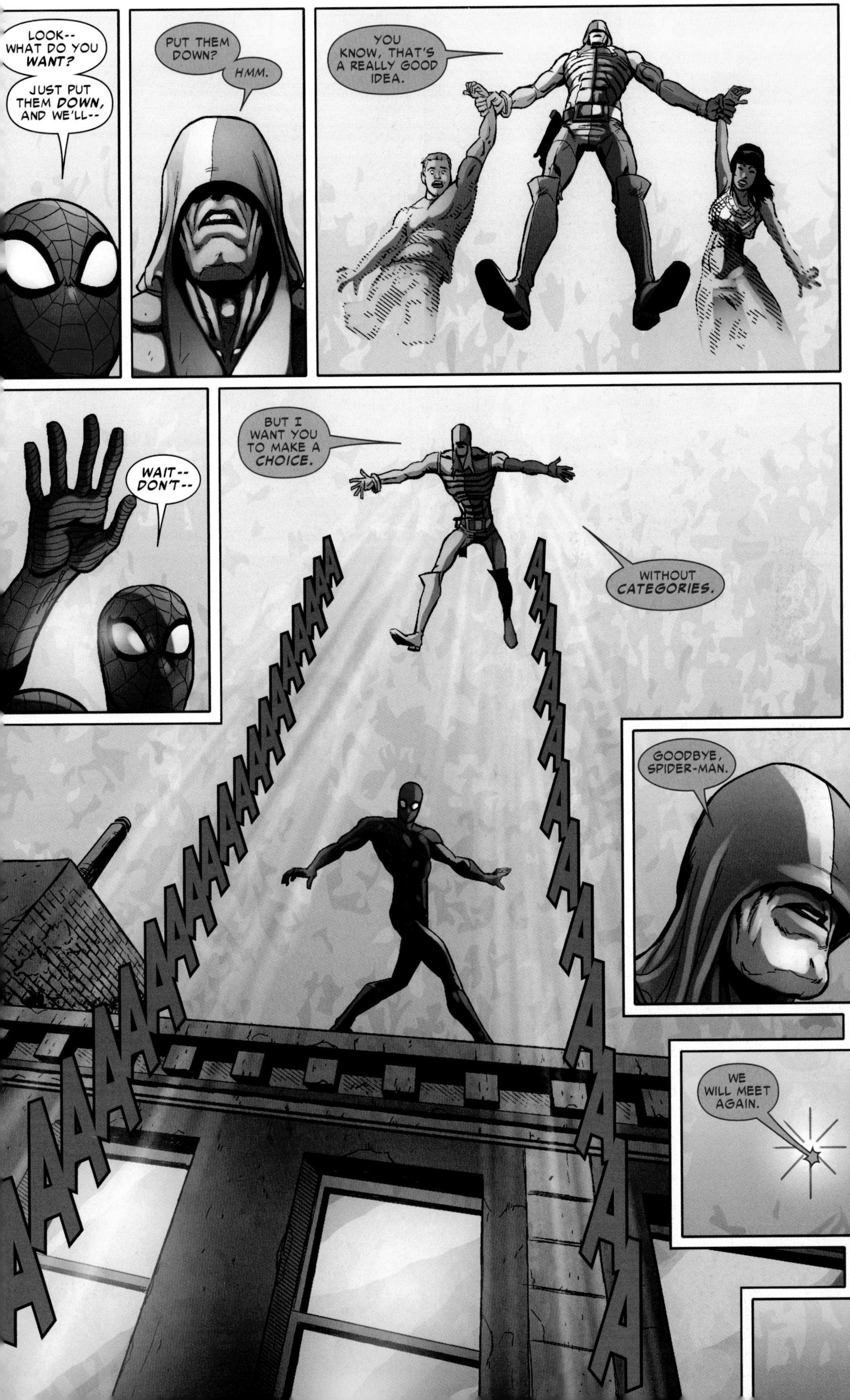
LOOK-- WHAT DO YOU WANT?
JUST PUT THEM DOWN, AND WE'LL--
PUT THEM DOWN?
HMM.
YOU KNOW, THAT'S A REALLY GOOD IDEA.
WAIT-- DON'T--
BUT I WANT YOU TO MAKE A CHOICE.
WITHOUT CATEGORIES.
AAAAAAAAAAAAAAAAAAAAAA
AAAAAAAAAAAAAAAAAAAAA
GOODBYE, SPIDER-MAN.
WE WILL MEET AGAIN.

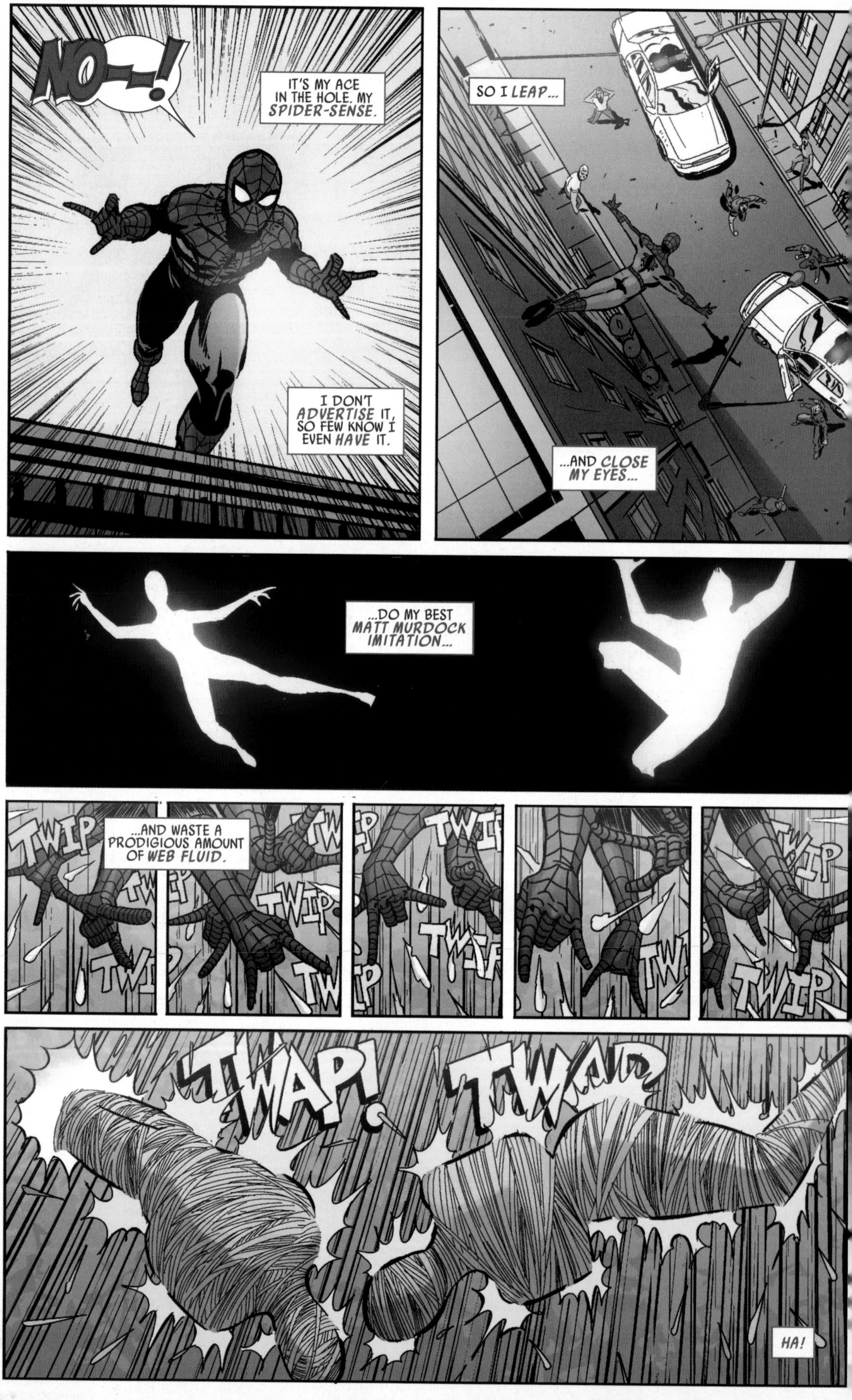
NO--!
IT'S MY ACE IN THE HOLE. MY SPIDER-SENSE.
I DON'T ADVERTISE IT, SO FEW KNOW I EVEN HAVE IT.
SO I LEAP...
...AND CLOSE MY EYES...
...DO MY BEST MATT MURDOCK IMITATION...
...AND WASTE A PRODIGIOUS AMOUNT OF WEB FLUID.
TWIP
TWIP
TWIP
TWIP
TWIP
TWIP
TWAP!
HA!

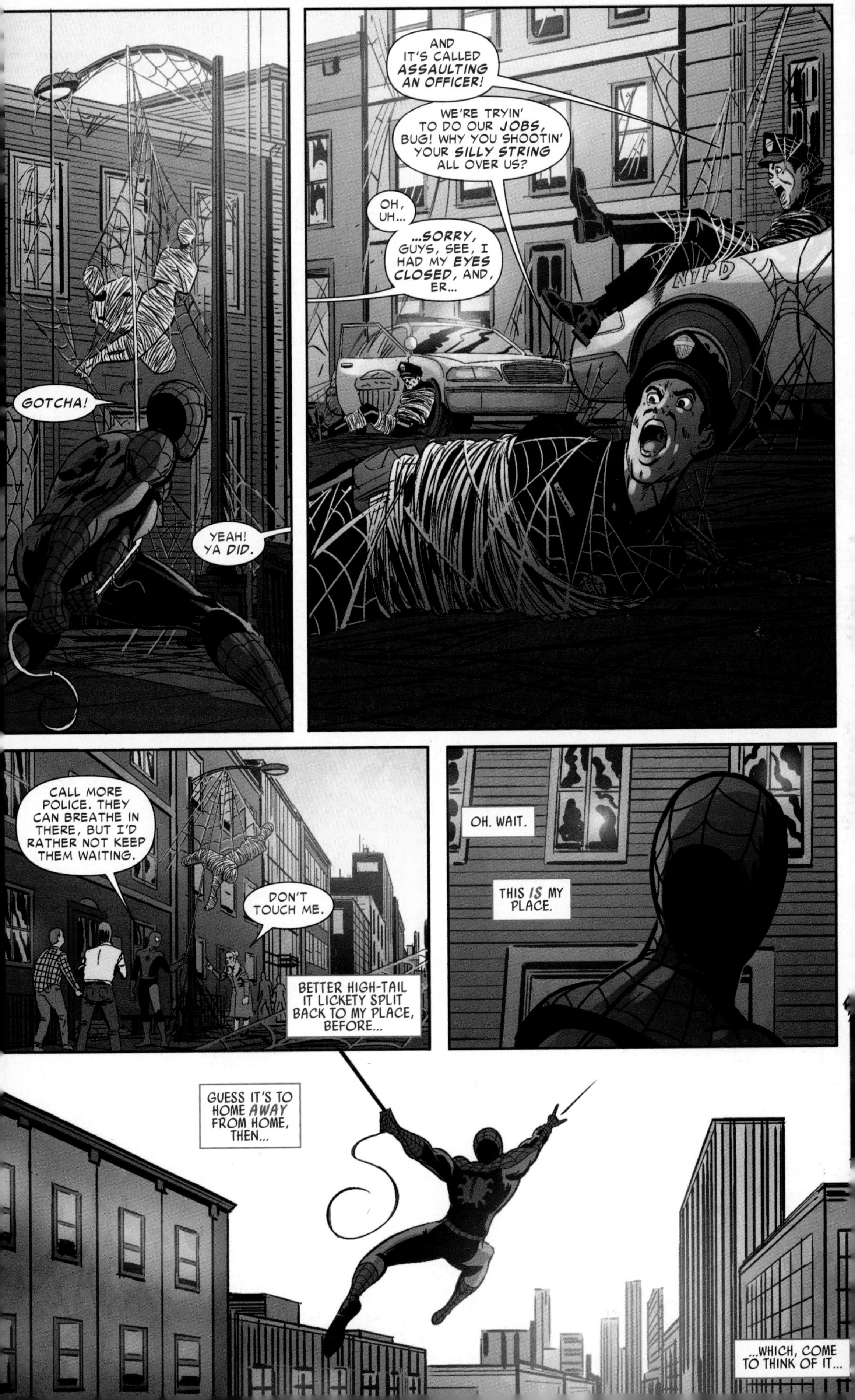
GOTCHA!
YEAH! YA DID.
AND IT'S CALLED ASSAULTING AN OFFICER!
WE'RE TRYIN' TO DO OUR JOBS, BUG! WHY YOU SHOOTIN' YOUR SILLY STRING ALL OVER US?
OH, UH...
...SORRY, GUYS, SEE, I HAD MY EYES CLOSED, AND, ER...
NYPD
CALL MORE POLICE. THEY CAN BREATHE IN THERE, BUT I'D RATHER NOT KEEP THEM WAITING.
DON'T TOUCH ME.
BETTER HIGH-TAIL IT LICKETY SPLIT BACK TO MY PLACE, BEFORE...
OH. WAIT.
THIS IS MY PLACE.
GUESS IT'S TO HOME AWAY FROM HOME, THEN...
...WHICH, COME TO THINK OF IT...

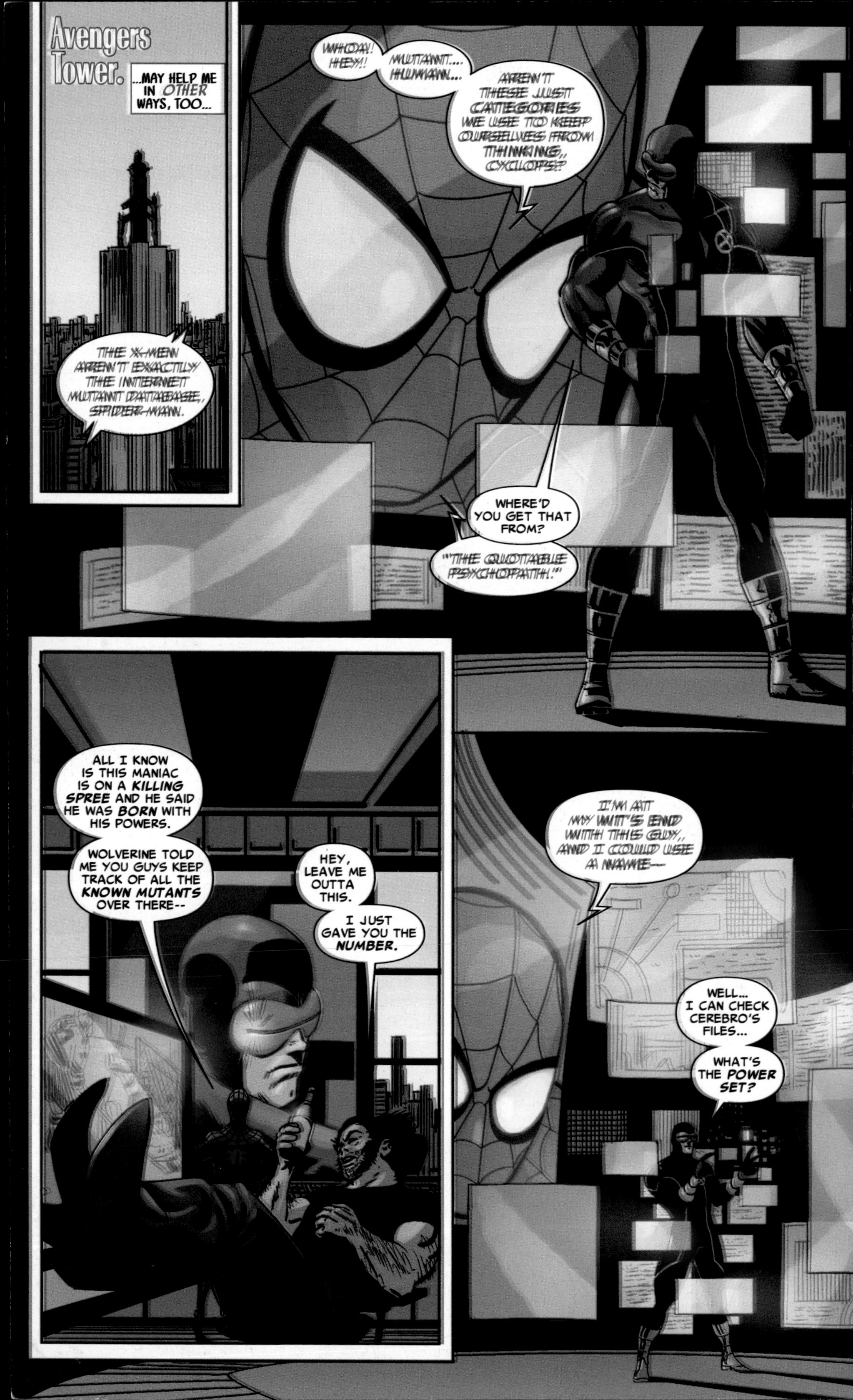
Avengers Tower.
...MAY HELP ME IN OTHER WAYS, TOO...
THE X-MEN AREN'T EXACTLY THE INTERNET MUTANT DATABASE, SPIDER-MAN.
WHOA! HEY!!
MUTANT... HUMAN...
AREN'T THESE JUST CATEGORIES WE USE TO KEEP OURSELVES FROM THINKING, CYCLOPS?
WHERE'D YOU GET THAT FROM?
"THE QUOTABLE PSYCHOPATH."
ALL I KNOW IS THIS MANIAC IS ON A KILLING SPREE AND HE SAID HE WAS BORN WITH HIS POWERS.
WOLVERINE TOLD ME YOU GUYS KEEP TRACK OF ALL THE KNOWN MUTANTS OVER THERE--
HEY, LEAVE ME OUTTA THIS.
I JUST GAVE YOU THE NUMBER.
I'M AT MY WIT'S END WITH THIS GUY, AND I COULD USE A NAME--
WELL... I CAN CHECK CEREBRO'S FILES...
WHAT'S THE POWER SET?

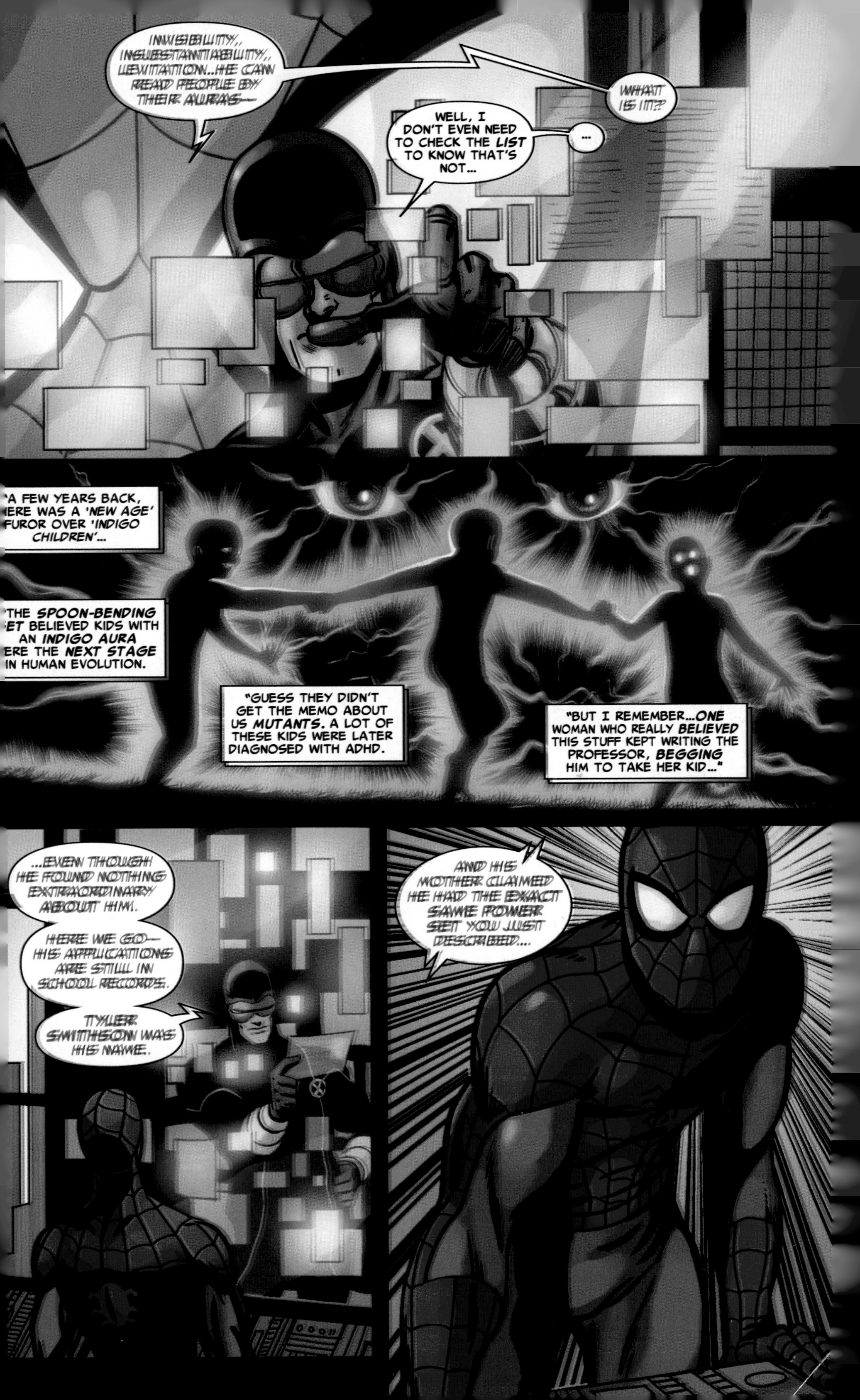

INVISIBILITY, INSUBSTANTIABILITY, LEVITATION... HE CAN READ PEOPLE BY THEIR AURAS--
WHAT IS IT?
WELL, I DON'T EVEN NEED TO CHECK THE LIST TO KNOW THAT'S NOT...
...
"A FEW YEARS BACK, HERE WAS A 'NEW AGE' FUROR OVER 'INDIGO CHILDREN'...
"THE SPOON-BENDING ET BELIEVED KIDS WITH AN INDIGO AURA ERE THE NEXT STAGE IN HUMAN EVOLUTION.
"GUESS THEY DIDN'T GET THE MEMO ABOUT US MUTANTS. A LOT OF THESE KIDS WERE LATER DIAGNOSED WITH ADHD.
"BUT I REMEMBER...ONE WOMAN WHO REALLY BELIEVED THIS STUFF KEPT WRITING THE PROFESSOR, BEGGING HIM TO TAKE HER KID..."
...EVEN THOUGH HE FOUND NOTHING EXTRAORDINARY ABOUT HIM.
HERE WE GO-- HIS APPLICATIONS ARE STILL IN SCHOOL RECORDS.
TYLER SMITHSON WAS HIS NAME.
AND HIS MOTHER CLAIMED HE HAD THE EXACT SAME POWER SET YOU JUST DESCRIBED...

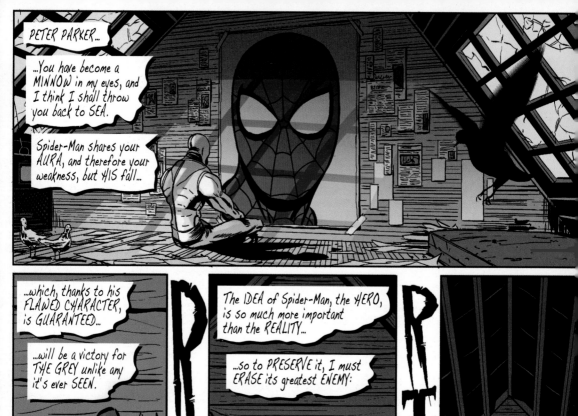

PETER PARKER...

...You have become a MINNOW in my eyes, and I think I shall throw you back to SEA.

Spider-Man shares your AURA, and therefore your weakness, but HIS fall...

...which, thanks to his FLAWED CHARACTER, is GUARANTEED...

...will be a victory for THE GREY unlike any it's ever SEEN.

The IDEA of Spider-Man, the HERO, is so much more important than the REALITY...

...so to PRESERVE it, I must ERASE its greatest ENEMY:

Spider-Man HIMSELF.

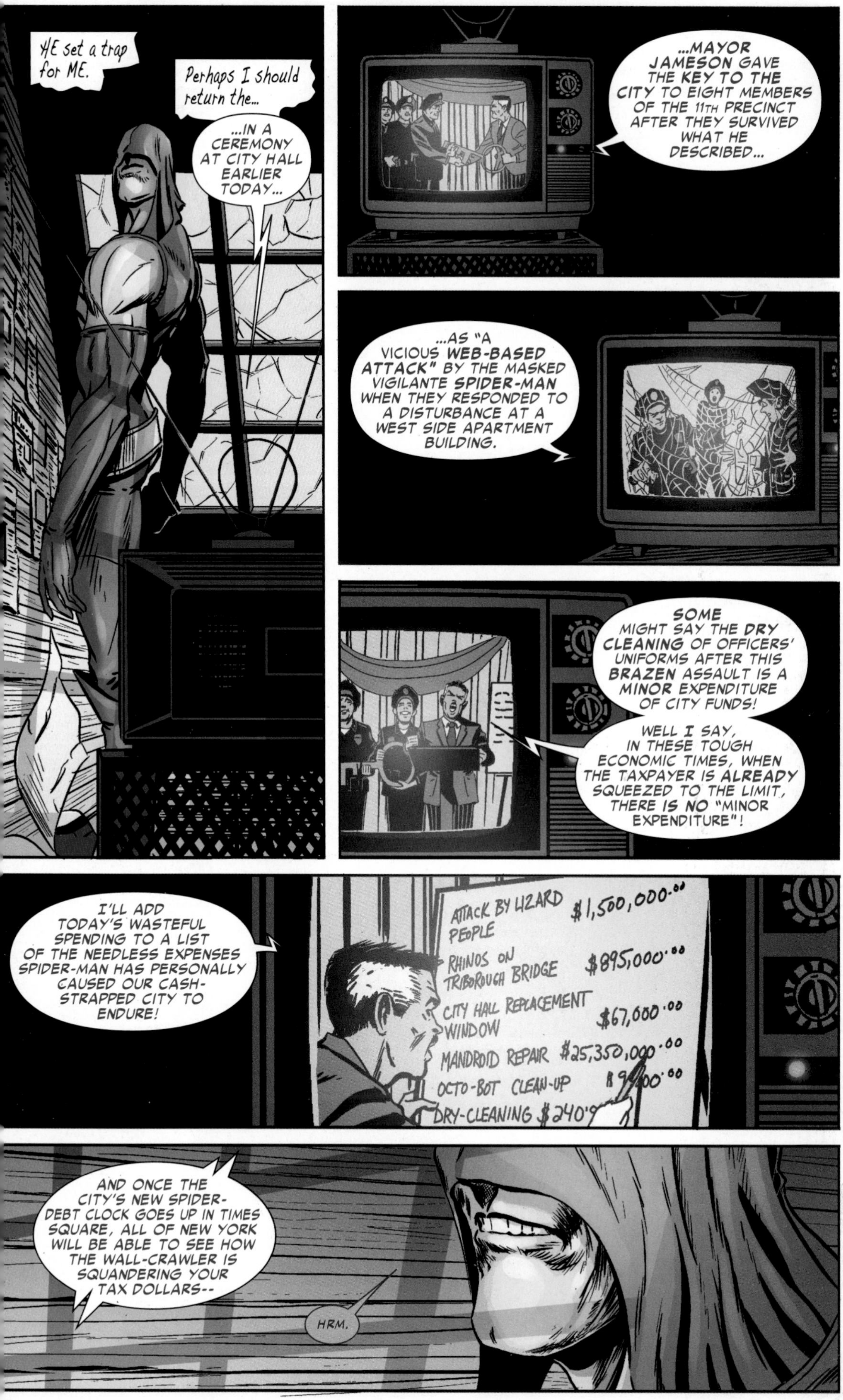

HE set a trap for ME.
Perhaps I should return the...
...IN A CEREMONY AT CITY HALL EARLIER TODAY...
...MAYOR JAMESON GAVE THE KEY TO THE CITY TO EIGHT MEMBERS OF THE 11TH PRECINCT AFTER THEY SURVIVED WHAT HE DESCRIBED...
...AS "A VICIOUS WEB-BASED ATTACK" BY THE MASKED VIGILANTE SPIDER-MAN WHEN THEY RESPONDED TO A DISTURBANCE AT A WEST SIDE APARTMENT BUILDING.
SOME MIGHT SAY THE DRY CLEANING OF OFFICERS' UNIFORMS AFTER THIS BRAZEN ASSAULT IS A MINOR EXPENDITURE OF CITY FUNDS!
WELL I SAY, IN THESE TOUGH ECONOMIC TIMES, WHEN THE TAXPAYER IS ALREADY SQUEEZED TO THE LIMIT, THERE IS NO "MINOR EXPENDITURE"!
I'LL ADD TODAY'S WASTEFUL SPENDING TO A LIST OF THE NEEDLESS EXPENSES SPIDER-MAN HAS PERSONALLY CAUSED OUR CASH-STRAPPED CITY TO ENDURE!
ATTACK BY LIZARD PEOPLE $1,500,000.00
RHINOS ON TRIBOROUGH BRIDGE $895,000.00
CITY HALL REPLACEMENT WINDOW $67,000.00
MANDROID REPAIR $25,350,000.00
OCTO-BOT CLEAN-UP
DRY-CLEANING $240
AND ONCE THE CITY'S NEW SPIDER-DEBT CLOCK GOES UP IN TIMES SQUARE, ALL OF NEW YORK WILL BE ABLE TO SEE HOW THE WALL-CRAWLER IS SQUANDERING YOUR TAX DOLLARS--
HRM.

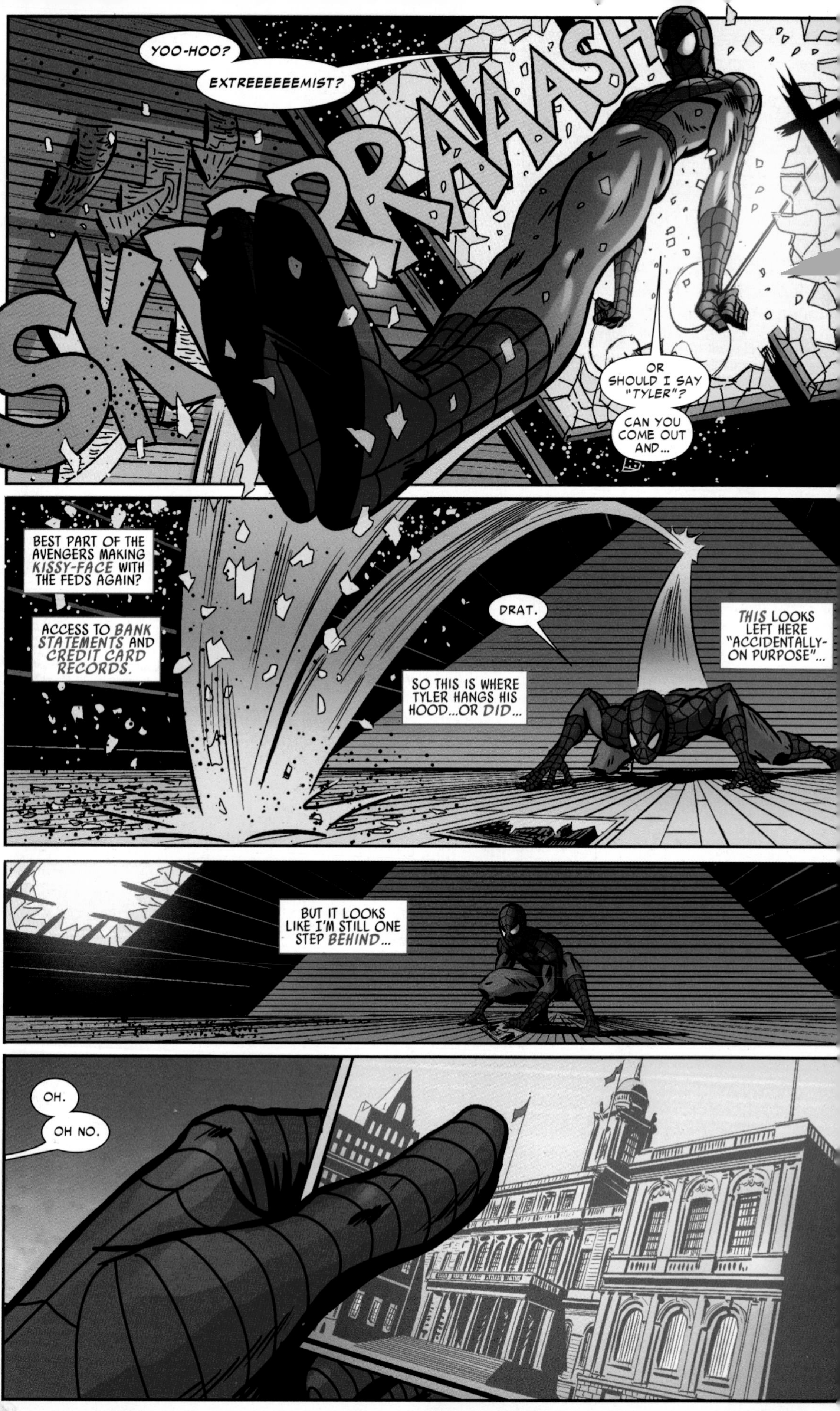
YOO-HOO?
EXTREEEEEEEMIST?
SKRRAAASH
OR SHOULD I SAY "TYLER"?
CAN YOU COME OUT AND...
BEST PART OF THE AVENGERS MAKING KISSY-FACE WITH THE FEDS AGAIN?
ACCESS TO BANK STATEMENTS AND CREDIT CARD RECORDS.
DRAT.
SO THIS IS WHERE TYLER HANGS HIS HOOD...OR DID...
THIS LOOKS LEFT HERE "ACCIDENTALLY-ON PURPOSE"...
BUT IT LOOKS LIKE I'M STILL ONE STEP BEHIND...
OH.
OH NO.

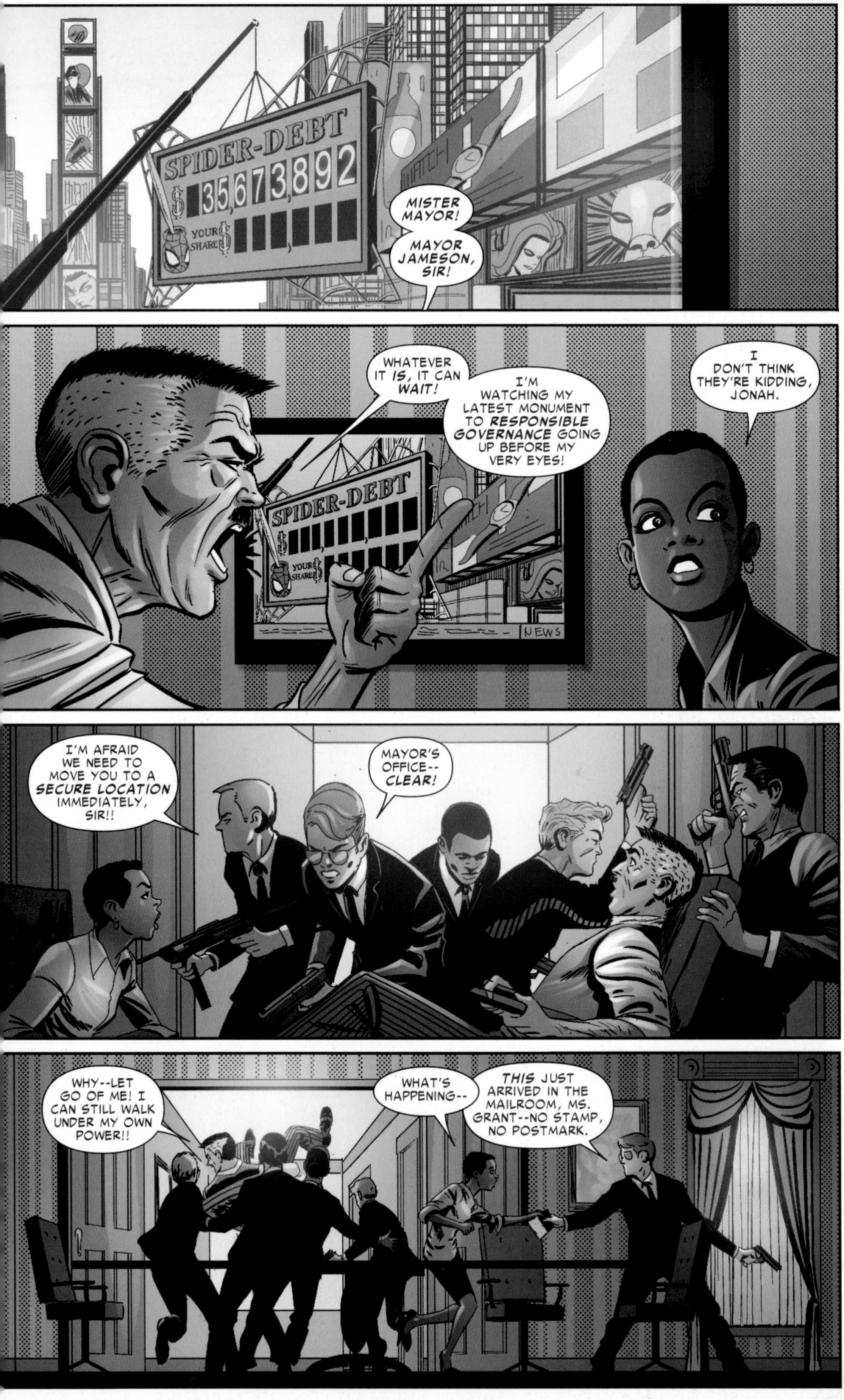
SPIDER-DEBT
$ 35,673,892
YOUR SHARE $
MISTER MAYOR!
MAYOR JAMESON, SIR!
WHATEVER IT IS, IT CAN WAIT!
I'M WATCHING MY LATEST MONUMENT TO RESPONSIBLE GOVERNANCE GOING UP BEFORE MY VERY EYES!
SPIDER-DEBT
YOUR SHARE $
NEWS
I DON'T THINK THEY'RE KIDDING, JONAH.
I'M AFRAID WE NEED TO MOVE YOU TO A SECURE LOCATION IMMEDIATELY, SIR!!
MAYOR'S OFFICE-- CLEAR!
WHY--LET GO OF ME! I CAN STILL WALK UNDER MY OWN POWER!!
WHAT'S HAPPENING--
THIS JUST ARRIVED IN THE MAILROOM, MS. GRANT--NO STAMP, NO POSTMARK.

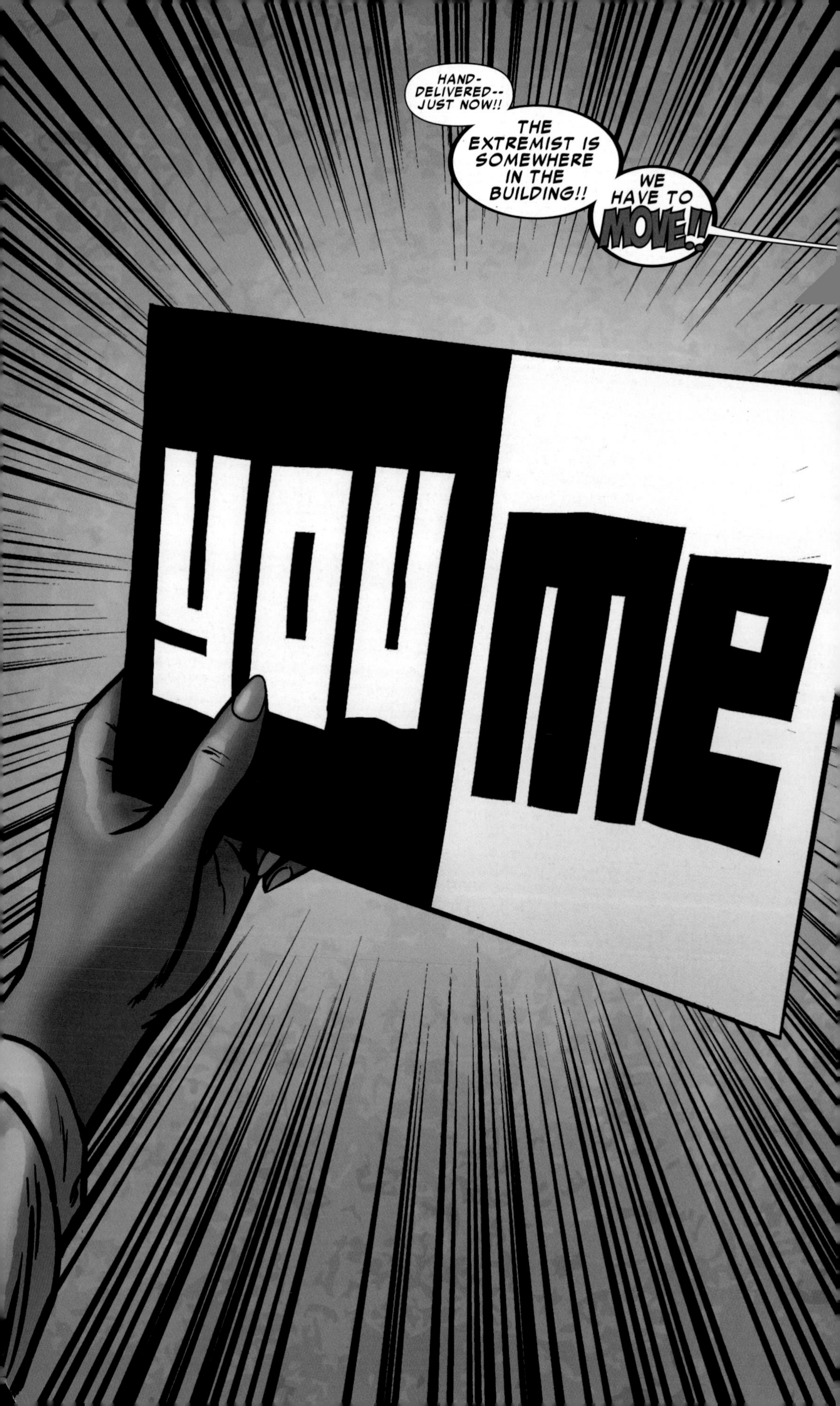
HAND-DELIVERED--JUST NOW!!
THE EXTREMIST IS SOMEWHERE IN THE BUILDING!!
WE HAVE TO MOVE!!
YOU
ME

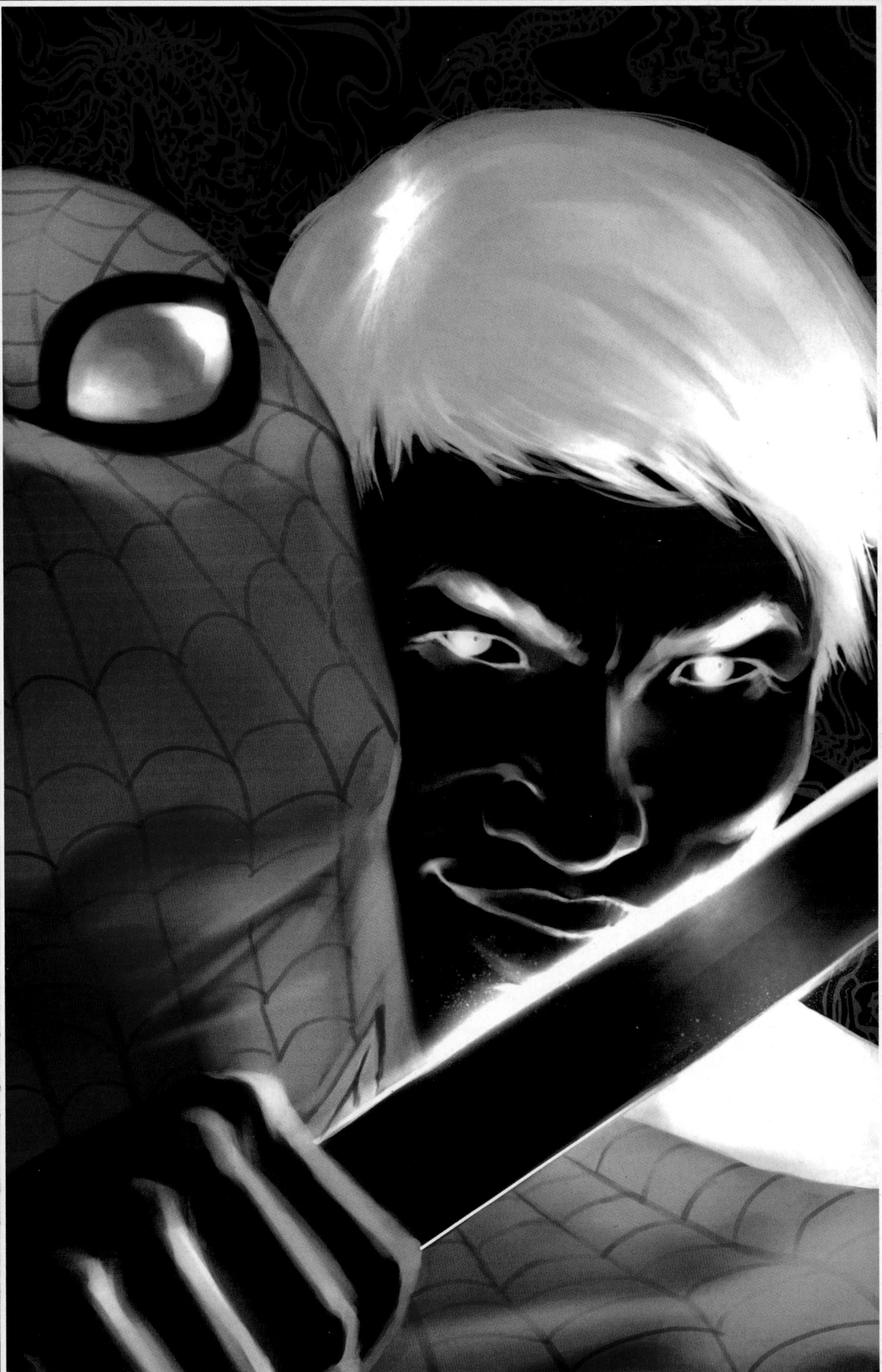

WEB OF SPIDER-MAN #10

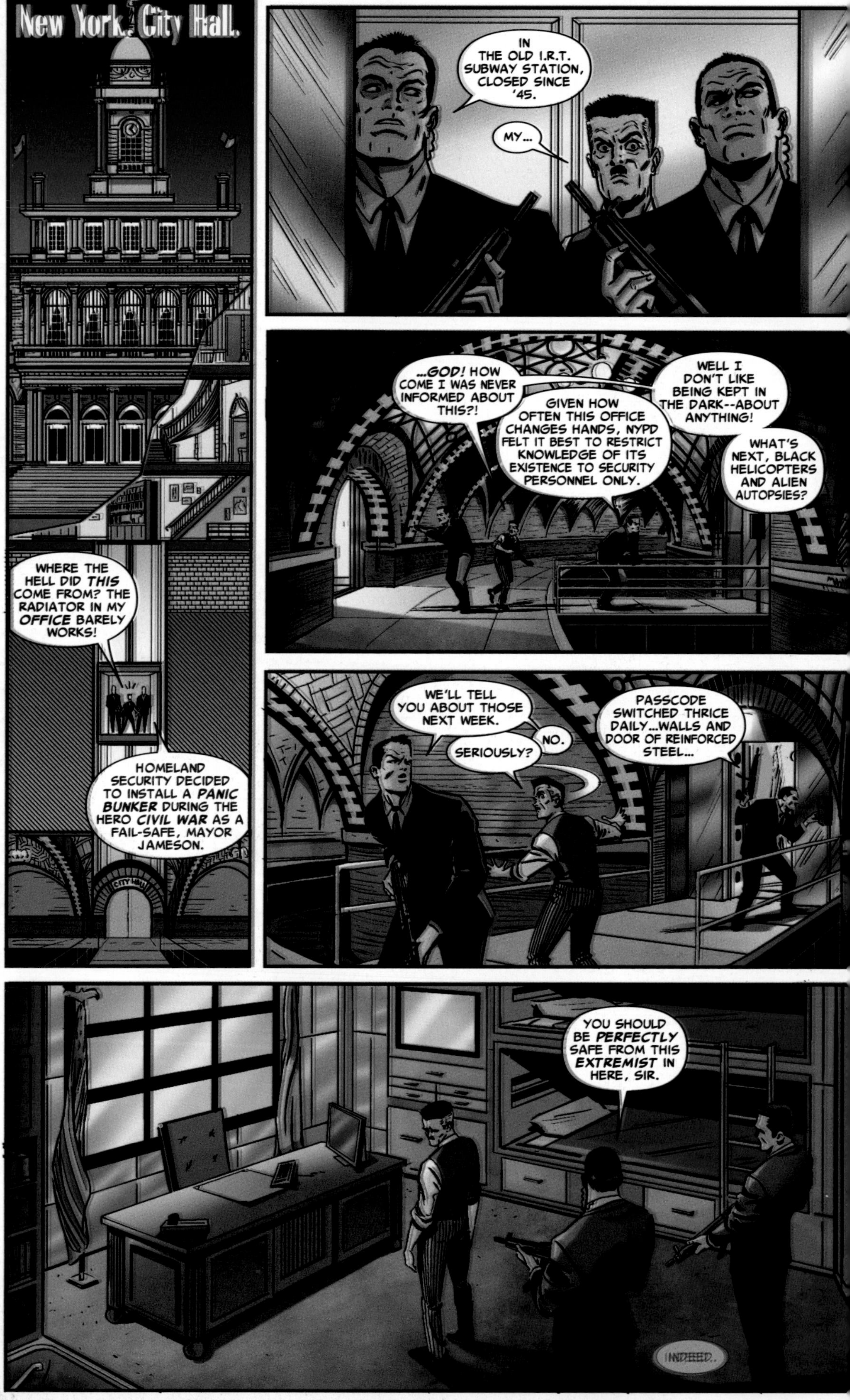
New York. City Hall.
IN THE OLD I.R.T. SUBWAY STATION, CLOSED SINCE '45.
MY...
WHERE THE HELL DID THIS COME FROM? THE RADIATOR IN MY OFFICE BARELY WORKS!
HOMELAND SECURITY DECIDED TO INSTALL A PANIC BUNKER DURING THE HERO CIVIL WAR AS A FAIL-SAFE, MAYOR JAMESON.
CITY HALL
...GOD! HOW COME I WAS NEVER INFORMED ABOUT THIS?!
GIVEN HOW OFTEN THIS OFFICE CHANGES HANDS, NYPD FELT IT BEST TO RESTRICT KNOWLEDGE OF ITS EXISTENCE TO SECURITY PERSONNEL ONLY.
WELL I DON'T LIKE BEING KEPT IN THE DARK--ABOUT ANYTHING!
WHAT'S NEXT, BLACK HELICOPTERS AND ALIEN AUTOPSIES?
WE'LL TELL YOU ABOUT THOSE NEXT WEEK.
SERIOUSLY?
NO.
PASSCODE SWITCHED THRICE DAILY...WALLS AND DOOR OF REINFORCED STEEL...
YOU SHOULD BE PERFECTLY SAFE FROM THIS EXTREMIST IN HERE, SIR.
INDEEED.

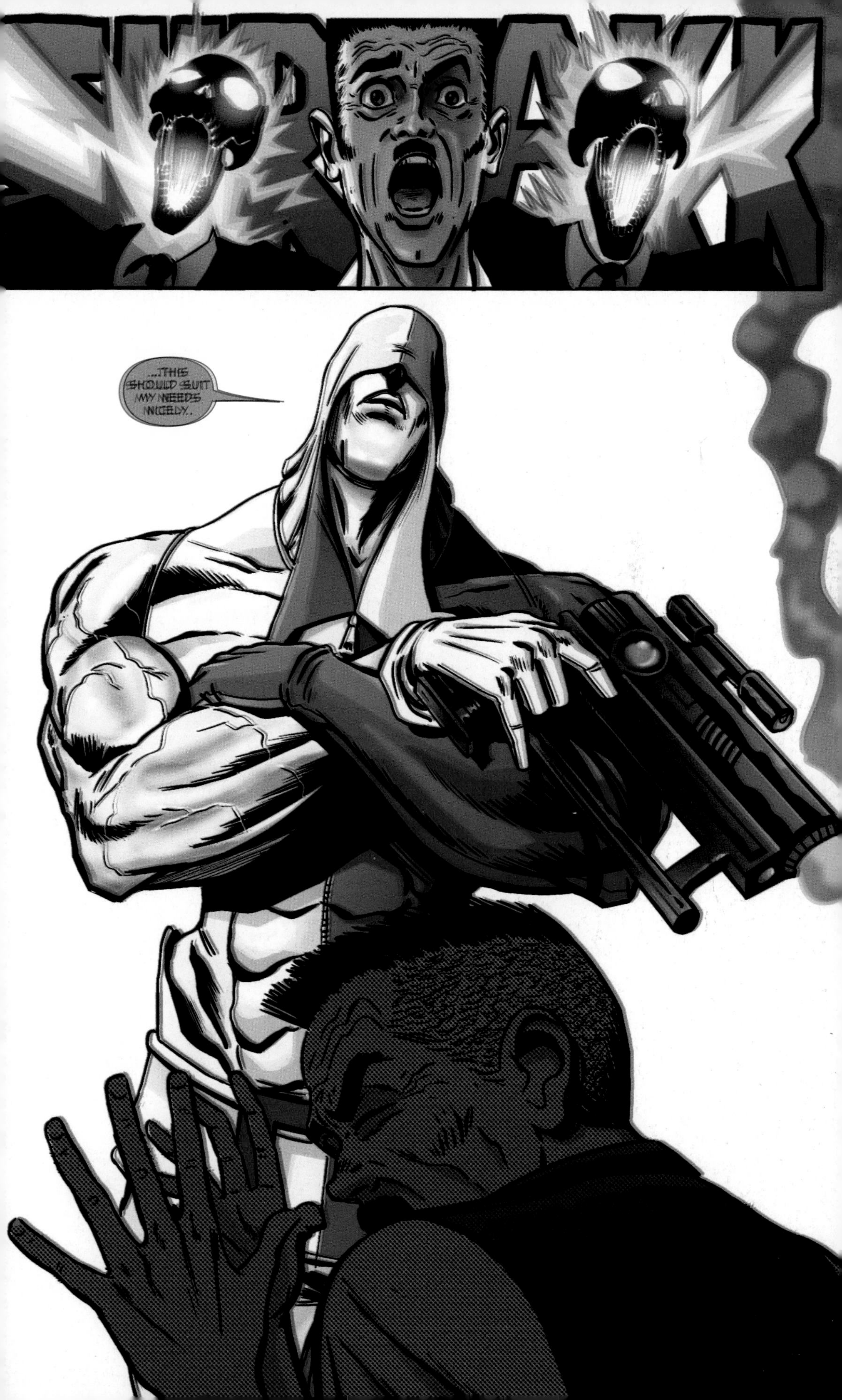
...THIS SHOULD SUIT MY NEEDS NICELY..

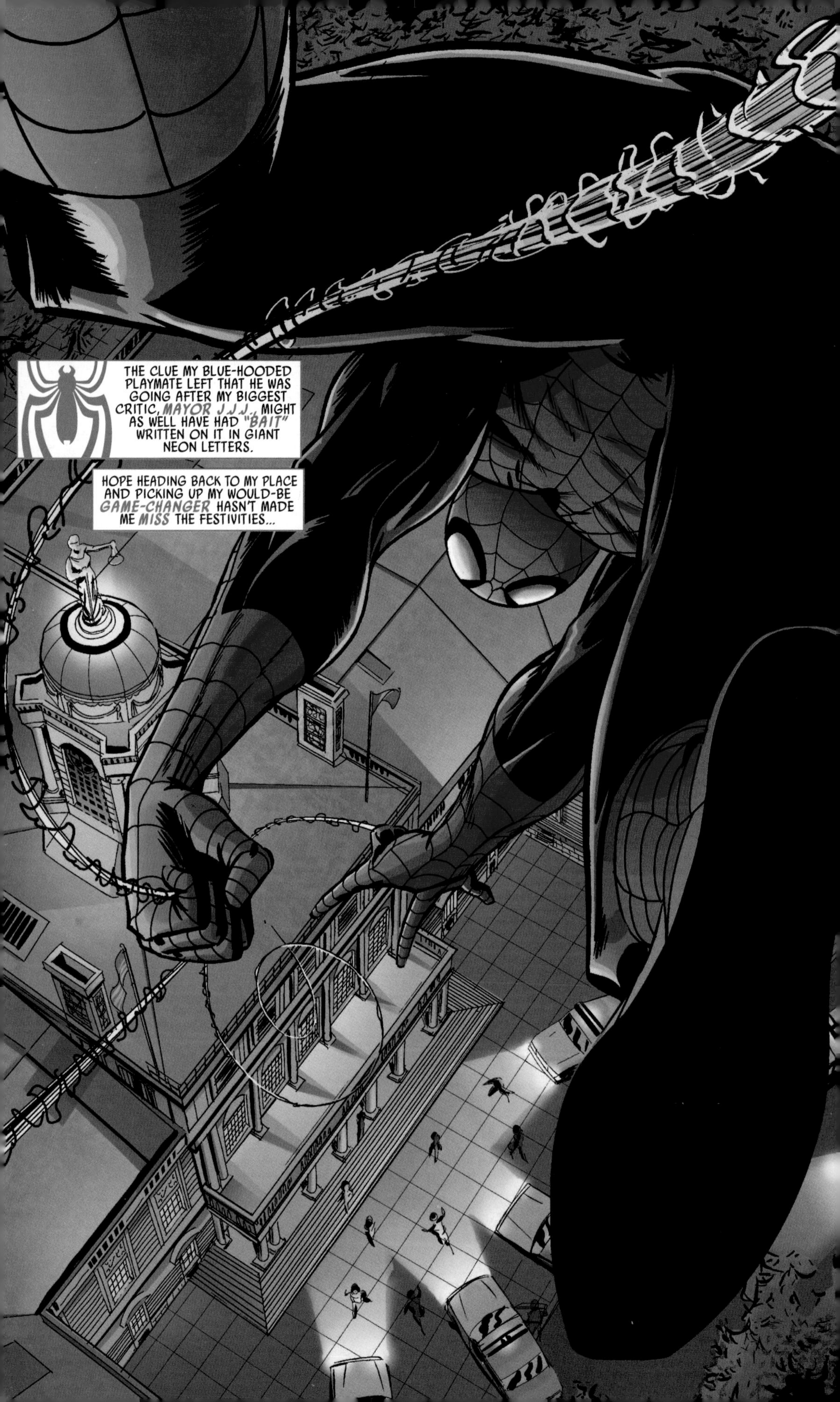
THE CLUE MY BLUE-HOODED PLAYMATE LEFT THAT HE WAS GOING AFTER MY BIGGEST CRITIC, MAYOR J.J.J., MIGHT AS WELL HAVE HAD "BAIT" WRITTEN ON IT IN GIANT NEON LETTERS.
HOPE HEADING BACK TO MY PLACE AND PICKING UP MY WOULD-BE GAME-CHANGER HASN'T MADE ME MISS THE FESTIVITIES...

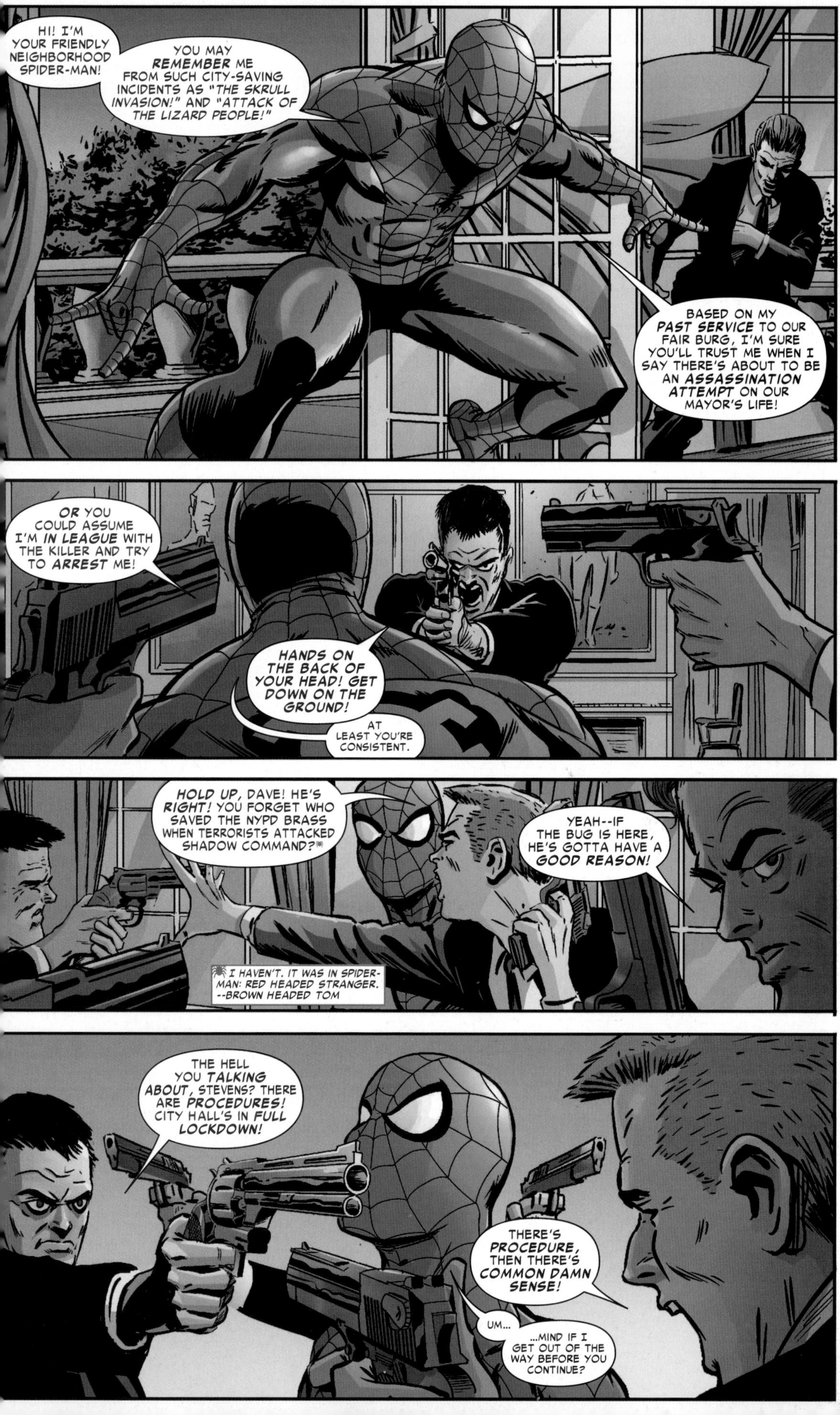
HI! I'M YOUR FRIENDLY NEIGHBORHOOD SPIDER-MAN!
YOU MAY REMEMBER ME FROM SUCH CITY-SAVING INCIDENTS AS "THE SKRULL INVASION!" AND "ATTACK OF THE LIZARD PEOPLE!"
BASED ON MY PAST SERVICE TO OUR FAIR BURG, I'M SURE YOU'LL TRUST ME WHEN I SAY THERE'S ABOUT TO BE AN ASSASSINATION ATTEMPT ON OUR MAYOR'S LIFE!
OR YOU COULD ASSUME I'M IN LEAGUE WITH THE KILLER AND TRY TO ARREST ME!
HANDS ON THE BACK OF YOUR HEAD! GET DOWN ON THE GROUND!
AT LEAST YOU'RE CONSISTENT.
HOLD UP, DAVE! HE'S RIGHT! YOU FORGET WHO SAVED THE NYPD BRASS WHEN TERRORISTS ATTACKED SHADOW COMMAND?
YEAH--IF THE BUG IS HERE, HE'S GOTTA HAVE A GOOD REASON!
I HAVEN'T. IT WAS IN SPIDER-MAN: RED HEADED STRANGER. --BROWN HEADED TOM
THE HELL YOU TALKING ABOUT, STEVENS? THERE ARE PROCEDURES! CITY HALL'S IN FULL LOCKDOWN!
THERE'S PROCEDURE, THEN THERE'S COMMON DAMN SENSE!
UM...
...MIND IF I GET OUT OF THE WAY BEFORE YOU CONTINUE?

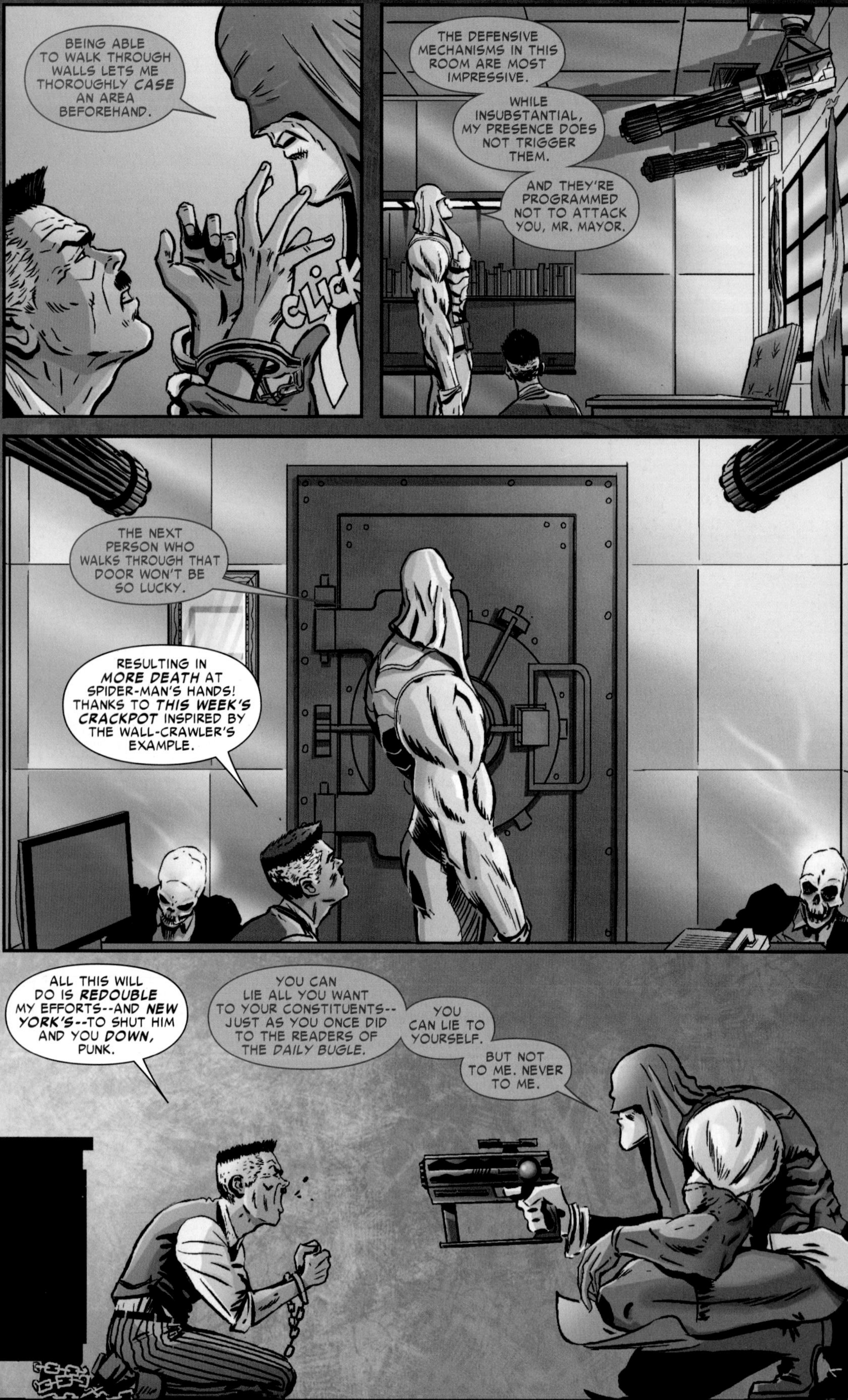
BEING ABLE TO WALK THROUGH WALLS LETS ME THOROUGHLY CASE AN AREA BEFOREHAND.
CLICK
THE DEFENSIVE MECHANISMS IN THIS ROOM ARE MOST IMPRESSIVE.
WHILE INSUBSTANTIAL, MY PRESENCE DOES NOT TRIGGER THEM.
AND THEY'RE PROGRAMMED NOT TO ATTACK YOU, MR. MAYOR.
THE NEXT PERSON WHO WALKS THROUGH THAT DOOR WON'T BE SO LUCKY.
RESULTING IN MORE DEATH AT SPIDER-MAN'S HANDS! THANKS TO THIS WEEK'S CRACKPOT INSPIRED BY THE WALL-CRAWLER'S EXAMPLE.
ALL THIS WILL DO IS REDOUBLE MY EFFORTS--AND NEW YORK'S--TO SHUT HIM AND YOU DOWN, PUNK.
YOU CAN LIE ALL YOU WANT TO YOUR CONSTITUENTS-- JUST AS YOU ONCE DID TO THE READERS OF THE DAILY BUGLE.
YOU CAN LIE TO YOURSELF.
BUT NOT TO ME. NEVER TO ME.

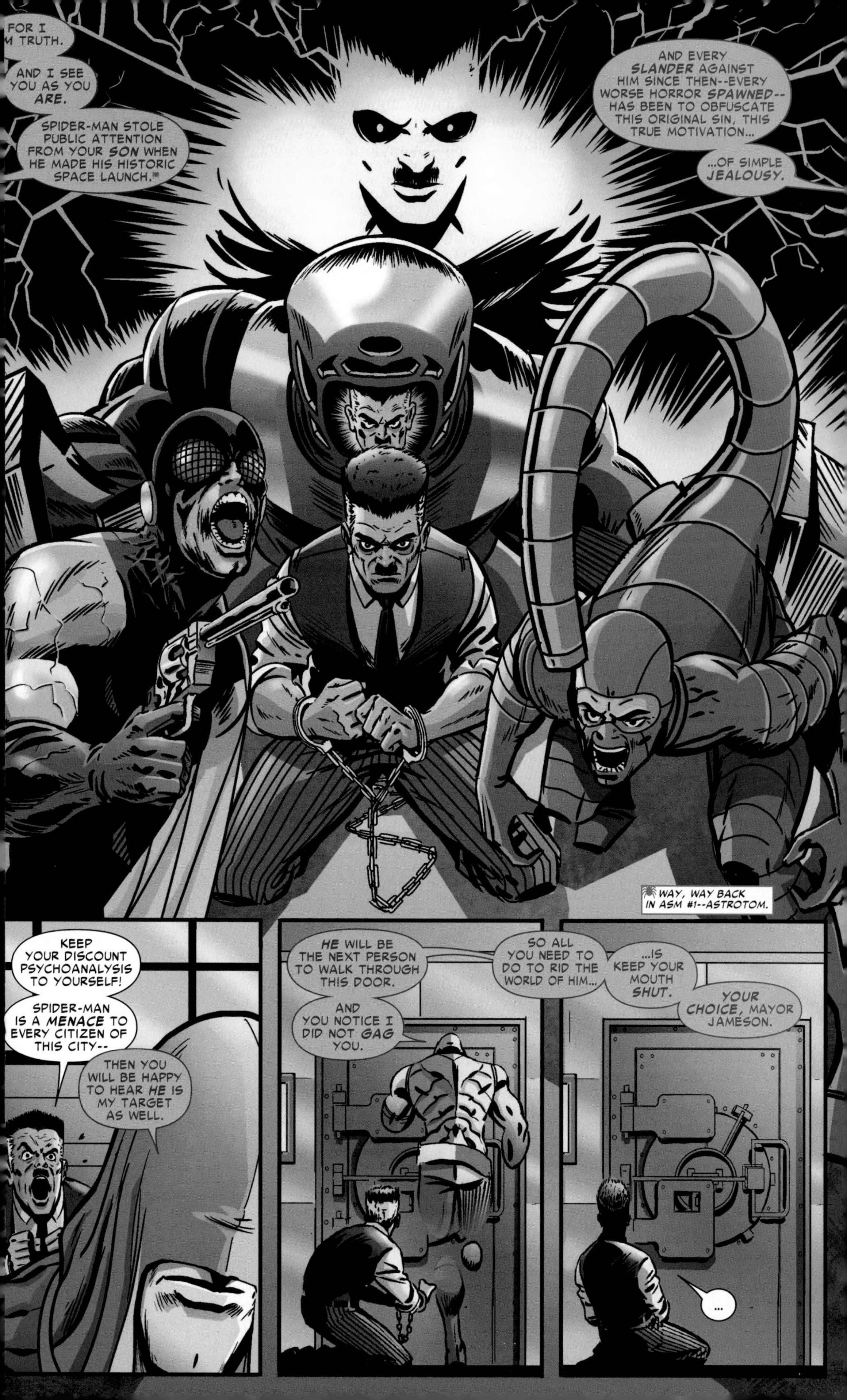

FOR I
M TRUTH.
AND I SEE YOU AS YOU ARE.
SPIDER-MAN STOLE PUBLIC ATTENTION FROM YOUR SON WHEN HE MADE HIS HISTORIC SPACE LAUNCH.*
AND EVERY SLANDER AGAINST HIM SINCE THEN--EVERY WORSE HORROR SPAWNED--HAS BEEN TO OBFUSCATE THIS ORIGINAL SIN, THIS TRUE MOTIVATION...
...OF SIMPLE JEALOUSY.
*WAY, WAY BACK IN ASM #1--ASTROTOM.
KEEP YOUR DISCOUNT PSYCHOANALYSIS TO YOURSELF!
SPIDER-MAN IS A MENACE TO EVERY CITIZEN OF THIS CITY--
THEN YOU WILL BE HAPPY TO HEAR HE IS MY TARGET AS WELL.
HE WILL BE THE NEXT PERSON TO WALK THROUGH THIS DOOR.
AND YOU NOTICE I DID NOT GAG YOU.
SO ALL YOU NEED TO DO TO RID THE WORLD OF HIM...
...IS KEEP YOUR MOUTH SHUT.
YOUR CHOICE, MAYOR JAMESON.
...

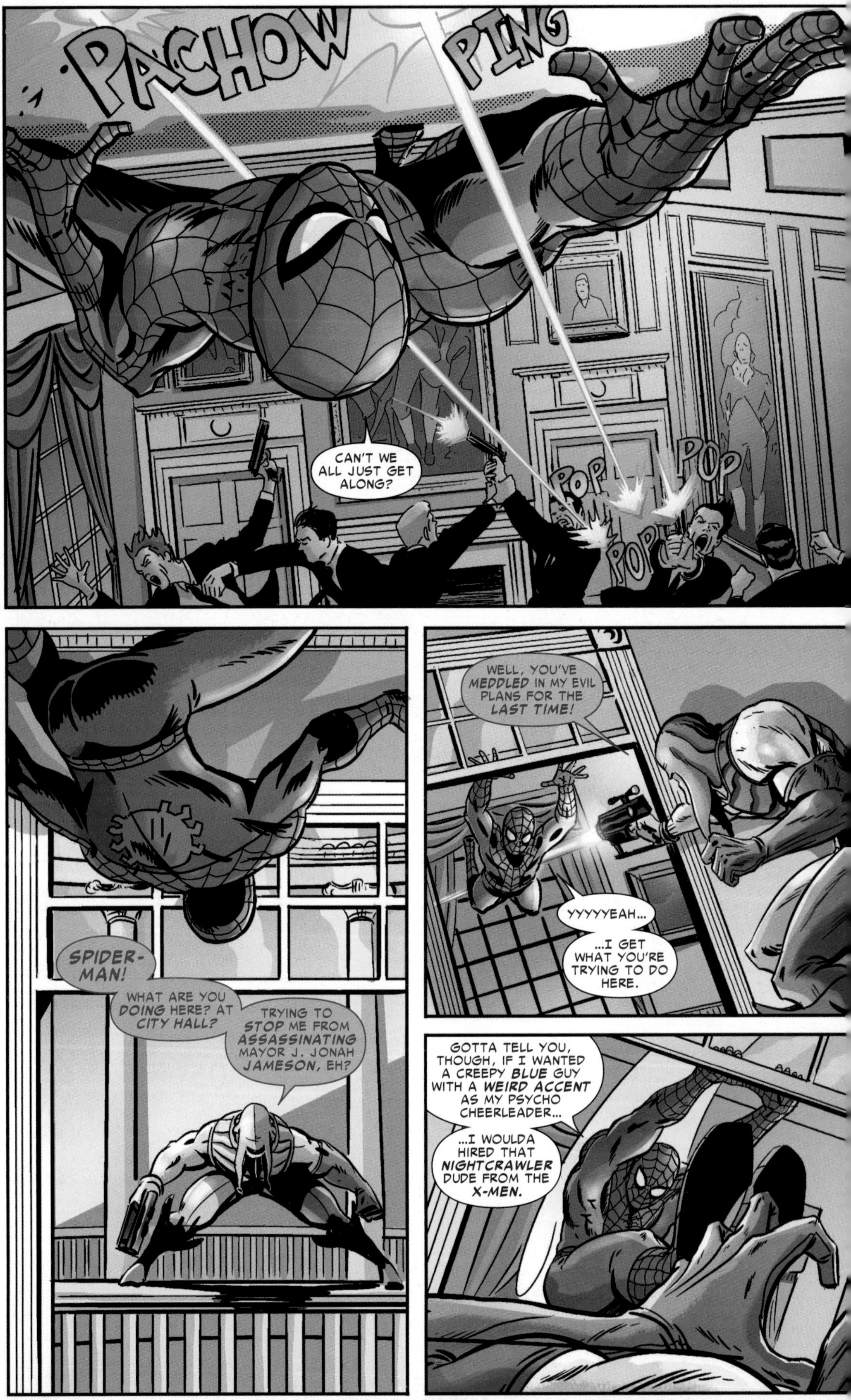
PACHOW
PING
CAN'T WE ALL JUST GET ALONG?
POP
POP
POP
SPIDER-MAN!
WHAT ARE YOU DOING HERE? AT CITY HALL?
TRYING TO STOP ME FROM ASSASSINATING MAYOR J. JONAH JAMESON, EH?
WELL, YOU'VE MEDDLED IN MY EVIL PLANS FOR THE LAST TIME!
YYYYYEAH...
...I GET WHAT YOU'RE TRYING TO DO HERE.
GOTTA TELL YOU, THOUGH, IF I WANTED A CREEPY BLUE GUY WITH A WEIRD ACCENT AS MY PSYCHO CHEERLEADER...
...I WOULDA HIRED THAT NIGHTCRAWLER DUDE FROM THE X-MEN.

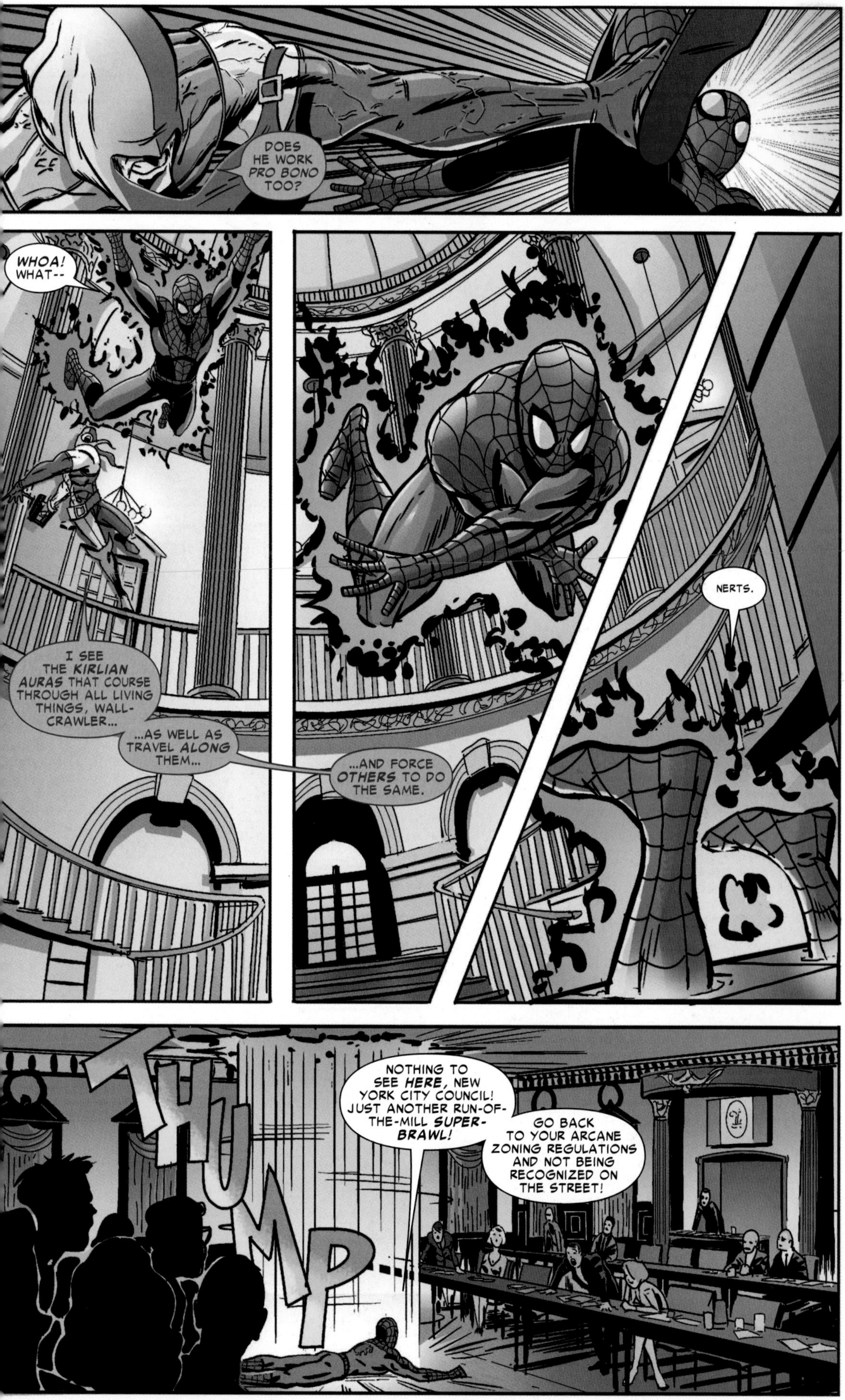

DOES HE WORK *PRO BONO* TOO?
WHOA! WHAT--
I SEE THE *KIRLIAN AURAS* THAT COURSE THROUGH ALL LIVING THINGS, WALL-CRAWLER...
...AS WELL AS TRAVEL *ALONG* THEM...
...AND FORCE *OTHERS* TO DO THE SAME.
NERTS.
THUMP...
NOTHING TO SEE *HERE*, NEW YORK CITY COUNCIL! JUST ANOTHER RUN-OF-THE-MILL *SUPER-BRAWL!*
GO BACK TO YOUR ARCANE ZONING REGULATIONS AND NOT BEING RECOGNIZED ON THE STREET!

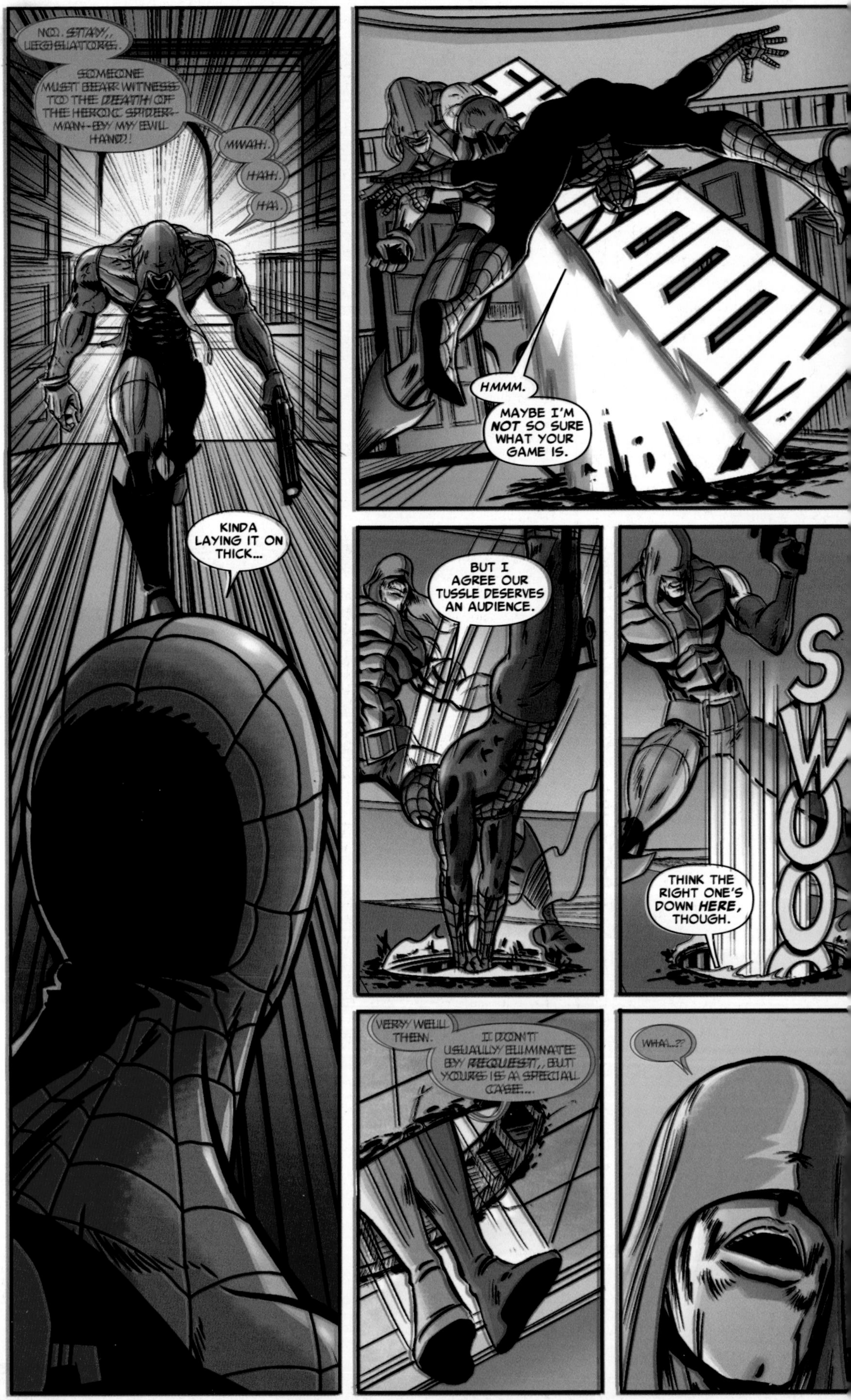
NO. STAY, LEGISLATORS.
SOMEONE MUST BEAR WITNESS TO THE DEATH OF THE HEROIC SPIDER-MAN--BY MY EVIL HAND!
MWAH.
HAH.
HA.
KINDA LAYING IT ON THICK...
HMMM.
MAYBE I'M NOT SO SURE WHAT YOUR GAME IS.
BUT I AGREE OUR TUSSLE DESERVES AN AUDIENCE.
SWOO
THINK THE RIGHT ONE'S DOWN HERE, THOUGH.
VERY WELL, THEN.
I DON'T USUALLY ELIMINATE BY REQUEST, BUT YOURS IS A SPECIAL CASE...
WHA...??

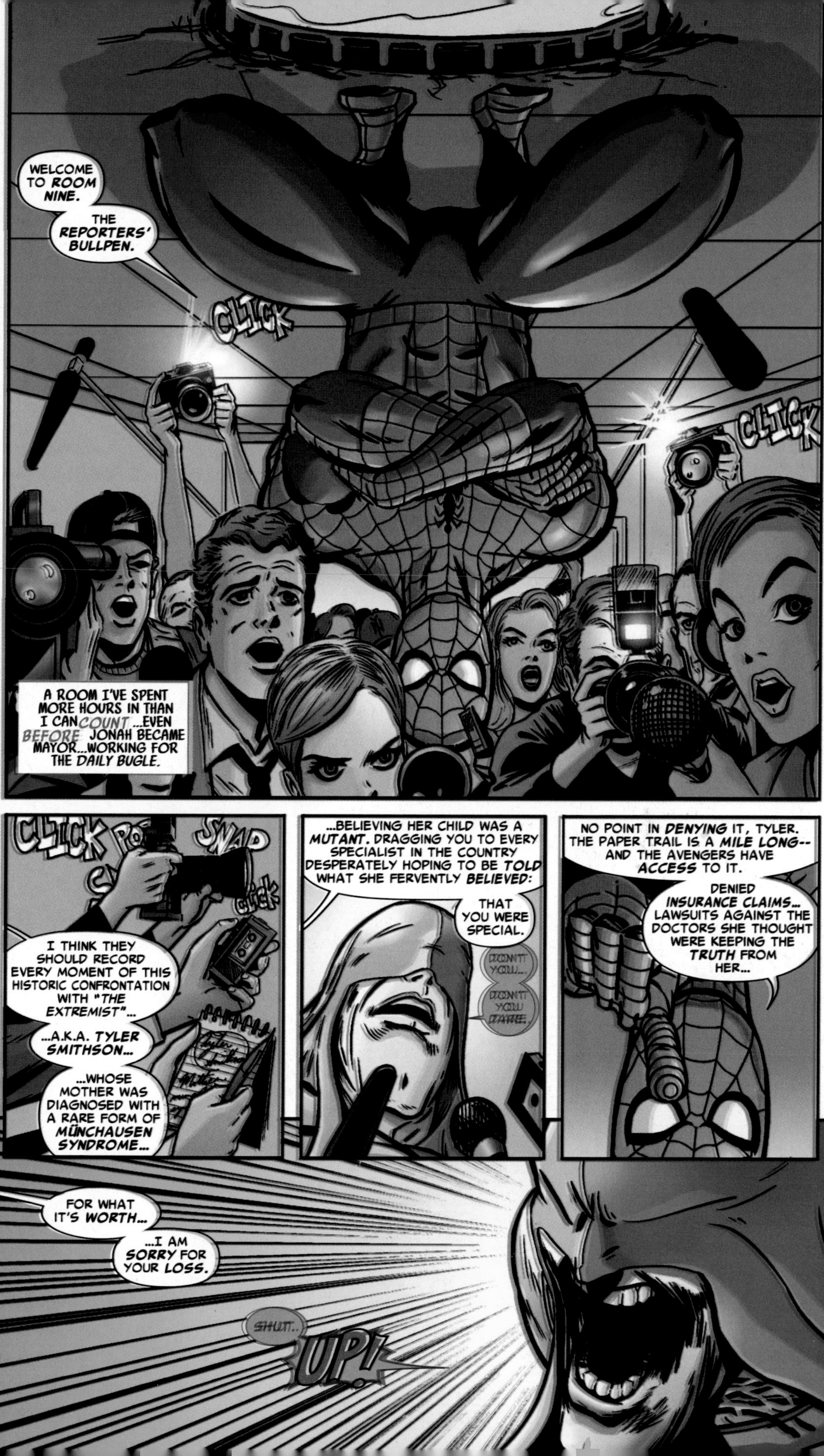
WELCOME TO ROOM NINE.
THE REPORTERS' BULLPEN.
CLICK
CLICK
A ROOM I'VE SPENT MORE HOURS IN THAN I CAN COUNT ...EVEN BEFORE JONAH BECAME MAYOR...WORKING FOR THE DAILY BUGLE.
CLICK
SNAP
CLICK
I THINK THEY SHOULD RECORD EVERY MOMENT OF THIS HISTORIC CONFRONTATION WITH "THE EXTREMIST"...
...A.K.A. TYLER SMITHSON...
...WHOSE MOTHER WAS DIAGNOSED WITH A RARE FORM OF MÜNCHAUSEN SYNDROME...
...BELIEVING HER CHILD WAS A MUTANT. DRAGGING YOU TO EVERY SPECIALIST IN THE COUNTRY DESPERATELY HOPING TO BE TOLD WHAT SHE FERVENTLY BELIEVED:
THAT YOU WERE SPECIAL.
DON'T YOU...
DON'T YOU DARE.
NO POINT IN DENYING IT, TYLER. THE PAPER TRAIL IS A MILE LONG-- AND THE AVENGERS HAVE ACCESS TO IT.
DENIED INSURANCE CLAIMS... LAWSUITS AGAINST THE DOCTORS SHE THOUGHT WERE KEEPING THE TRUTH FROM HER...
FOR WHAT IT'S WORTH...
...I AM SORRY FOR YOUR LOSS.
SHUT...
UP!

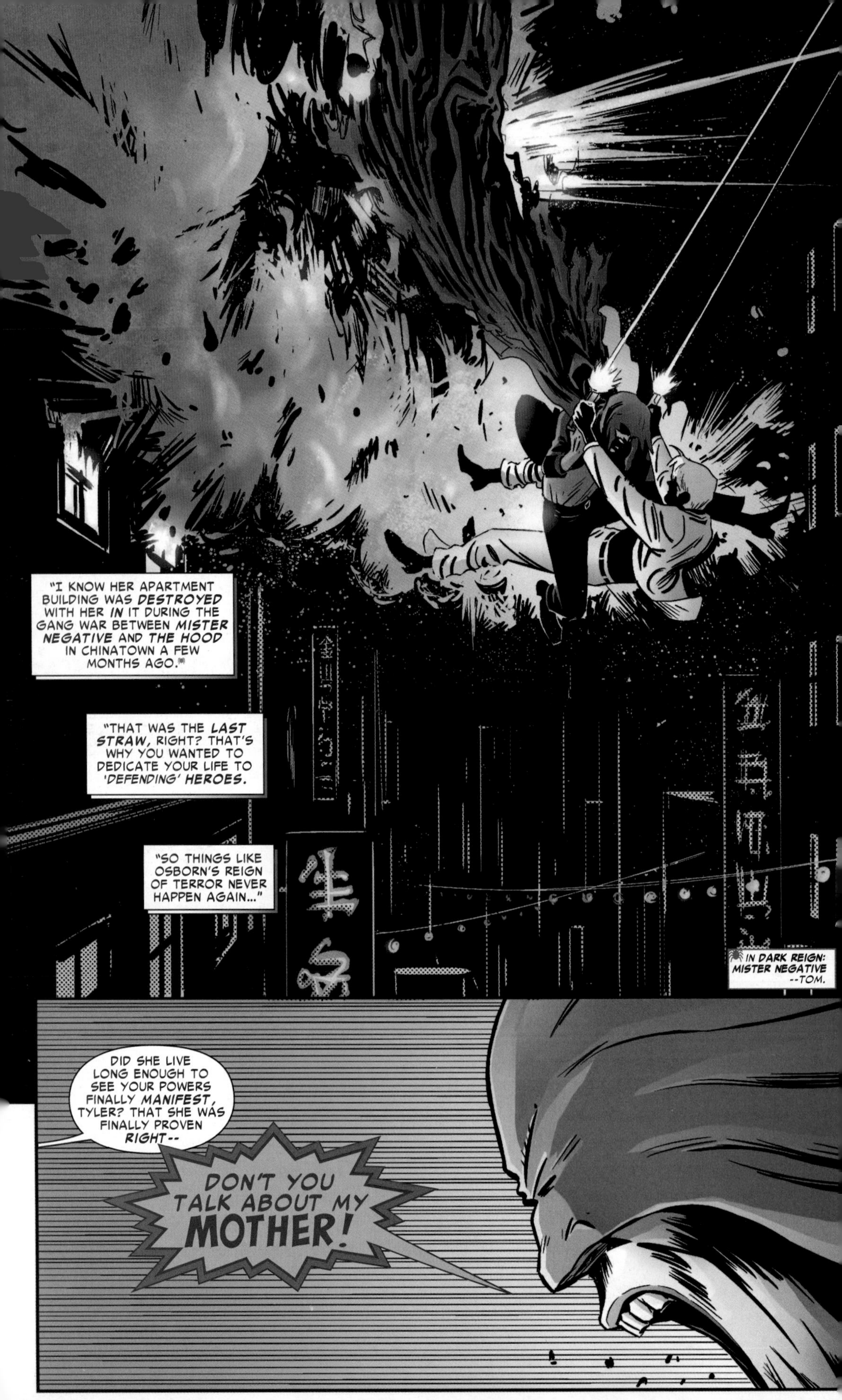
"I KNOW HER APARTMENT BUILDING WAS DESTROYED WITH HER IN IT DURING THE GANG WAR BETWEEN MISTER NEGATIVE AND THE HOOD IN CHINATOWN A FEW MONTHS AGO.*
"THAT WAS THE LAST STRAW, RIGHT? THAT'S WHY YOU WANTED TO DEDICATE YOUR LIFE TO 'DEFENDING' HEROES.
"SO THINGS LIKE OSBORN'S REIGN OF TERROR NEVER HAPPEN AGAIN..."
*IN DARK REIGN: MISTER NEGATIVE --TOM.
DID SHE LIVE LONG ENOUGH TO SEE YOUR POWERS FINALLY MANIFEST, TYLER? THAT SHE WAS FINALLY PROVEN RIGHT--
DON'T YOU TALK ABOUT MY MOTHER!

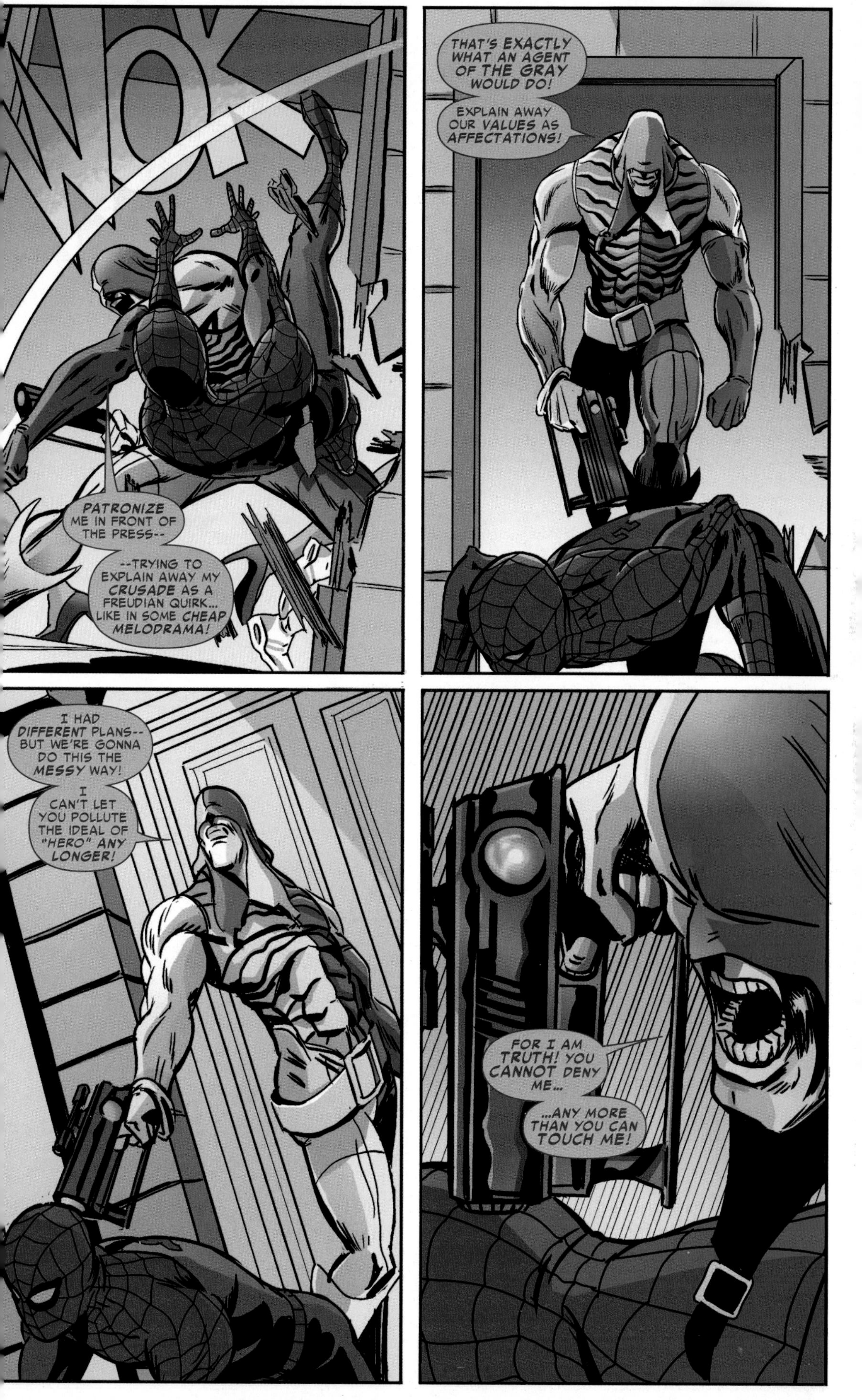

PATRONIZE ME IN FRONT OF THE PRESS--
--TRYING TO EXPLAIN AWAY MY CRUSADE AS A FREUDIAN QUIRK... LIKE IN SOME CHEAP MELODRAMA!
THAT'S EXACTLY WHAT AN AGENT OF THE GRAY WOULD DO!
EXPLAIN AWAY OUR VALUES AS AFFECTATIONS!
I HAD DIFFERENT PLANS-- BUT WE'RE GONNA DO THIS THE MESSY WAY!
I CAN'T LET YOU POLLUTE THE IDEAL OF "HERO" ANY LONGER!
FOR I AM TRUTH! YOU CANNOT DENY ME...
...ANY MORE THAN YOU CAN TOUCH ME!

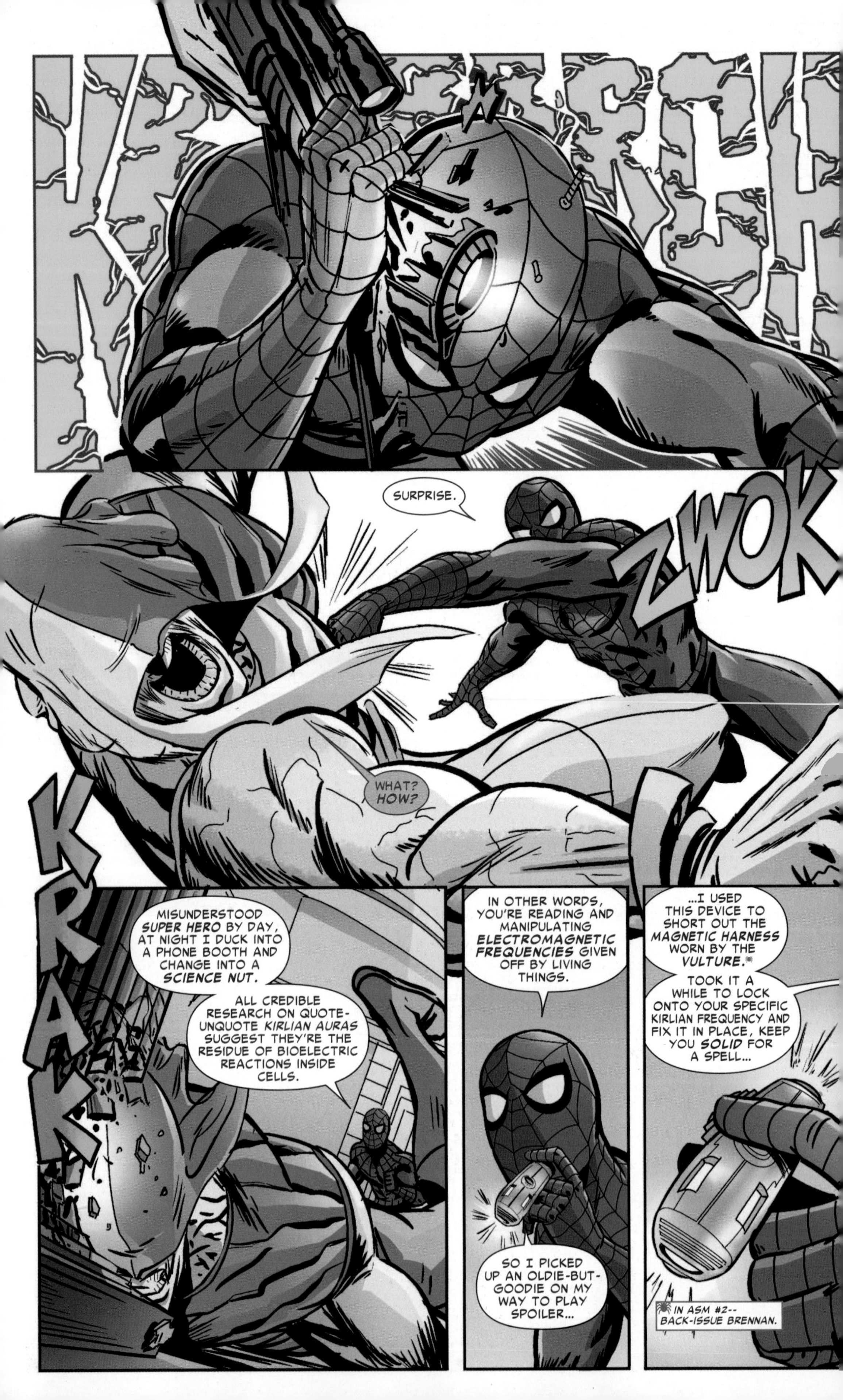
KRRRRSSSSCHHH
SURPRISE.
ZWOK
WHAT? HOW?
KRAKA
MISUNDERSTOOD SUPER HERO BY DAY, AT NIGHT I DUCK INTO A PHONE BOOTH AND CHANGE INTO A SCIENCE NUT.
ALL CREDIBLE RESEARCH ON QUOTE-UNQUOTE KIRLIAN AURAS SUGGEST THEY'RE THE RESIDUE OF BIOELECTRIC REACTIONS INSIDE CELLS.
IN OTHER WORDS, YOU'RE READING AND MANIPULATING ELECTROMAGNETIC FREQUENCIES GIVEN OFF BY LIVING THINGS.
SO I PICKED UP AN OLDIE-BUT-GOODIE ON MY WAY TO PLAY SPOILER...
...I USED THIS DEVICE TO SHORT OUT THE MAGNETIC HARNESS WORN BY THE VULTURE.
TOOK IT A WHILE TO LOCK ONTO YOUR SPECIFIC KIRLIAN FREQUENCY AND FIX IT IN PLACE, KEEP YOU SOLID FOR A SPELL...
IN ASM #2-- BACK-ISSUE BRENNAN.

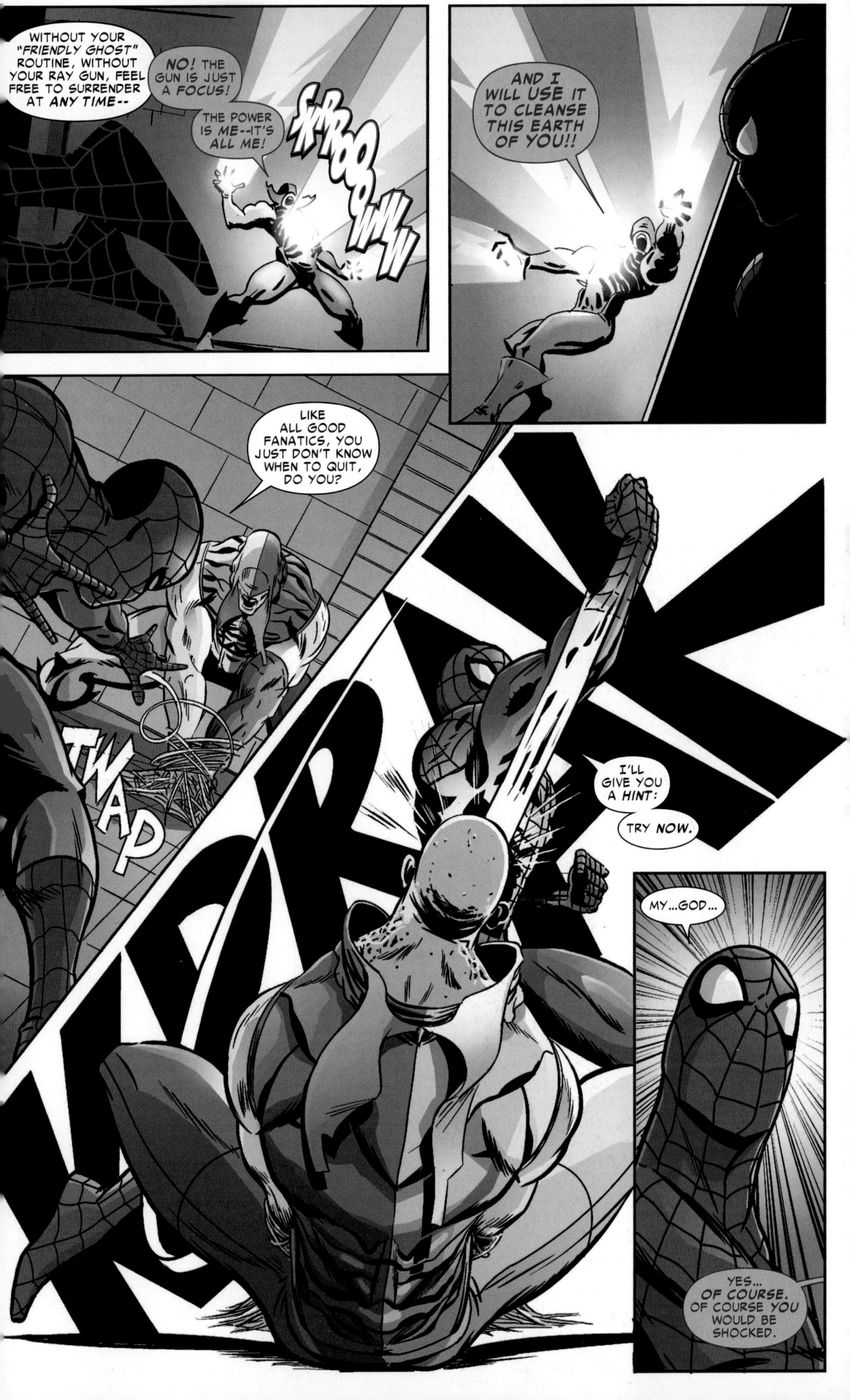

WITHOUT YOUR "FRIENDLY GHOST" ROUTINE, WITHOUT YOUR RAY GUN, FEEL FREE TO SURRENDER AT ANY TIME--
NO! THE GUN IS JUST A FOCUS!
THE POWER IS ME--IT'S ALL ME!
SKRROOOWWW
AND I WILL USE IT TO CLEANSE THIS EARTH OF YOU!!
LIKE ALL GOOD FANATICS, YOU JUST DON'T KNOW WHEN TO QUIT, DO YOU?
TWAP
I'LL GIVE YOU A HINT:
TRY NOW.
MY...GOD...
YES... OF COURSE. OF COURSE YOU WOULD BE SHOCKED.

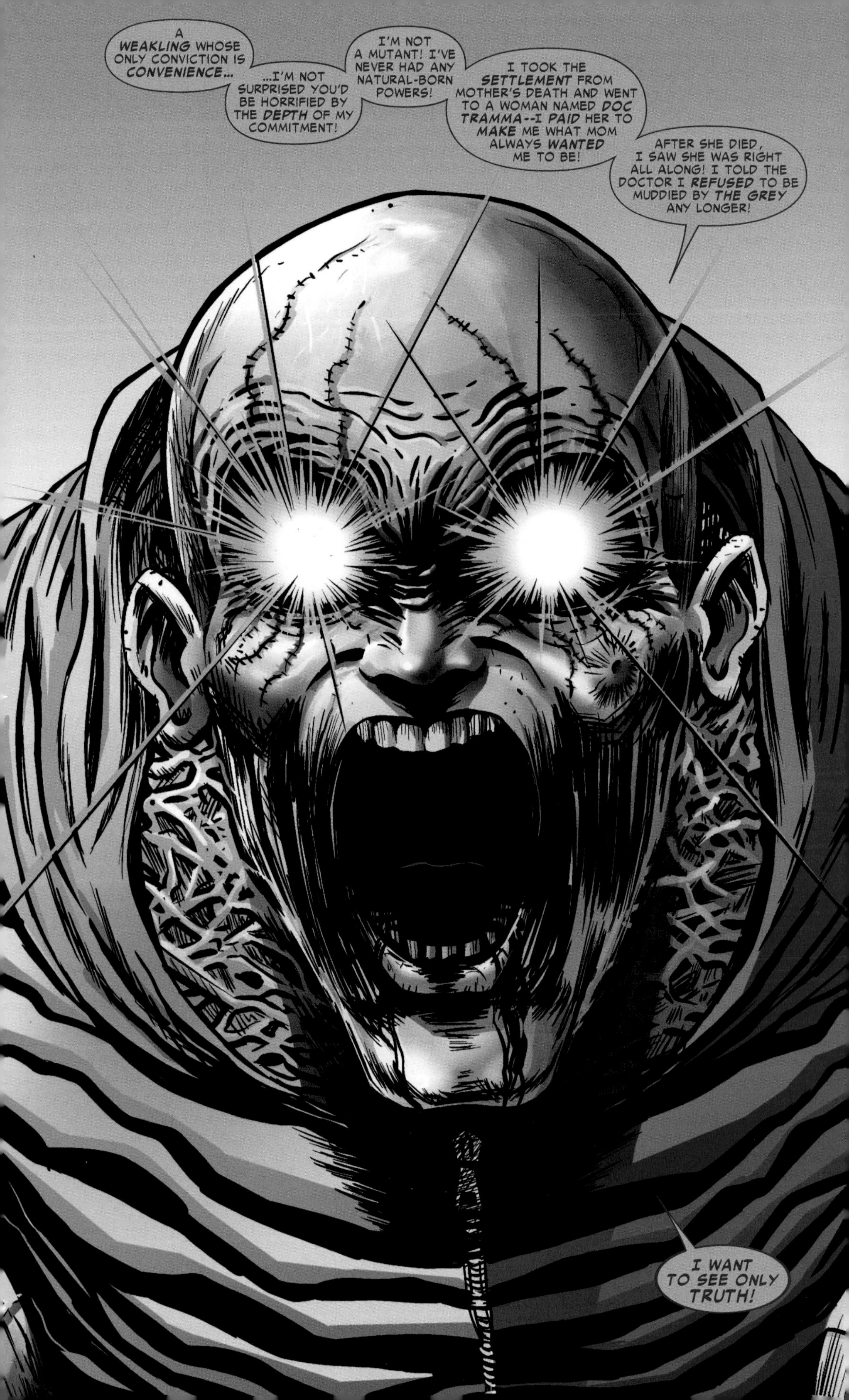
A WEAKLING WHOSE ONLY CONVICTION IS CONVENIENCE...
...I'M NOT SURPRISED YOU'D BE HORRIFIED BY THE DEPTH OF MY COMMITMENT!
I'M NOT A MUTANT! I'VE NEVER HAD ANY NATURAL-BORN POWERS!
I TOOK THE SETTLEMENT FROM MOTHER'S DEATH AND WENT TO A WOMAN NAMED DOC TRAMMA--I PAID HER TO MAKE ME WHAT MOM ALWAYS WANTED ME TO BE!
AFTER SHE DIED, I SAW SHE WAS RIGHT ALL ALONG! I TOLD THE DOCTOR I REFUSED TO BE MUDDIED BY THE GREY ANY LONGER!
I WANT TO SEE ONLY TRUTH!

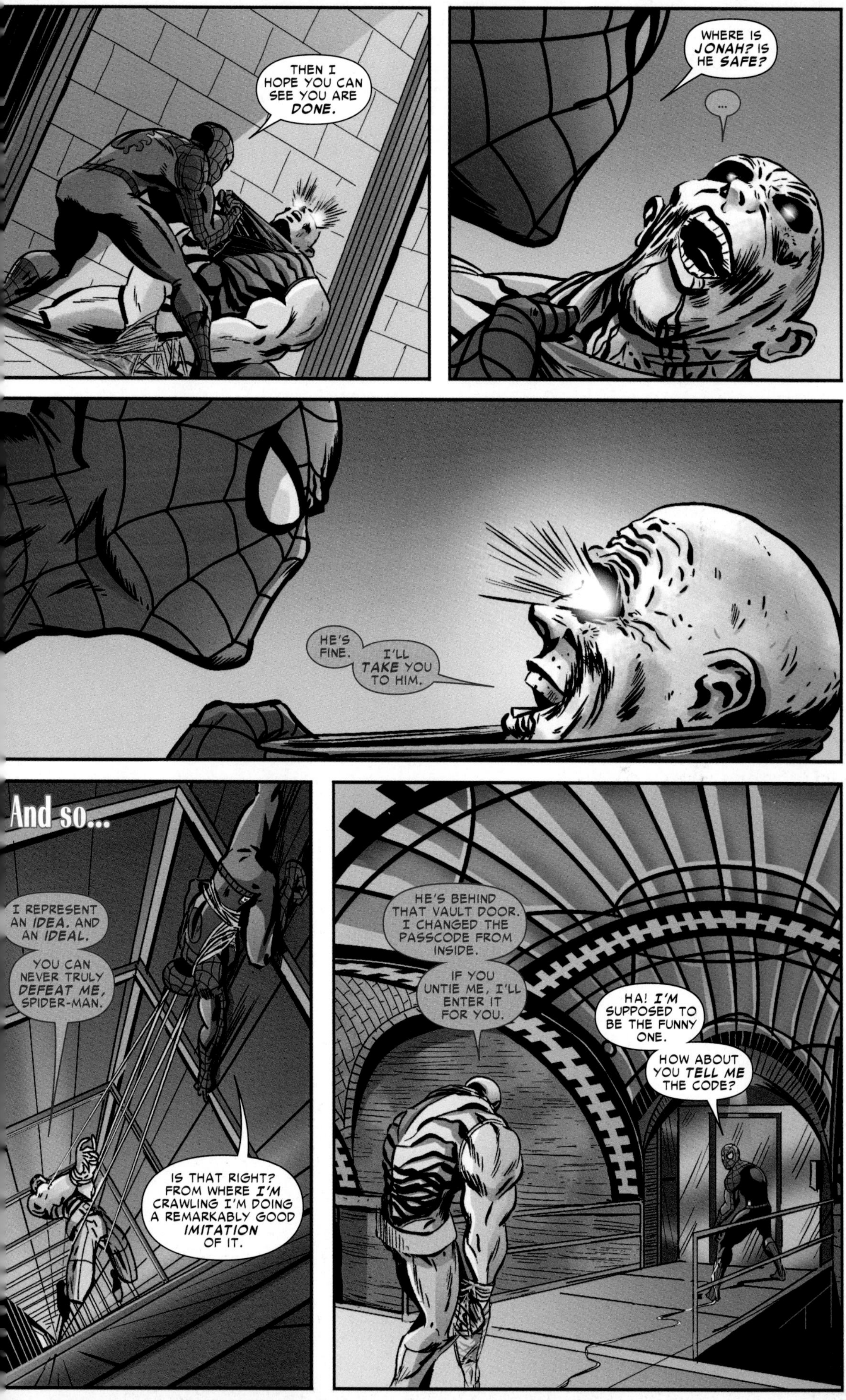
THEN I HOPE YOU CAN SEE YOU ARE DONE.
WHERE IS JONAH? IS HE SAFE?
...
HE'S FINE.
I'LL TAKE YOU TO HIM.
And so...
I REPRESENT AN IDEA. AND AN IDEAL.
YOU CAN NEVER TRULY DEFEAT ME, SPIDER-MAN.
IS THAT RIGHT? FROM WHERE I'M CRAWLING I'M DOING A REMARKABLY GOOD IMITATION OF IT.
HE'S BEHIND THAT VAULT DOOR. I CHANGED THE PASSCODE FROM INSIDE.
IF YOU UNTIE ME, I'LL ENTER IT FOR YOU.
HA! I'M SUPPOSED TO BE THE FUNNY ONE.
HOW ABOUT YOU TELL ME THE CODE?

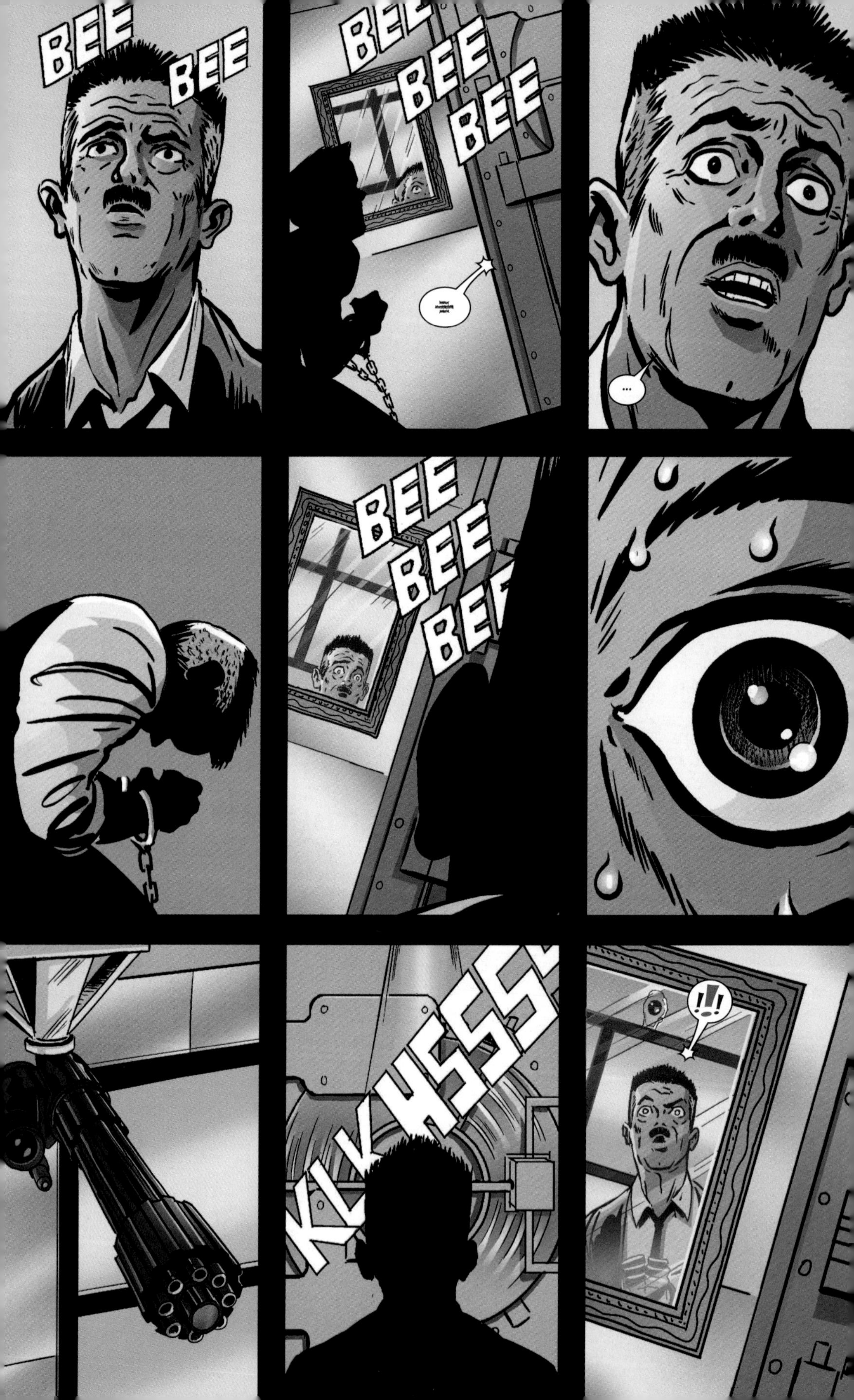
BEE
BEE
BEE
BEE
BEE
...
BEE
BEE
KLIK
HSSSS
!!

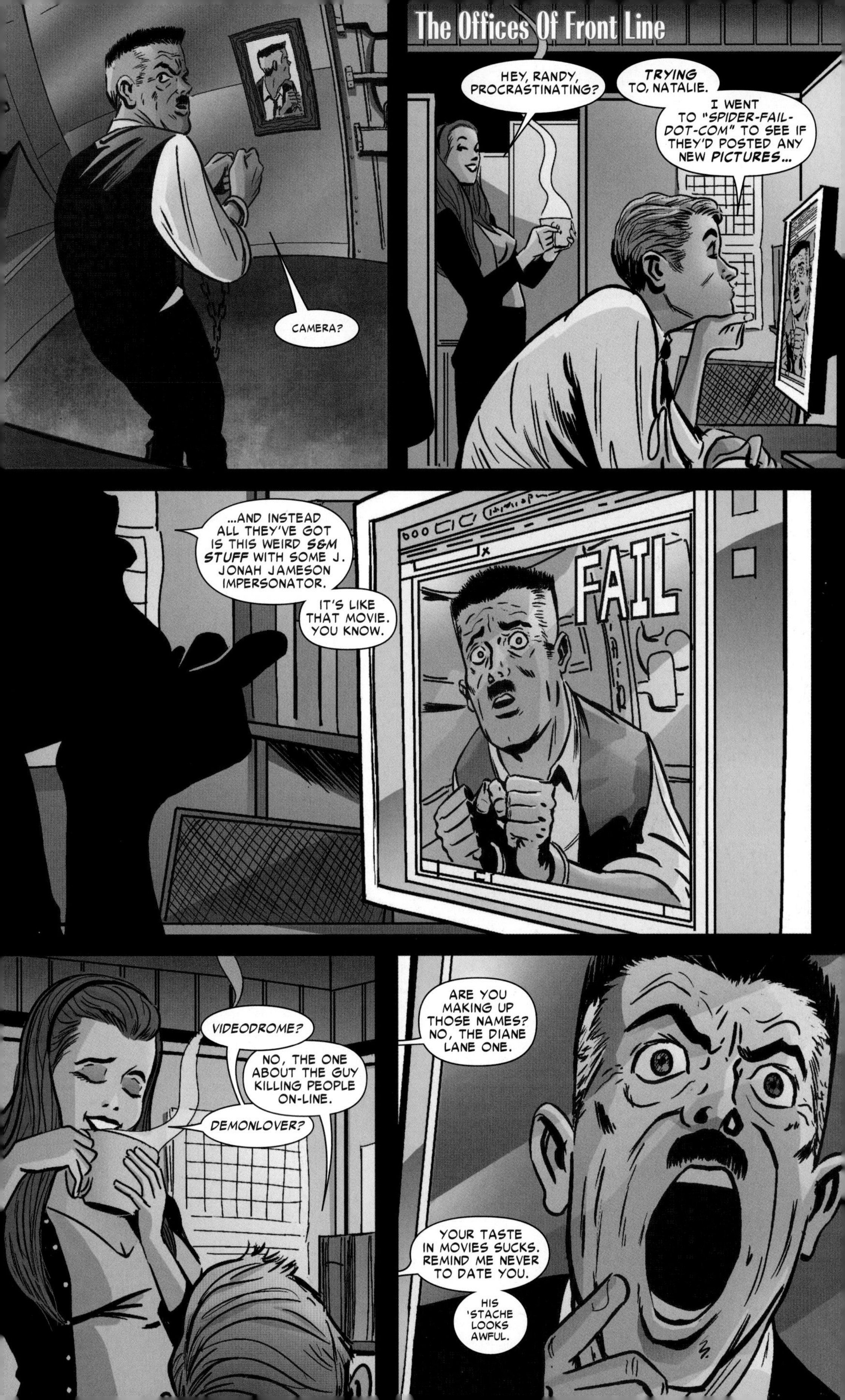
CAMERA?
The Offices Of Front Line
HEY, RANDY, PROCRASTINATING?
TRYING TO, NATALIE.
I WENT TO "SPIDER-FAIL-DOT-COM" TO SEE IF THEY'D POSTED ANY NEW PICTURES...
...AND INSTEAD ALL THEY'VE GOT IS THIS WEIRD S&M STUFF WITH SOME J. JONAH JAMESON IMPERSONATOR.
IT'S LIKE THAT MOVIE. YOU KNOW.
FAIL
VIDEODROME?
NO, THE ONE ABOUT THE GUY KILLING PEOPLE ON-LINE.
DEMONLOVER?
ARE YOU MAKING UP THOSE NAMES? NO, THE DIANE LANE ONE.
YOUR TASTE IN MOVIES SUCKS. REMIND ME NEVER TO DATE YOU.
HIS 'STACHE LOOKS AWFUL.

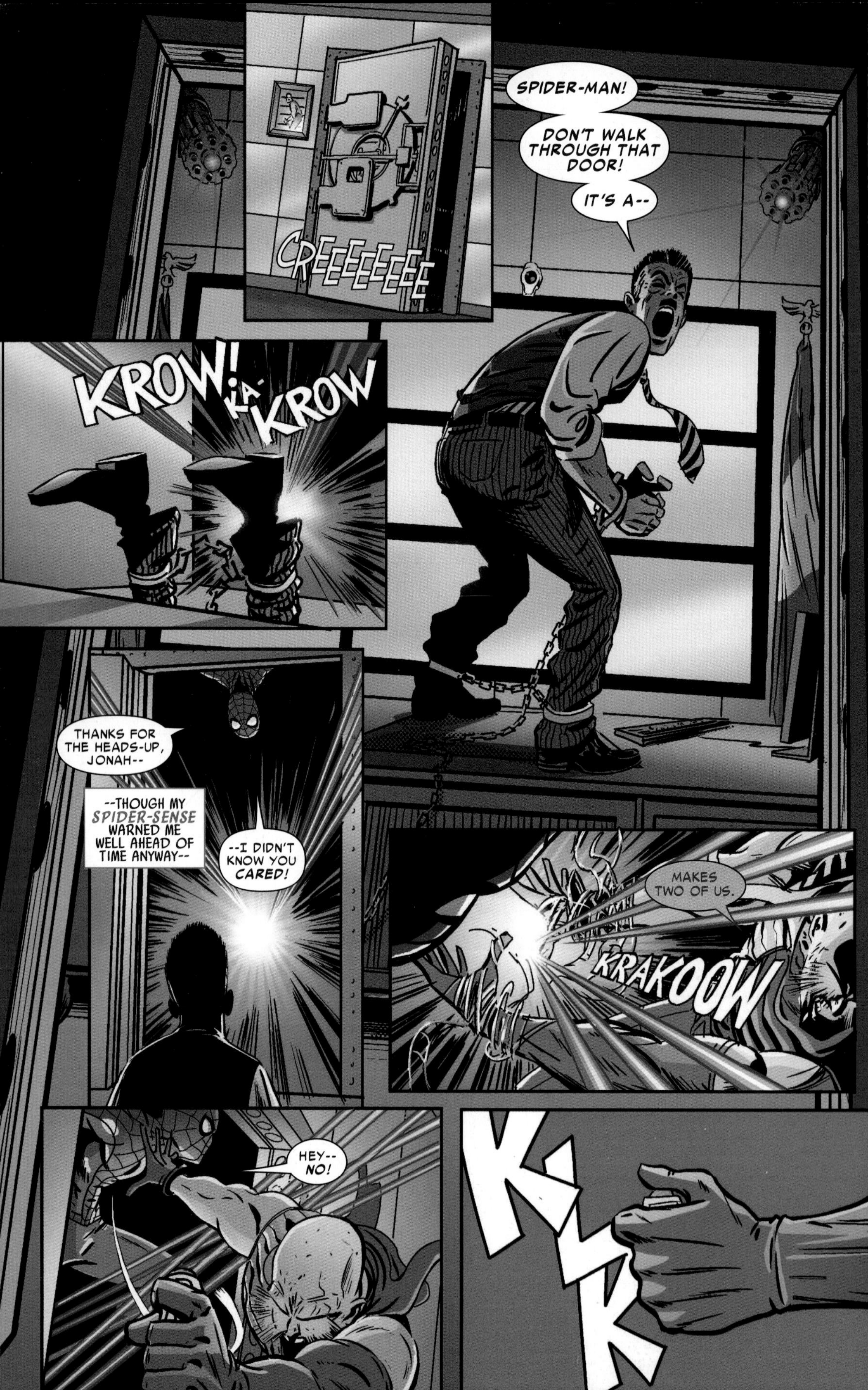
CREEEEEEEEE
SPIDER-MAN!
DON'T WALK THROUGH THAT DOOR!
IT'S A--
KROW! KA-KROW
THANKS FOR THE HEADS-UP, JONAH--
--THOUGH MY SPIDER-SENSE WARNED ME WELL AHEAD OF TIME ANYWAY--
--I DIDN'T KNOW YOU CARED!
MAKES TWO OF US.
KRAKOOW
HEY-- NO!
KLIK

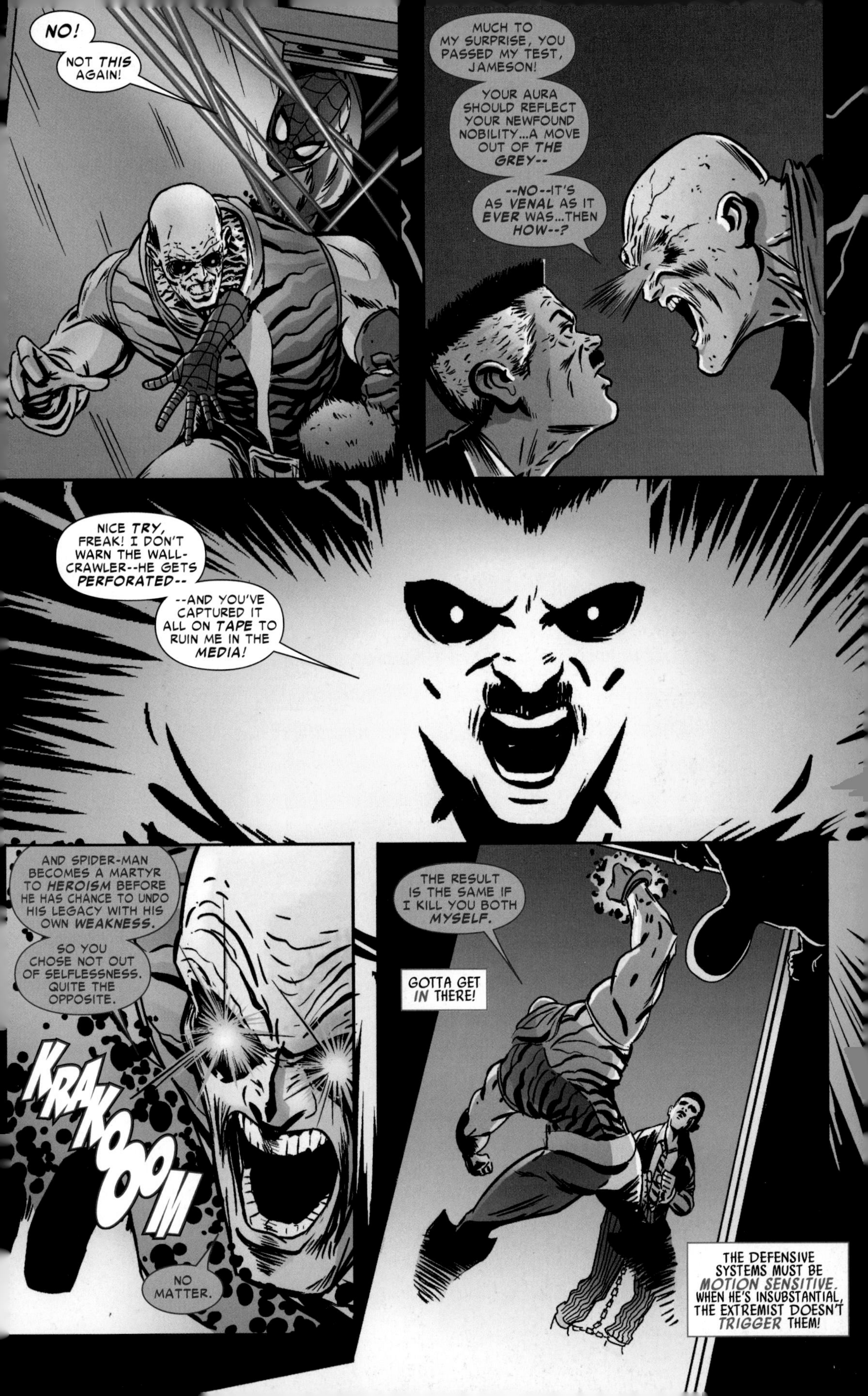
NO!
NOT THIS AGAIN!
MUCH TO MY SURPRISE, YOU PASSED MY TEST, JAMESON!
YOUR AURA SHOULD REFLECT YOUR NEWFOUND NOBILITY...A MOVE OUT OF THE GREY--
--NO--IT'S AS VENAL AS IT EVER WAS...THEN HOW--?
NICE TRY, FREAK! I DON'T WARN THE WALL-CRAWLER--HE GETS PERFORATED--
--AND YOU'VE CAPTURED IT ALL ON TAPE TO RUIN ME IN THE MEDIA!
AND SPIDER-MAN BECOMES A MARTYR TO HEROISM BEFORE HE HAS CHANCE TO UNDO HIS LEGACY WITH HIS OWN WEAKNESS.
SO YOU CHOSE NOT OUT OF SELFLESSNESS. QUITE THE OPPOSITE.
KRAKOOOM
NO MATTER.
THE RESULT IS THE SAME IF I KILL YOU BOTH MYSELF.
GOTTA GET IN THERE!
THE DEFENSIVE SYSTEMS MUST BE MOTION SENSITIVE. WHEN HE'S INSUBSTANTIAL, THE EXTREMIST DOESN'T TRIGGER THEM!

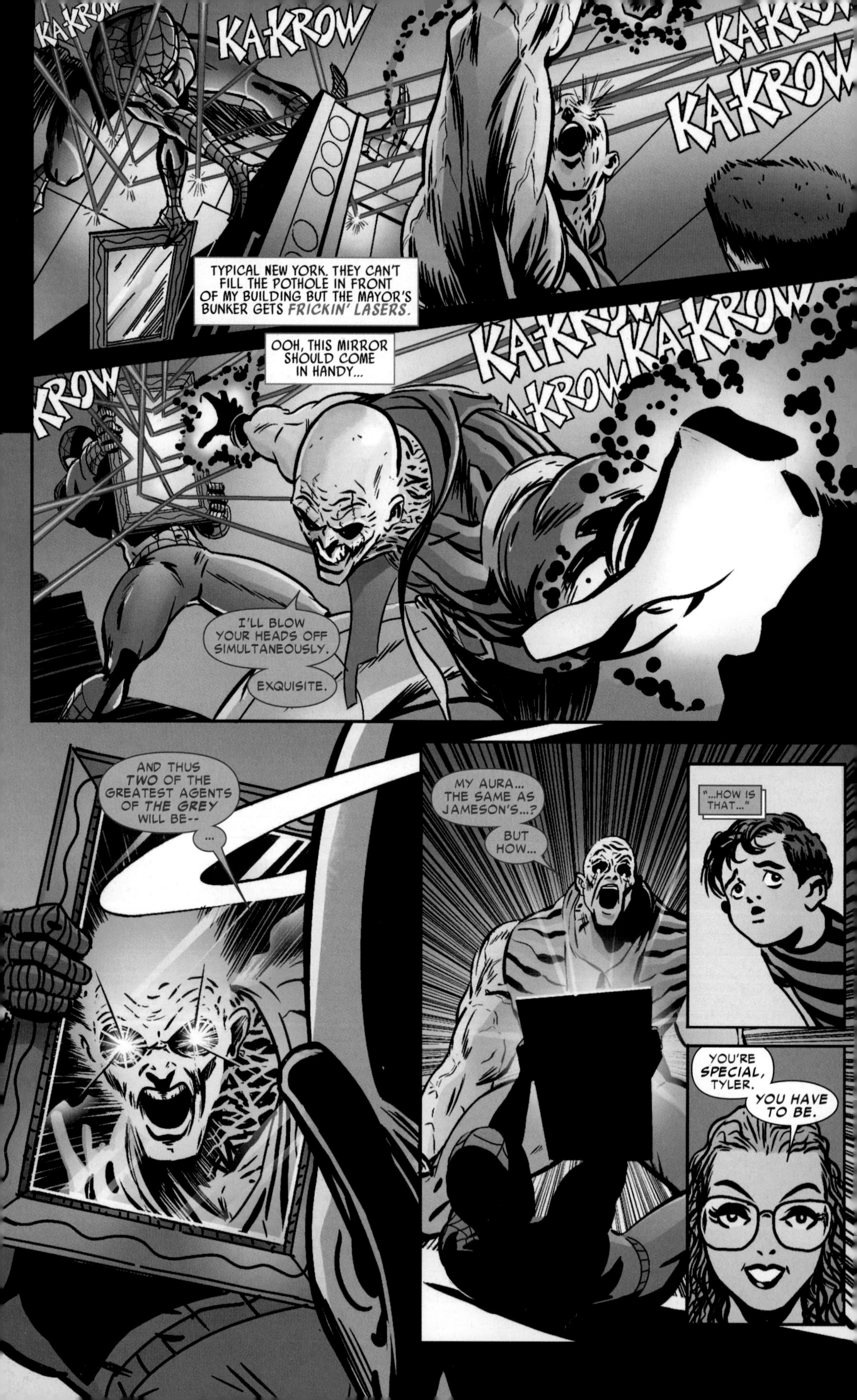
KA-KROW
KA-KROW
KA-KROW
KA-KROW
TYPICAL NEW YORK. THEY CAN'T FILL THE POTHOLE IN FRONT OF MY BUILDING BUT THE MAYOR'S BUNKER GETS FRICKIN' LASERS.
OOH, THIS MIRROR SHOULD COME IN HANDY...
KROW
KA-KROW
KA-KROW
KA-KROW
I'LL BLOW YOUR HEADS OFF SIMULTANEOUSLY.
EXQUISITE.
AND THUS TWO OF THE GREATEST AGENTS OF THE GREY WILL BE--
...
MY AURA... THE SAME AS JAMESON'S...?
BUT HOW...
"...HOW IS THAT..."
YOU'RE SPECIAL, TYLER.
YOU HAVE TO BE.

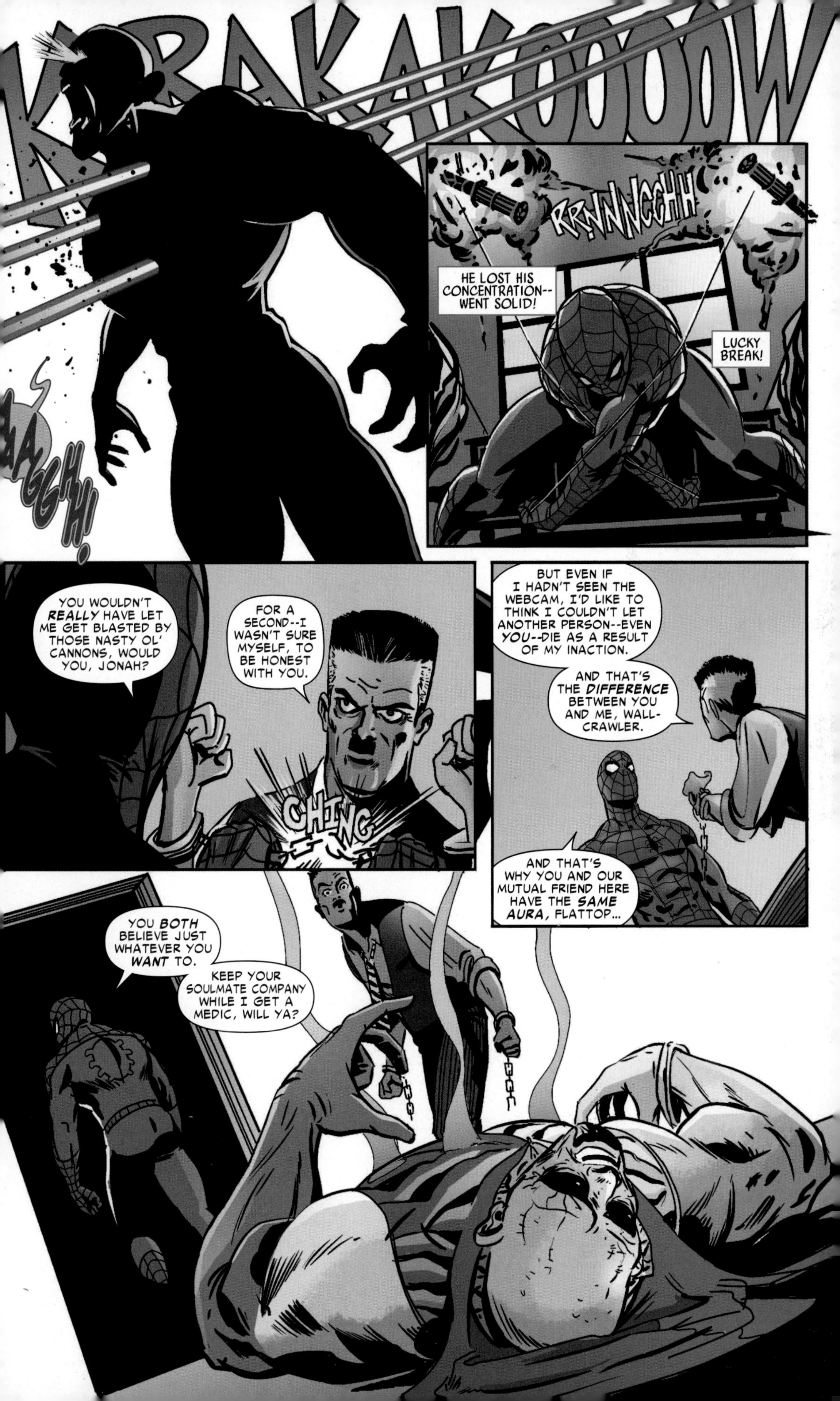

KRAKAKOOOOW
AAAGHH!
RRNNNCCHH
HE LOST HIS CONCENTRATION--WENT SOLID!
LUCKY BREAK!
YOU WOULDN'T REALLY HAVE LET ME GET BLASTED BY THOSE NASTY OL' CANNONS, WOULD YOU, JONAH?
FOR A SECOND--I WASN'T SURE MYSELF, TO BE HONEST WITH YOU.
CHING
BUT EVEN IF I HADN'T SEEN THE WEBCAM, I'D LIKE TO THINK I COULDN'T LET ANOTHER PERSON--EVEN YOU--DIE AS A RESULT OF MY INACTION.
AND THAT'S THE DIFFERENCE BETWEEN YOU AND ME, WALL-CRAWLER.
AND THAT'S WHY YOU AND OUR MUTUAL FRIEND HERE HAVE THE SAME AURA, FLATTOP...
YOU BOTH BELIEVE JUST WHATEVER YOU WANT TO.
KEEP YOUR SOULMATE COMPANY WHILE I GET A MEDIC, WILL YA?

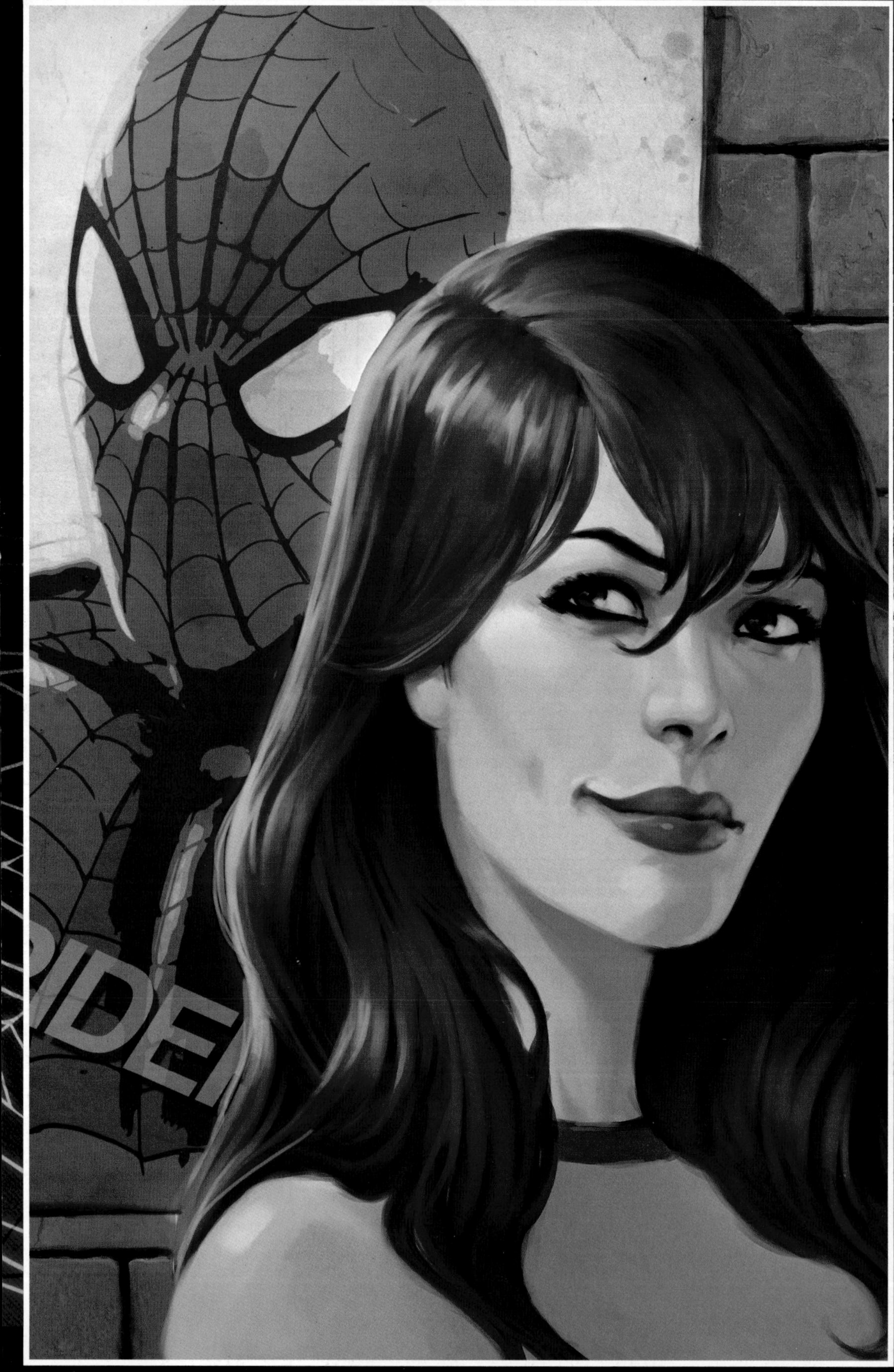

WEB OF SPIDER-MAN #11

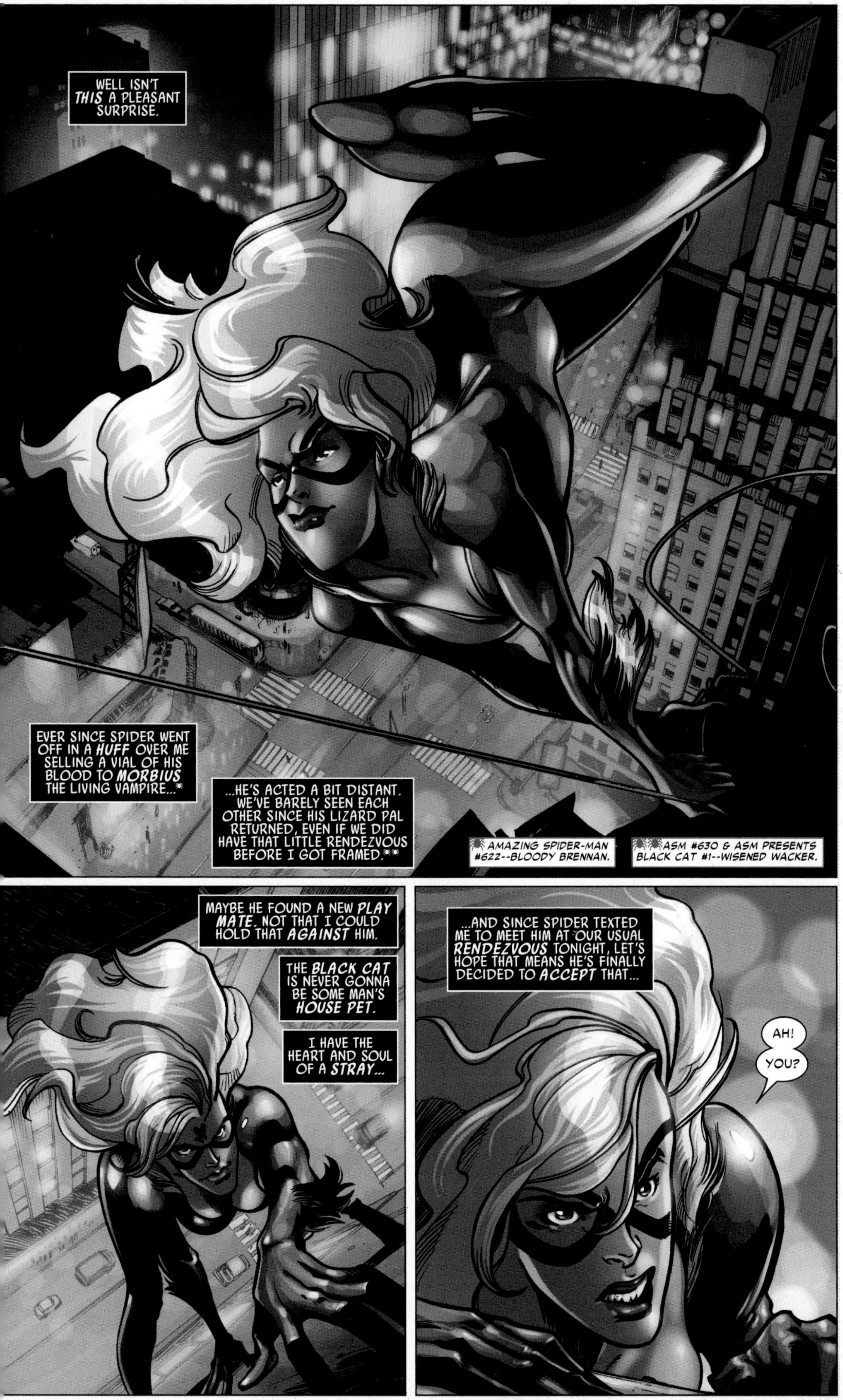
WELL ISN'T THIS A PLEASANT SURPRISE.
EVER SINCE SPIDER WENT OFF IN A HUFF OVER ME SELLING A VIAL OF HIS BLOOD TO MORBIUS THE LIVING VAMPIRE...*
...HE'S ACTED A BIT DISTANT. WE'VE BARELY SEEN EACH OTHER SINCE HIS LIZARD PAL RETURNED, EVEN IF WE DID HAVE THAT LITTLE RENDEZVOUS BEFORE I GOT FRAMED.**
*AMAZING SPIDER-MAN #622--BLOODY BRENNAN.
**ASM #630 & ASM PRESENTS BLACK CAT #1--WISENED WACKER.
MAYBE HE FOUND A NEW PLAY MATE. NOT THAT I COULD HOLD THAT AGAINST HIM.
THE BLACK CAT IS NEVER GONNA BE SOME MAN'S HOUSE PET.
I HAVE THE HEART AND SOUL OF A STRAY...
...AND SINCE SPIDER TEXTED ME TO MEET HIM AT OUR USUAL RENDEZVOUS TONIGHT, LET'S HOPE THAT MEANS HE'S FINALLY DECIDED TO ACCEPT THAT...
AH!
YOU?

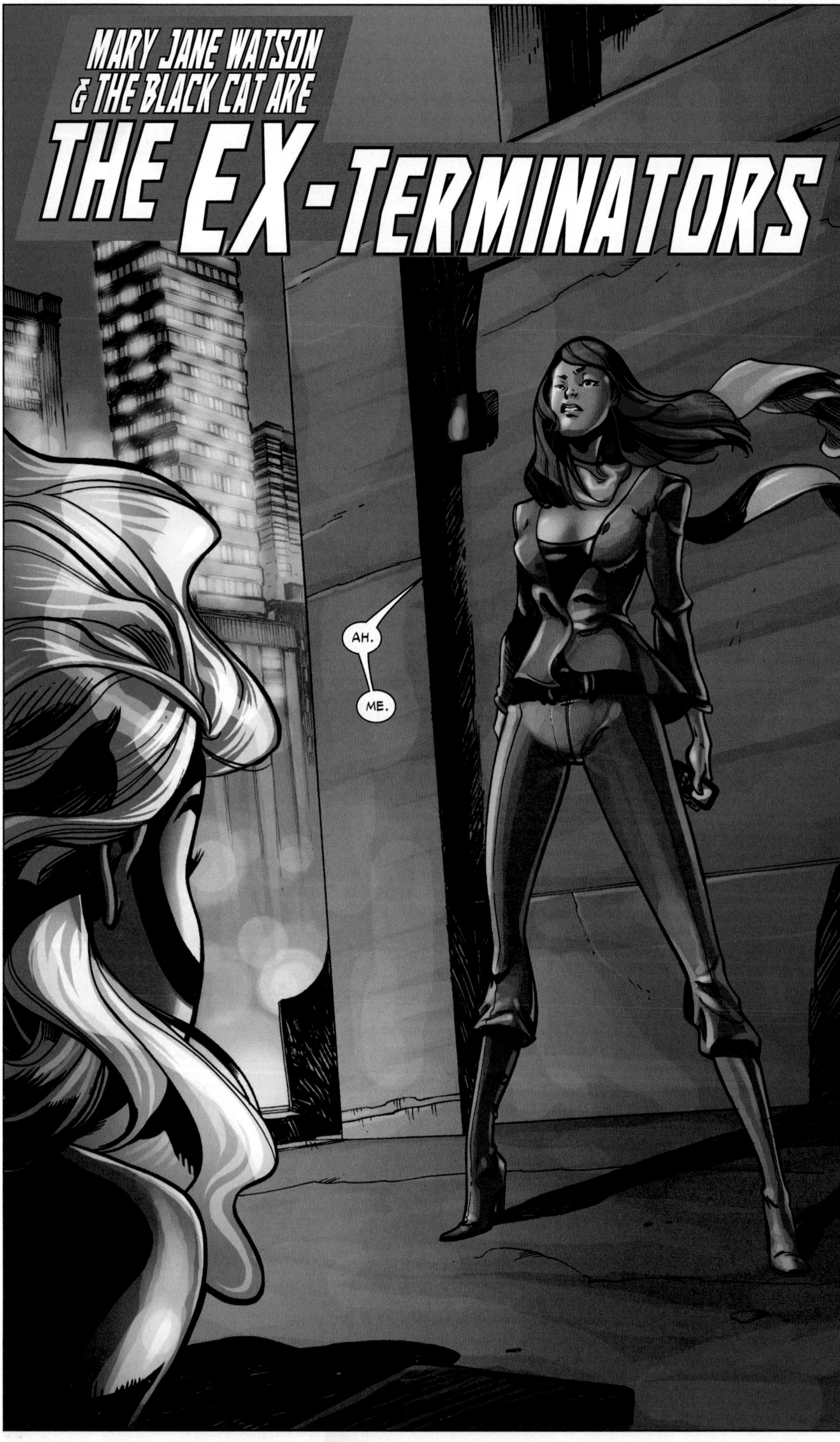

MARY JANE WATSON
& THE BLACK CAT ARE
THE EX-TERMINATORS
AH.
ME.

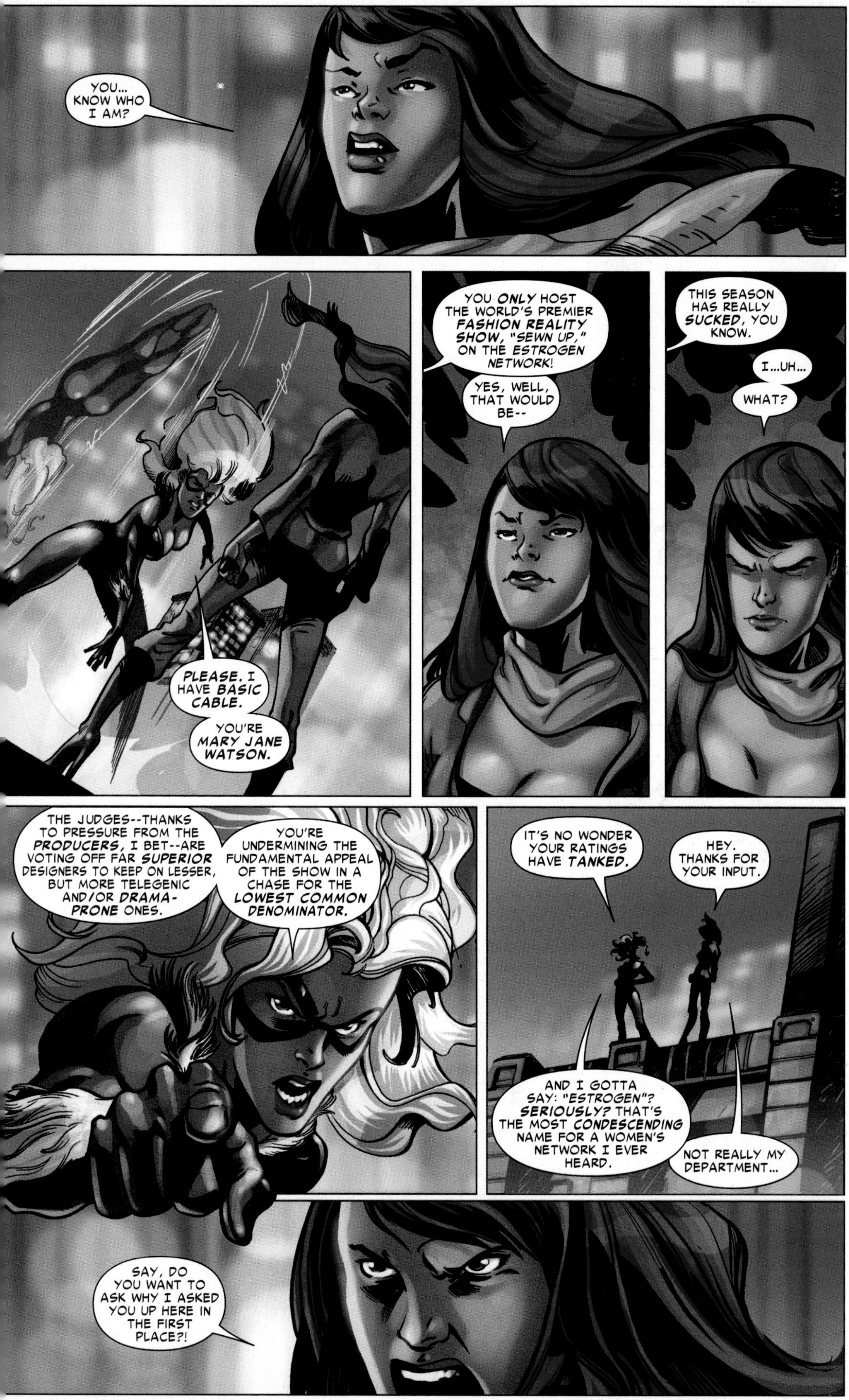
YOU... KNOW WHO I AM?
PLEASE. I HAVE BASIC CABLE.
YOU'RE MARY JANE WATSON.
YOU ONLY HOST THE WORLD'S PREMIER FASHION REALITY SHOW, "SEWN UP," ON THE ESTROGEN NETWORK!
YES, WELL, THAT WOULD BE--
THIS SEASON HAS REALLY SUCKED, YOU KNOW.
I...UH...
WHAT?
THE JUDGES--THANKS TO PRESSURE FROM THE PRODUCERS, I BET--ARE VOTING OFF FAR SUPERIOR DESIGNERS TO KEEP ON LESSER, BUT MORE TELEGENIC AND/OR DRAMA-PRONE ONES.
YOU'RE UNDERMINING THE FUNDAMENTAL APPEAL OF THE SHOW IN A CHASE FOR THE LOWEST COMMON DENOMINATOR.
IT'S NO WONDER YOUR RATINGS HAVE TANKED.
HEY. THANKS FOR YOUR INPUT.
AND I GOTTA SAY: "ESTROGEN"? SERIOUSLY? THAT'S THE MOST CONDESCENDING NAME FOR A WOMEN'S NETWORK I EVER HEARD.
NOT REALLY MY DEPARTMENT...
SAY, DO YOU WANT TO ASK WHY I ASKED YOU UP HERE IN THE FIRST PLACE?!

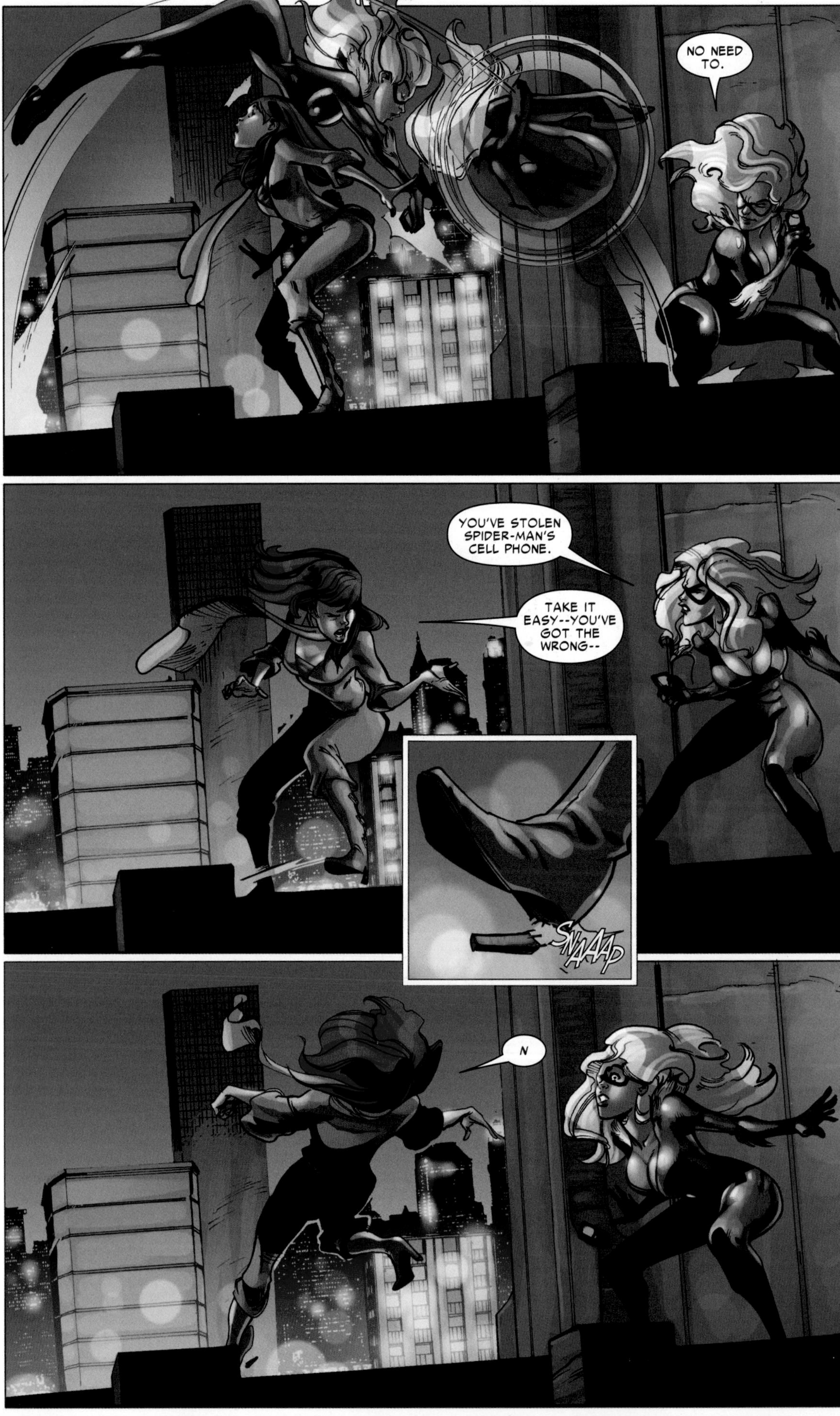
NO NEED TO.
YOU'VE STOLEN SPIDER-MAN'S CELL PHONE.
TAKE IT EASY--YOU'VE GOT THE WRONG--
SNAAAP
N

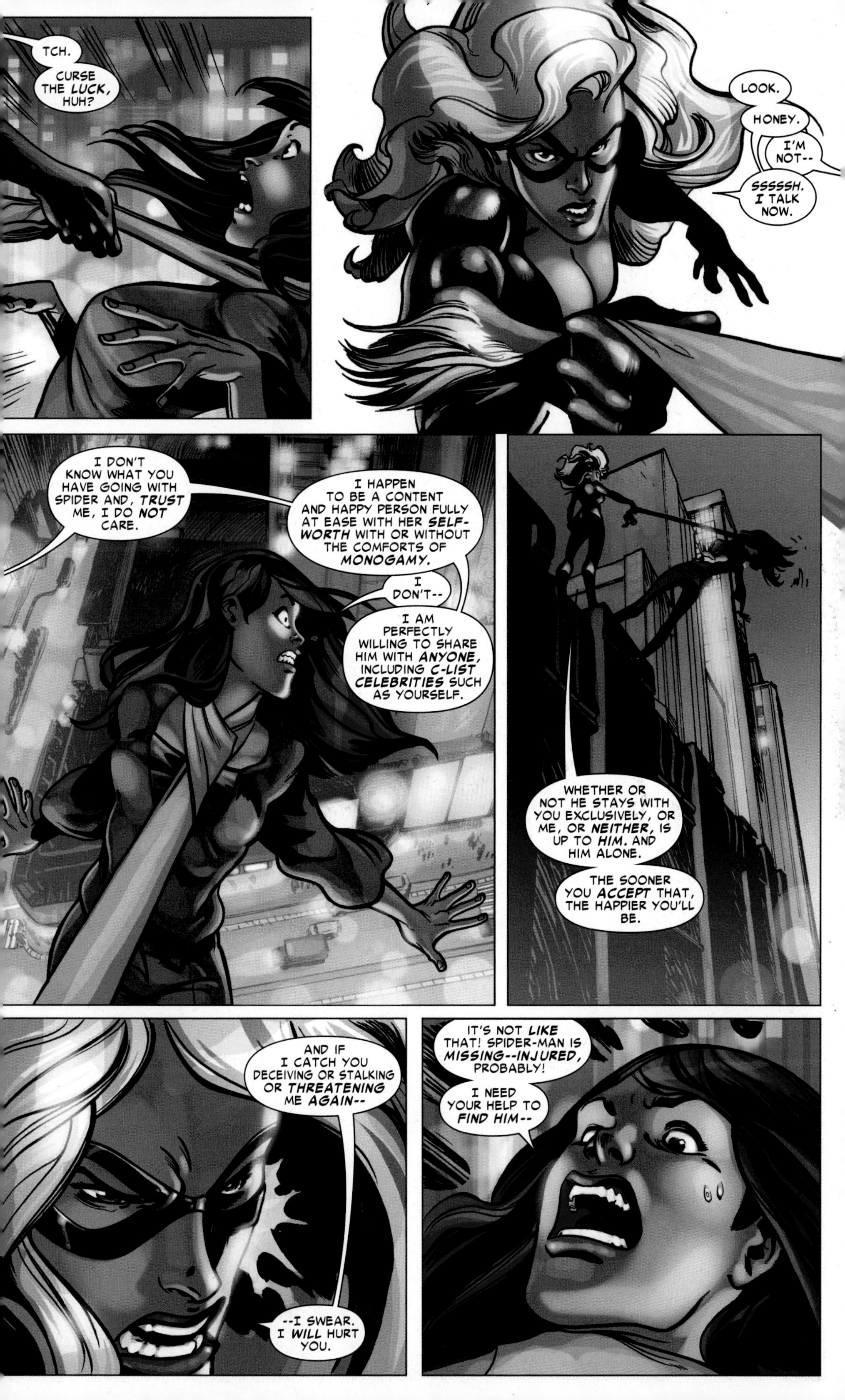
TCH.
CURSE THE LUCK, HUH?
LOOK.
HONEY.
I'M NOT--
SSSSSH. I TALK NOW.
I DON'T KNOW WHAT YOU HAVE GOING WITH SPIDER AND, TRUST ME, I DO NOT CARE.
I HAPPEN TO BE A CONTENT AND HAPPY PERSON FULLY AT EASE WITH HER SELF-WORTH WITH OR WITHOUT THE COMFORTS OF MONOGAMY.
I DON'T--
I AM PERFECTLY WILLING TO SHARE HIM WITH ANYONE, INCLUDING C-LIST CELEBRITIES SUCH AS YOURSELF.
WHETHER OR NOT HE STAYS WITH YOU EXCLUSIVELY, OR ME, OR NEITHER, IS UP TO HIM. AND HIM ALONE.
THE SOONER YOU ACCEPT THAT, THE HAPPIER YOU'LL BE.
AND IF I CATCH YOU DECEIVING OR STALKING OR THREATENING ME AGAIN--
--I SWEAR. I WILL HURT YOU.
IT'S NOT LIKE THAT! SPIDER-MAN IS MISSING--INJURED, PROBABLY!
I NEED YOUR HELP TO FIND HIM--

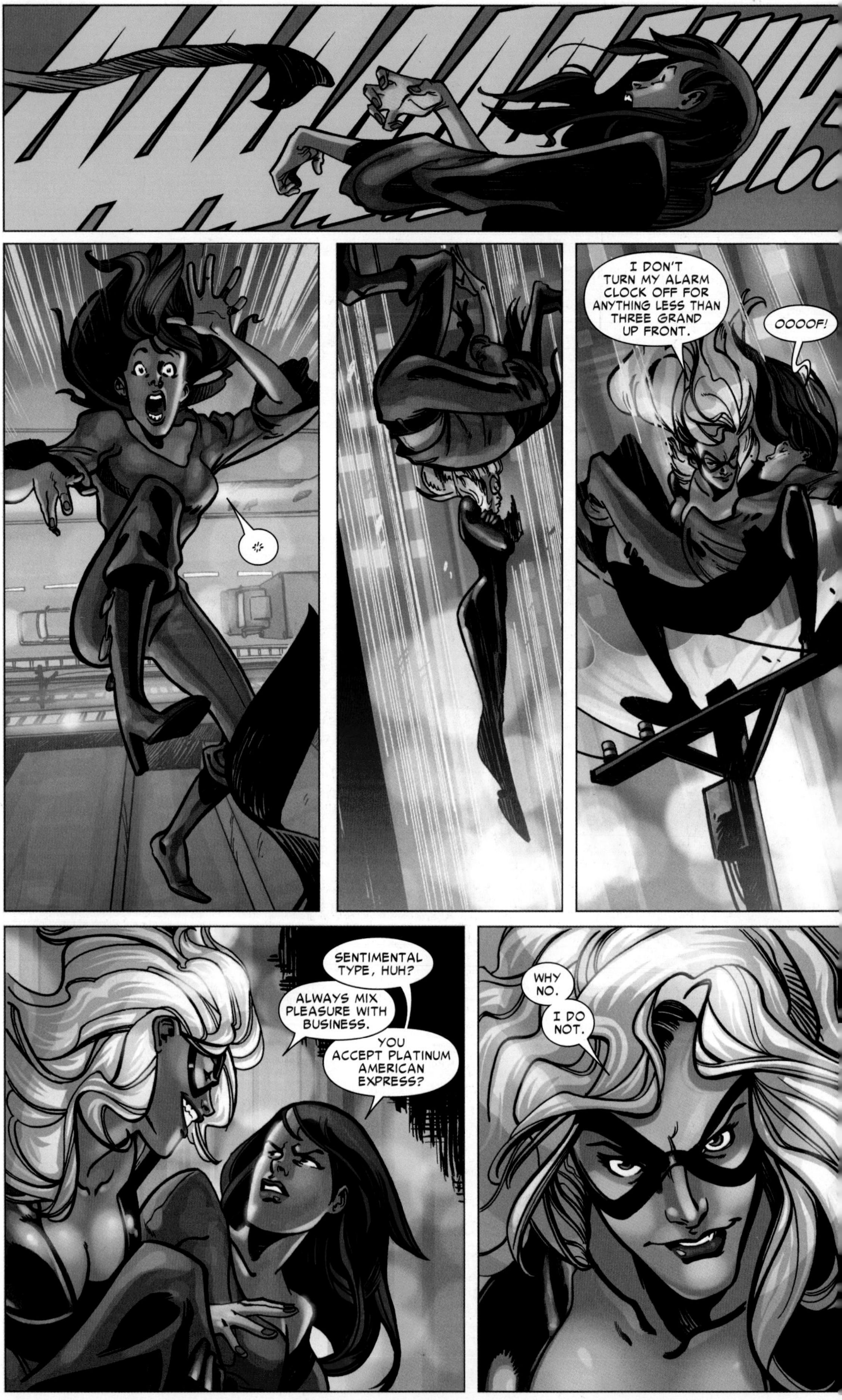
I DON'T TURN MY ALARM CLOCK OFF FOR ANYTHING LESS THAN THREE GRAND UP FRONT.
OOOOF!
SENTIMENTAL TYPE, HUH?
ALWAYS MIX PLEASURE WITH BUSINESS.
YOU ACCEPT PLATINUM AMERICAN EXPRESS?
WHY NO.
I DO NOT.

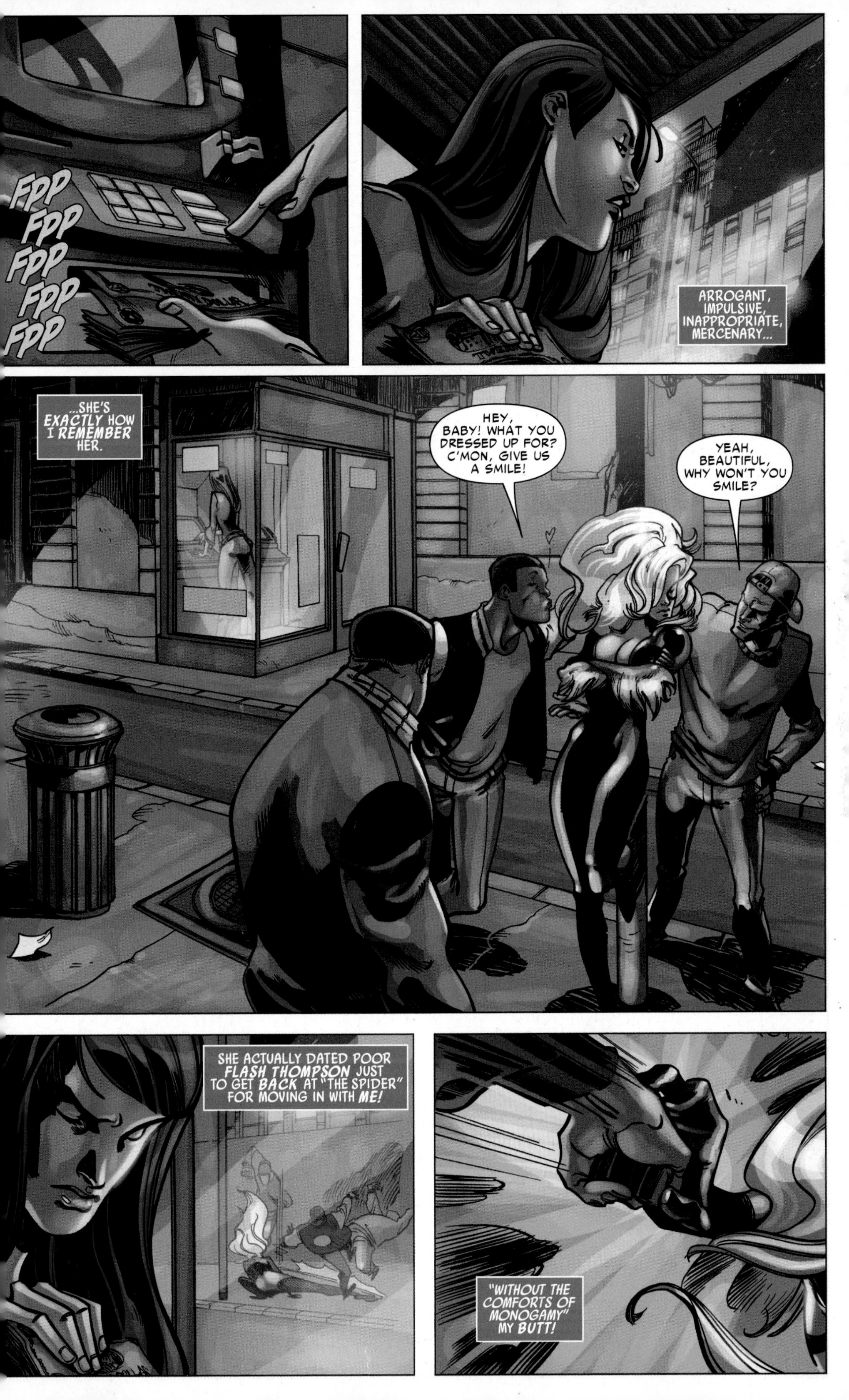
FPP FPP FPP FPP FPP
ARROGANT, IMPULSIVE, INAPPROPRIATE, MERCENARY...
...SHE'S EXACTLY HOW I REMEMBER HER.
HEY, BABY! WHAT YOU DRESSED UP FOR? C'MON, GIVE US A SMILE!
YEAH, BEAUTIFUL, WHY WON'T YOU SMILE?
SHE ACTUALLY DATED POOR FLASH THOMPSON JUST TO GET BACK AT "THE SPIDER" FOR MOVING IN WITH ME!
"WITHOUT THE COMFORTS OF MONOGAMY" MY BUTT!

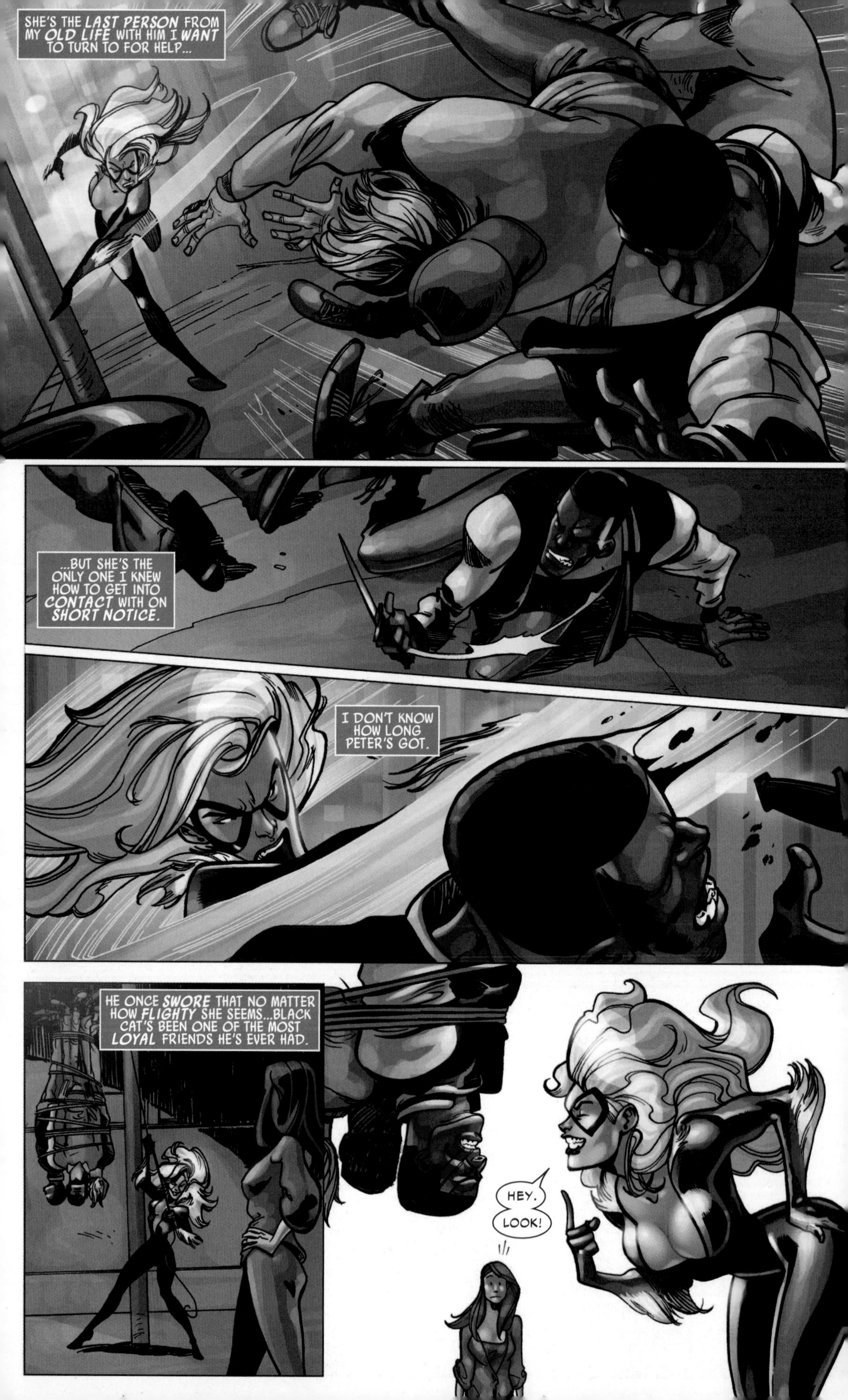
SHE'S THE LAST PERSON FROM MY OLD LIFE WITH HIM I WANT TO TURN TO FOR HELP...
...BUT SHE'S THE ONLY ONE I KNEW HOW TO GET INTO CONTACT WITH ON SHORT NOTICE.
I DON'T KNOW HOW LONG PETER'S GOT.
HE ONCE SWORE THAT NO MATTER HOW FLIGHTY SHE SEEMS...BLACK CAT'S BEEN ONE OF THE MOST LOYAL FRIENDS HE'S EVER HAD.
HEY.
LOOK!

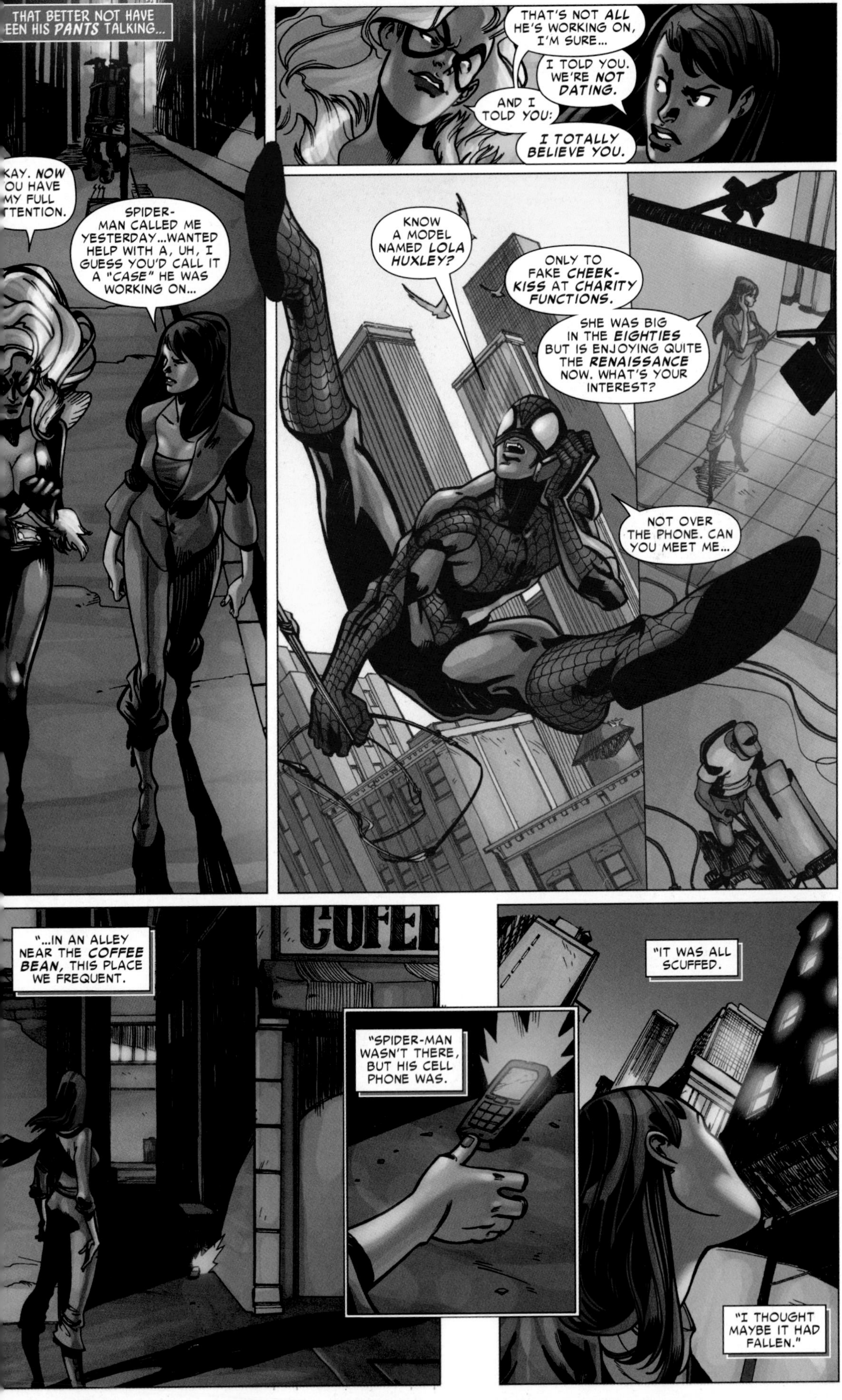
THAT BETTER NOT HAVE
EEN HIS PANTS TALKING...
THAT'S NOT ALL HE'S WORKING ON, I'M SURE...
I TOLD YOU. WE'RE NOT DATING.
AND I TOLD YOU:
I TOTALLY BELIEVE YOU.
KAY. NOW OU HAVE MY FULL TTENTION.
SPIDER-MAN CALLED ME YESTERDAY...WANTED HELP WITH A, UH, I GUESS YOU'D CALL IT A "CASE" HE WAS WORKING ON...
KNOW A MODEL NAMED LOLA HUXLEY?
ONLY TO FAKE CHEEK-KISS AT CHARITY FUNCTIONS.
SHE WAS BIG IN THE EIGHTIES BUT IS ENJOYING QUITE THE RENAISSANCE NOW. WHAT'S YOUR INTEREST?
NOT OVER THE PHONE. CAN YOU MEET ME...
"...IN AN ALLEY NEAR THE COFFEE BEAN, THIS PLACE WE FREQUENT.
COFFE
"SPIDER-MAN WASN'T THERE, BUT HIS CELL PHONE WAS.
"IT WAS ALL SCUFFED.
"I THOUGHT MAYBE IT HAD FALLEN."

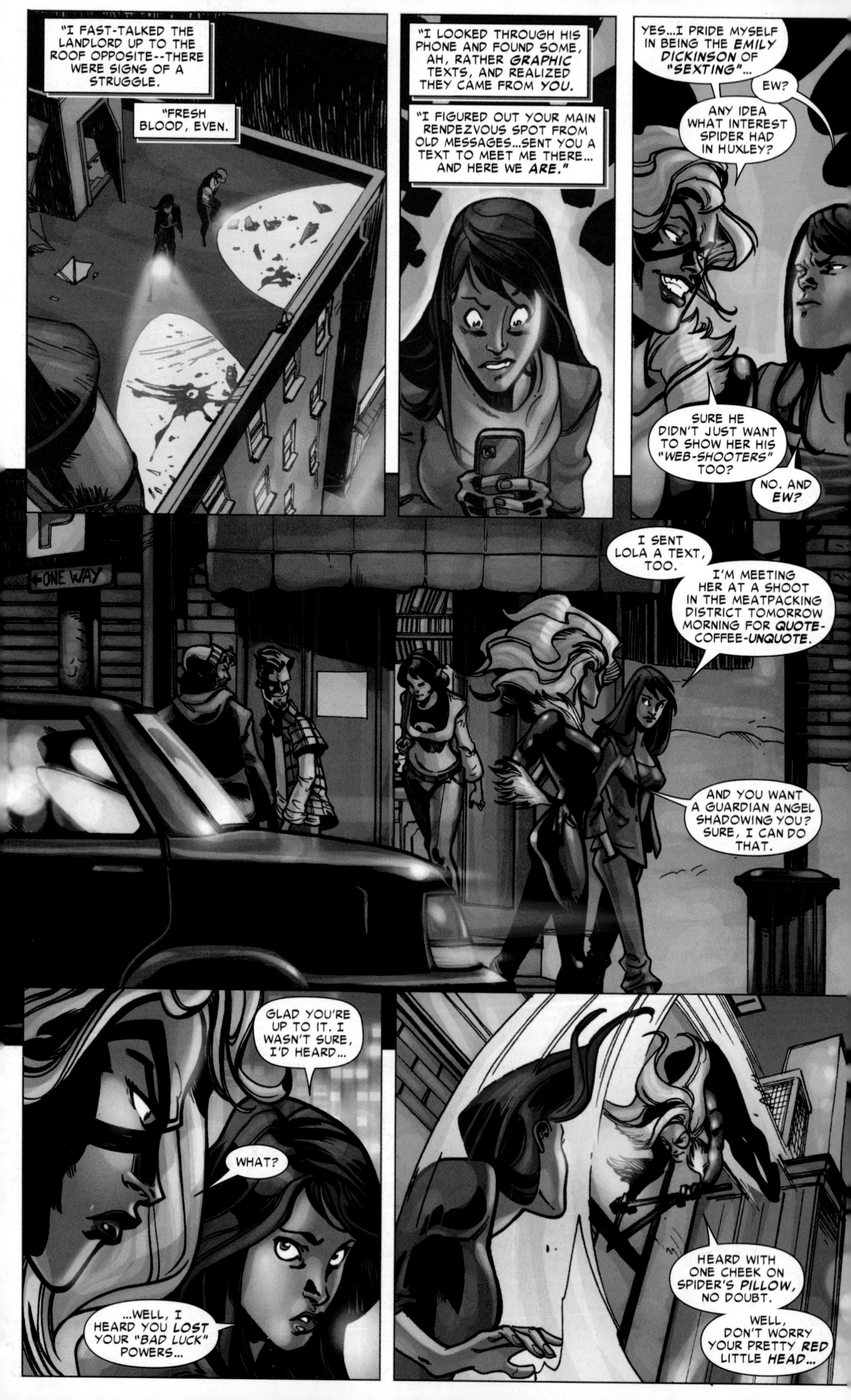
"I FAST-TALKED THE LANDLORD UP TO THE ROOF OPPOSITE--THERE WERE SIGNS OF A STRUGGLE.
"FRESH BLOOD, EVEN.
"I LOOKED THROUGH HIS PHONE AND FOUND SOME, AH, RATHER GRAPHIC TEXTS, AND REALIZED THEY CAME FROM YOU.
"I FIGURED OUT YOUR MAIN RENDEZVOUS SPOT FROM OLD MESSAGES...SENT YOU A TEXT TO MEET ME THERE... AND HERE WE ARE."
YES...I PRIDE MYSELF IN BEING THE EMILY DICKINSON OF "SEXTING"...
EW?
ANY IDEA WHAT INTEREST SPIDER HAD IN HUXLEY?
SURE HE DIDN'T JUST WANT TO SHOW HER HIS "WEB-SHOOTERS" TOO?
NO. AND EW?
ONE WAY
I SENT LOLA A TEXT, TOO.
I'M MEETING HER AT A SHOOT IN THE MEATPACKING DISTRICT TOMORROW MORNING FOR QUOTE-COFFEE-UNQUOTE.
AND YOU WANT A GUARDIAN ANGEL SHADOWING YOU? SURE, I CAN DO THAT.
GLAD YOU'RE UP TO IT. I WASN'T SURE, I'D HEARD...
WHAT?
...WELL, I HEARD YOU LOST YOUR "BAD LUCK" POWERS...
HEARD WITH ONE CHEEK ON SPIDER'S PILLOW, NO DOUBT.
WELL, DON'T WORRY YOUR PRETTY RED LITTLE HEAD...

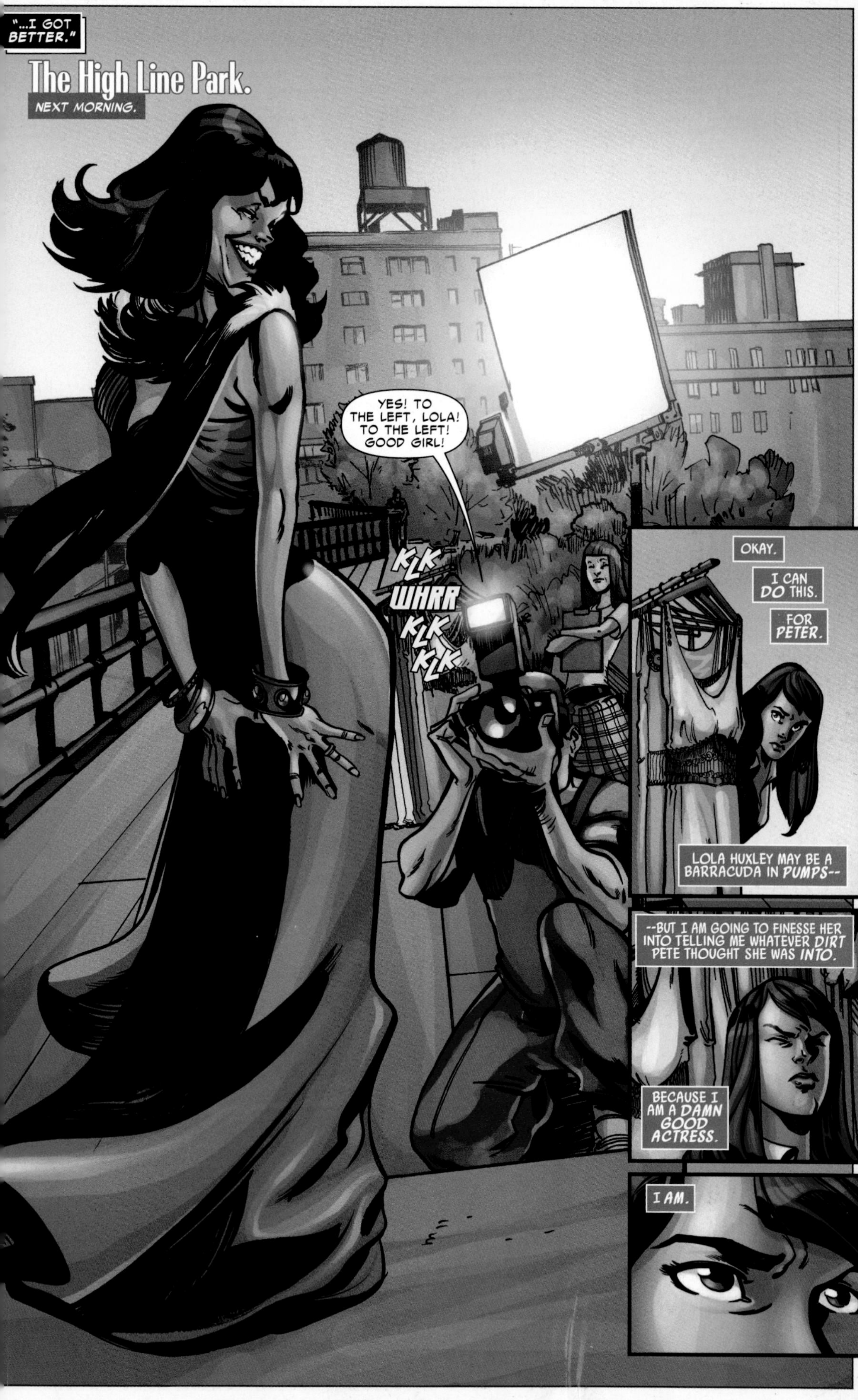
"...I GOT BETTER."
The High Line Park.
NEXT MORNING.
YES! TO THE LEFT, LOLA! TO THE LEFT! GOOD GIRL!
KLK
WHRR
KLK
KLK
OKAY.
I CAN DO THIS.
FOR PETER.
LOLA HUXLEY MAY BE A BARRACUDA IN PUMPS--
--BUT I AM GOING TO FINESSE HER INTO TELLING ME WHATEVER DIRT PETE THOUGHT SHE WAS INTO.
BECAUSE I AM A DAMN GOOD ACTRESS.
I AM.

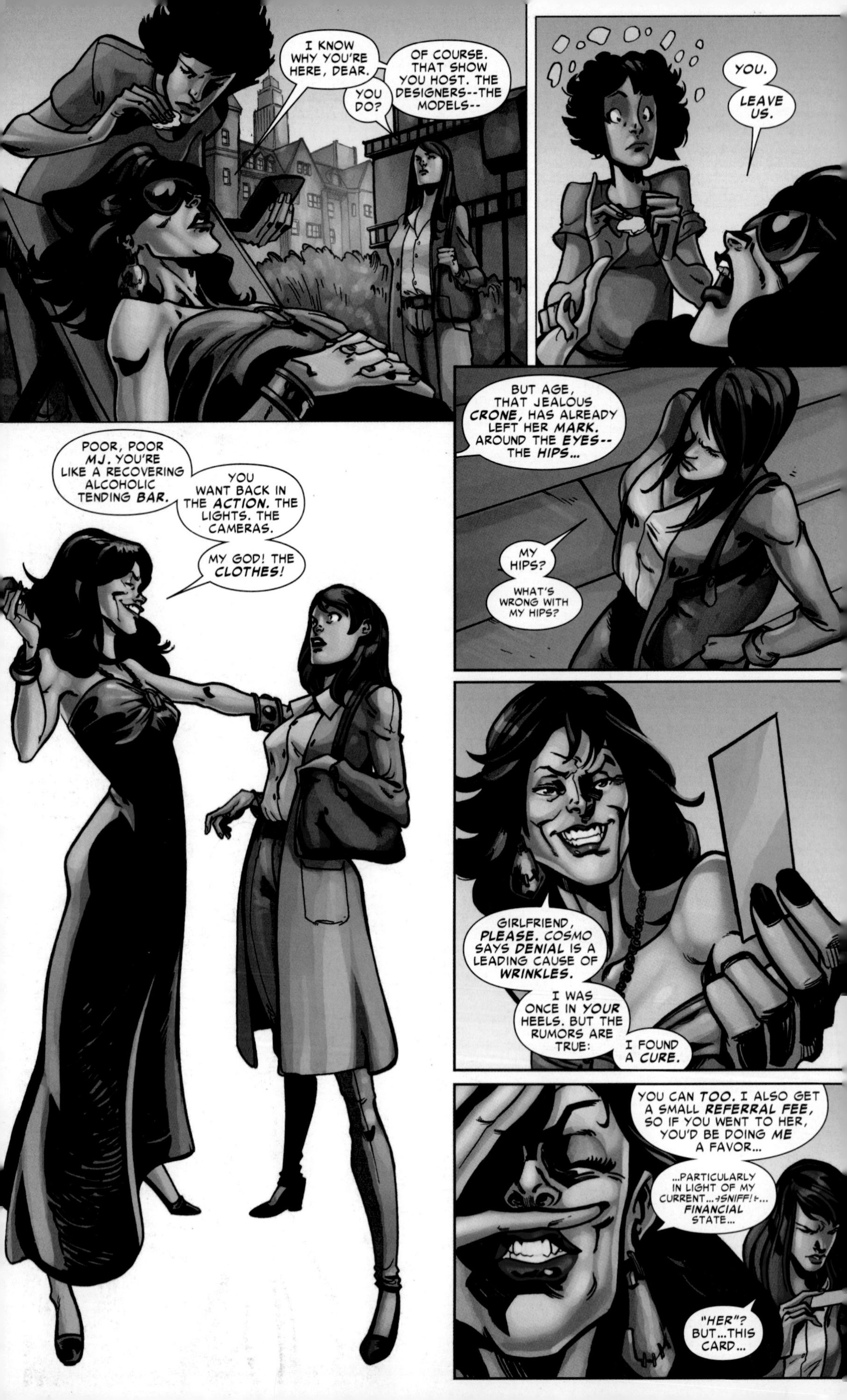
I KNOW WHY YOU'RE HERE, DEAR.
YOU DO?
OF COURSE. THAT SHOW YOU HOST. THE DESIGNERS--THE MODELS--
YOU.
LEAVE US.
BUT AGE, THAT JEALOUS CRONE, HAS ALREADY LEFT HER MARK. AROUND THE EYES-- THE HIPS...
MY HIPS?
WHAT'S WRONG WITH MY HIPS?
POOR, POOR MJ. YOU'RE LIKE A RECOVERING ALCOHOLIC TENDING BAR.
YOU WANT BACK IN THE ACTION. THE LIGHTS. THE CAMERAS.
MY GOD! THE CLOTHES!
GIRLFRIEND, PLEASE. COSMO SAYS DENIAL IS A LEADING CAUSE OF WRINKLES.
I WAS ONCE IN YOUR HEELS. BUT THE RUMORS ARE TRUE:
I FOUND A CURE.
YOU CAN TOO. I ALSO GET A SMALL REFERRAL FEE, SO IF YOU WENT TO HER, YOU'D BE DOING ME A FAVOR...
...PARTICULARLY IN LIGHT OF MY CURRENT... SNIFF! ... FINANCIAL STATE...
"HER"? BUT...THIS CARD...

...IT'S BLANK.

SPIDER, SPIDER, *SPIDER*...

...WHAT*EVER* AM I TO DO WITH YOU?

I WISH YOU'D SHOW A LITTLE MORE *IMAGINATION* THAN THE EX-CHEERLEADER, GIRL-NEXT-DOOR, *SEARS LINGERIE MODEL* TYPE.

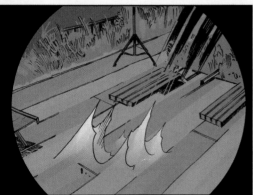

'LL ADMIT SHE HAS MORE *GUTS* THAN THE 'ERAGE BUBBLE-HEADED CLOTHESHORSE...

...BUT *STILL.*

YOU MADE THE SAFE CHOICE.

STORY OF YOUR LIFE.

WHAT THE WHAT?

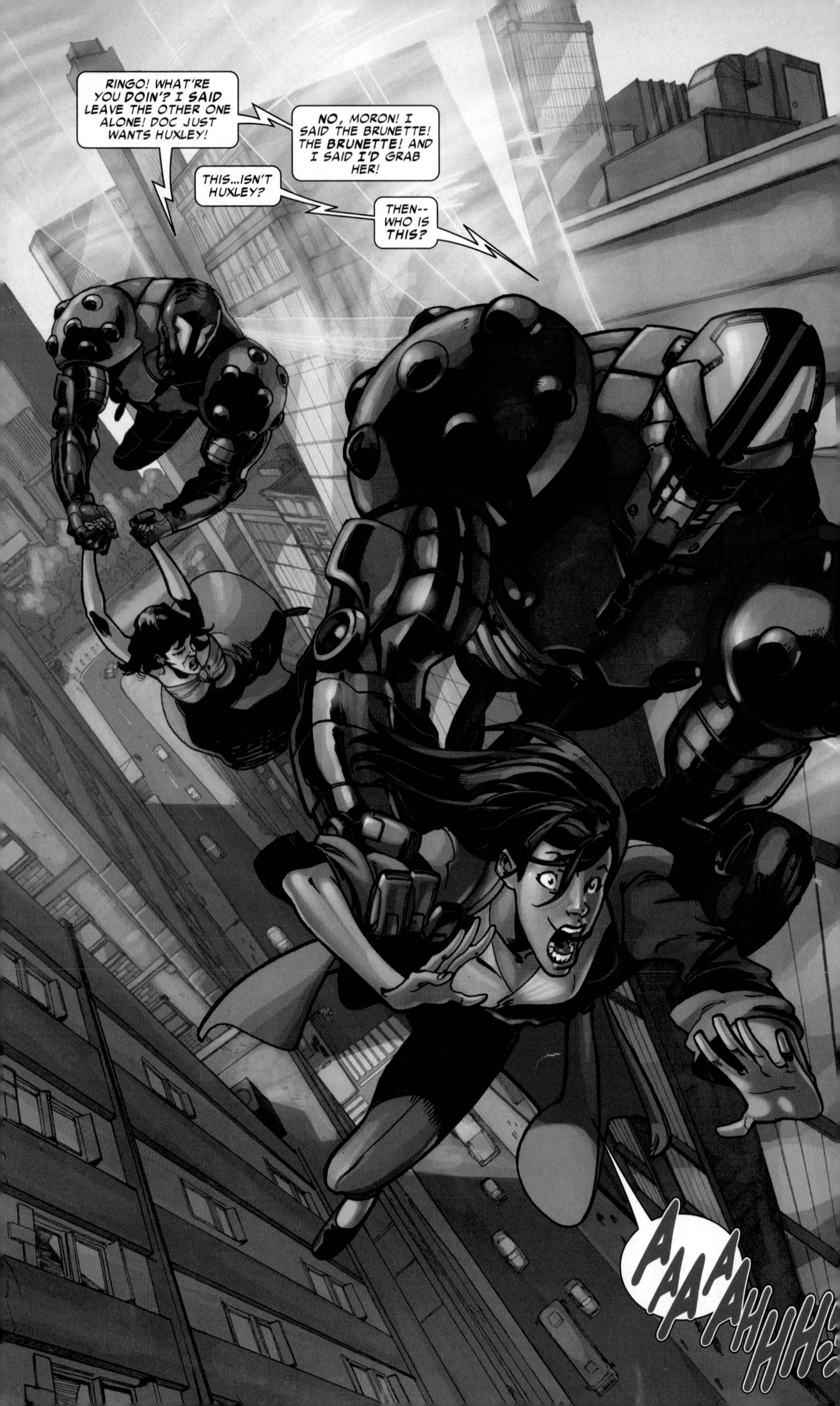
RINGO! WHAT'RE YOU DOIN'? I SAID LEAVE THE OTHER ONE ALONE! DOC JUST WANTS HUXLEY!
NO, MORON! I SAID THE BRUNETTE! THE BRUNETTE! AND I SAID I'D GRAB HER!
THIS...ISN'T HUXLEY?
THEN-- WHO IS THIS?
AAAAAHHHH

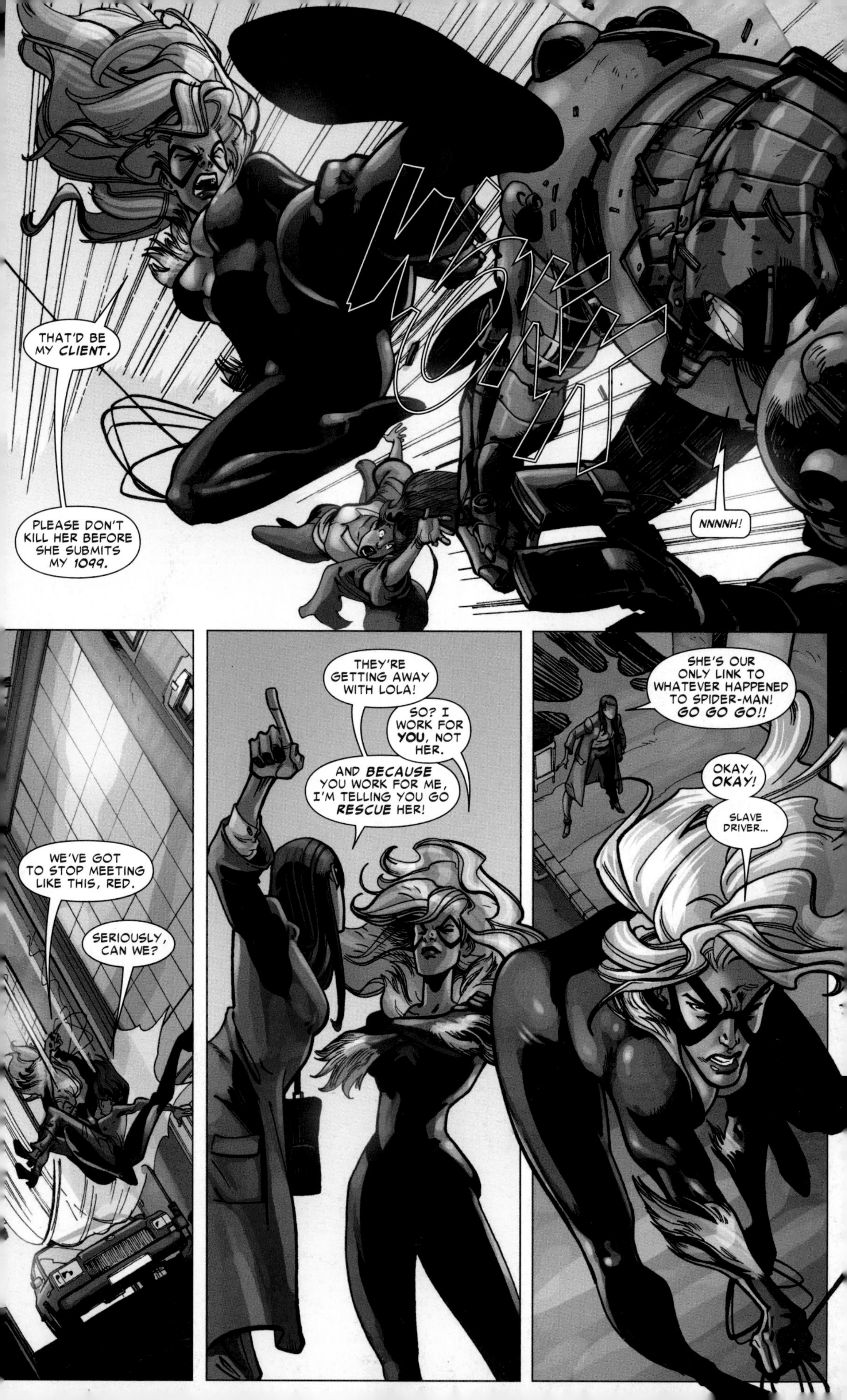
THAT'D BE MY CLIENT.
PLEASE DON'T KILL HER BEFORE SHE SUBMITS MY 1099.
NNNNH!
WE'VE GOT TO STOP MEETING LIKE THIS, RED.
SERIOUSLY, CAN WE?
THEY'RE GETTING AWAY WITH LOLA!
SO? I WORK FOR YOU, NOT HER.
AND BECAUSE YOU WORK FOR ME, I'M TELLING YOU GO RESCUE HER!
SHE'S OUR ONLY LINK TO WHATEVER HAPPENED TO SPIDER-MAN! GO GO GO!!
OKAY, OKAY!
SLAVE DRIVER...

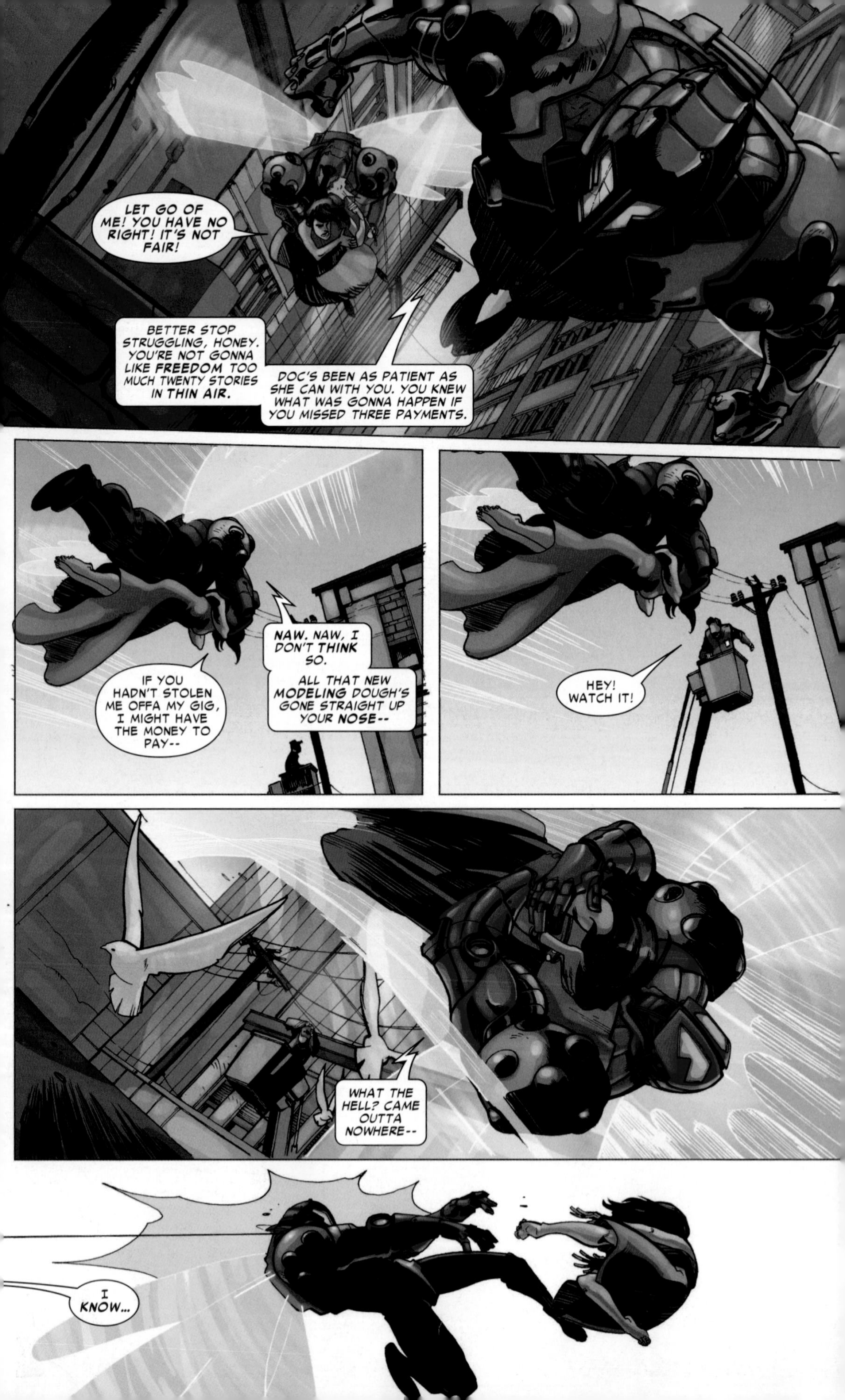
LET GO OF ME! YOU HAVE NO RIGHT! IT'S NOT FAIR!
BETTER STOP STRUGGLING, HONEY. YOU'RE NOT GONNA LIKE FREEDOM TOO MUCH TWENTY STORIES IN THIN AIR.
DOC'S BEEN AS PATIENT AS SHE CAN WITH YOU. YOU KNEW WHAT WAS GONNA HAPPEN IF YOU MISSED THREE PAYMENTS.
IF YOU HADN'T STOLEN ME OFFA MY GIG, I MIGHT HAVE THE MONEY TO PAY--
NAW. NAW, I DON'T THINK SO.
ALL THAT NEW MODELING DOUGH'S GONE STRAIGHT UP YOUR NOSE--
HEY! WATCH IT!
WHAT THE HELL? CAME OUTTA NOWHERE--
I KNOW...

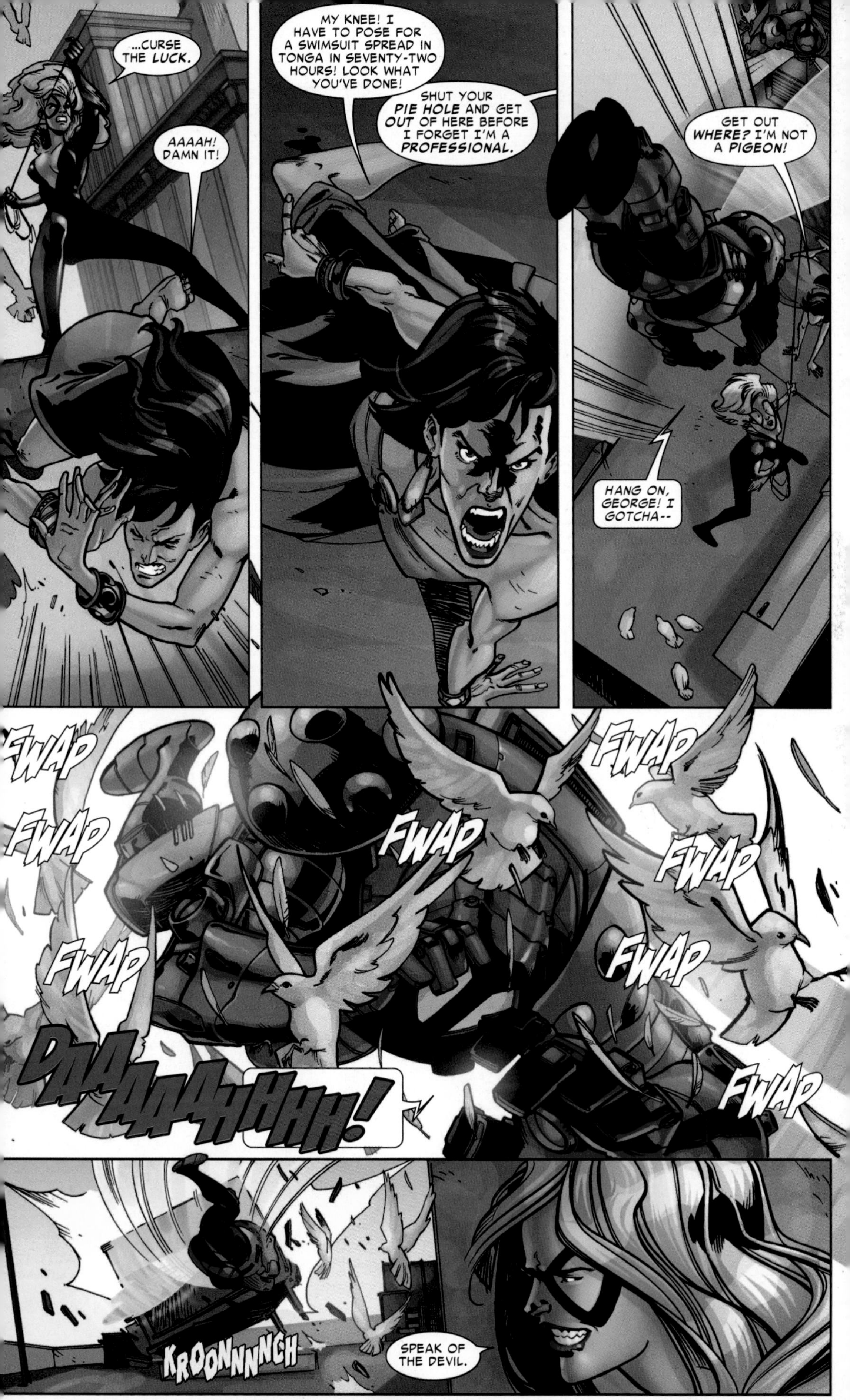
...CURSE THE LUCK.
AAAAH! DAMN IT!
MY KNEE! I HAVE TO POSE FOR A SWIMSUIT SPREAD IN TONGA IN SEVENTY-TWO HOURS! LOOK WHAT YOU'VE DONE!
SHUT YOUR PIE HOLE AND GET OUT OF HERE BEFORE I FORGET I'M A PROFESSIONAL.
GET OUT WHERE? I'M NOT A PIGEON!
HANG ON, GEORGE! I GOTCHA--
FWAP
FWAP
FWAP
FWAP
FWAP
FWAP
FWAP
DAAAAAAAHHHH!
KROONNNNCH
SPEAK OF THE DEVIL.

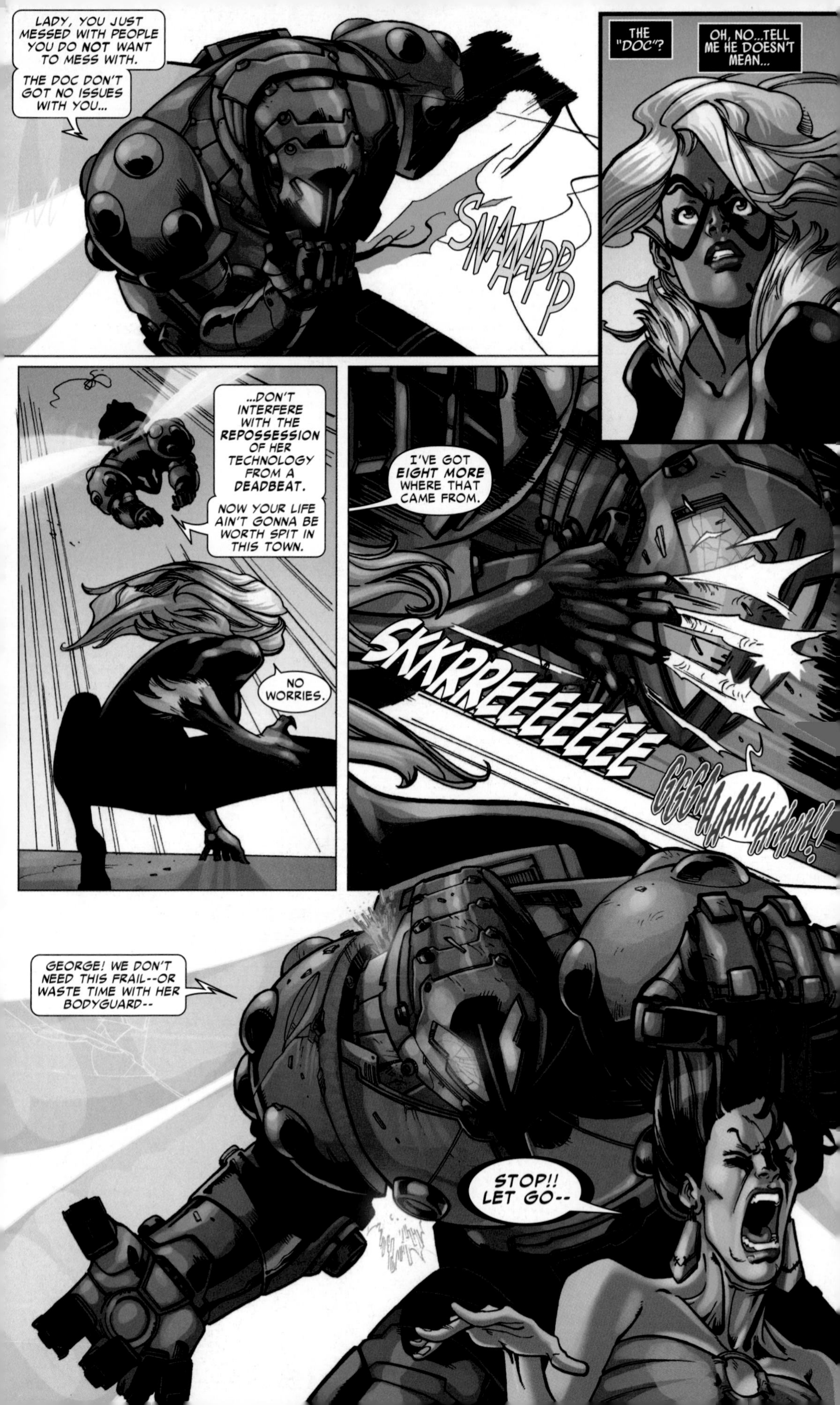
LADY, YOU JUST MESSED WITH PEOPLE YOU DO NOT WANT TO MESS WITH.
THE DOC DON'T GOT NO ISSUES WITH YOU...
SNAAAPP
THE "DOC"?
OH, NO...TELL ME HE DOESN'T MEAN...
...DON'T INTERFERE WITH THE REPOSSESSION OF HER TECHNOLOGY FROM A DEADBEAT.
NOW YOUR LIFE AIN'T GONNA BE WORTH SPIT IN THIS TOWN.
NO WORRIES.
I'VE GOT EIGHT MORE WHERE THAT CAME FROM.
SKKRREEEEEEEE
GEORGE! WE DON'T NEED THIS FRAIL--OR WASTE TIME WITH HER BODYGUARD--
STOP!! LET GO--

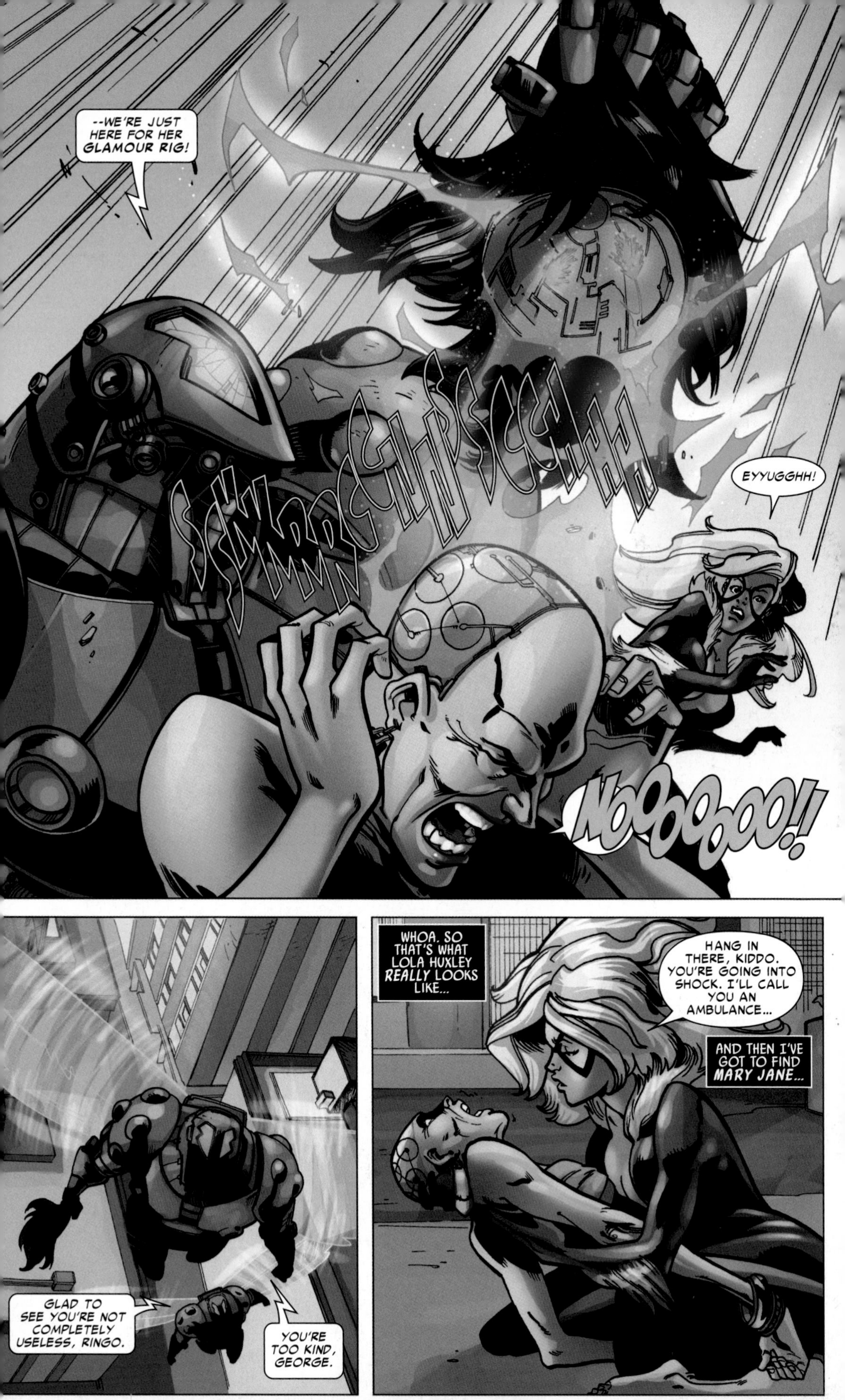
--WE'RE JUST HERE FOR HER GLAMOUR RIG!
EYYUGGHH!
NOOOOOOO!!
GLAD TO SEE YOU'RE NOT COMPLETELY USELESS, RINGO.
YOU'RE TOO KIND, GEORGE.
WHOA. SO THAT'S WHAT LOLA HUXLEY REALLY LOOKS LIKE...
HANG IN THERE, KIDDO. YOU'RE GOING INTO SHOCK. I'LL CALL YOU AN AMBULANCE...
AND THEN I'VE GOT TO FIND MARY JANE...

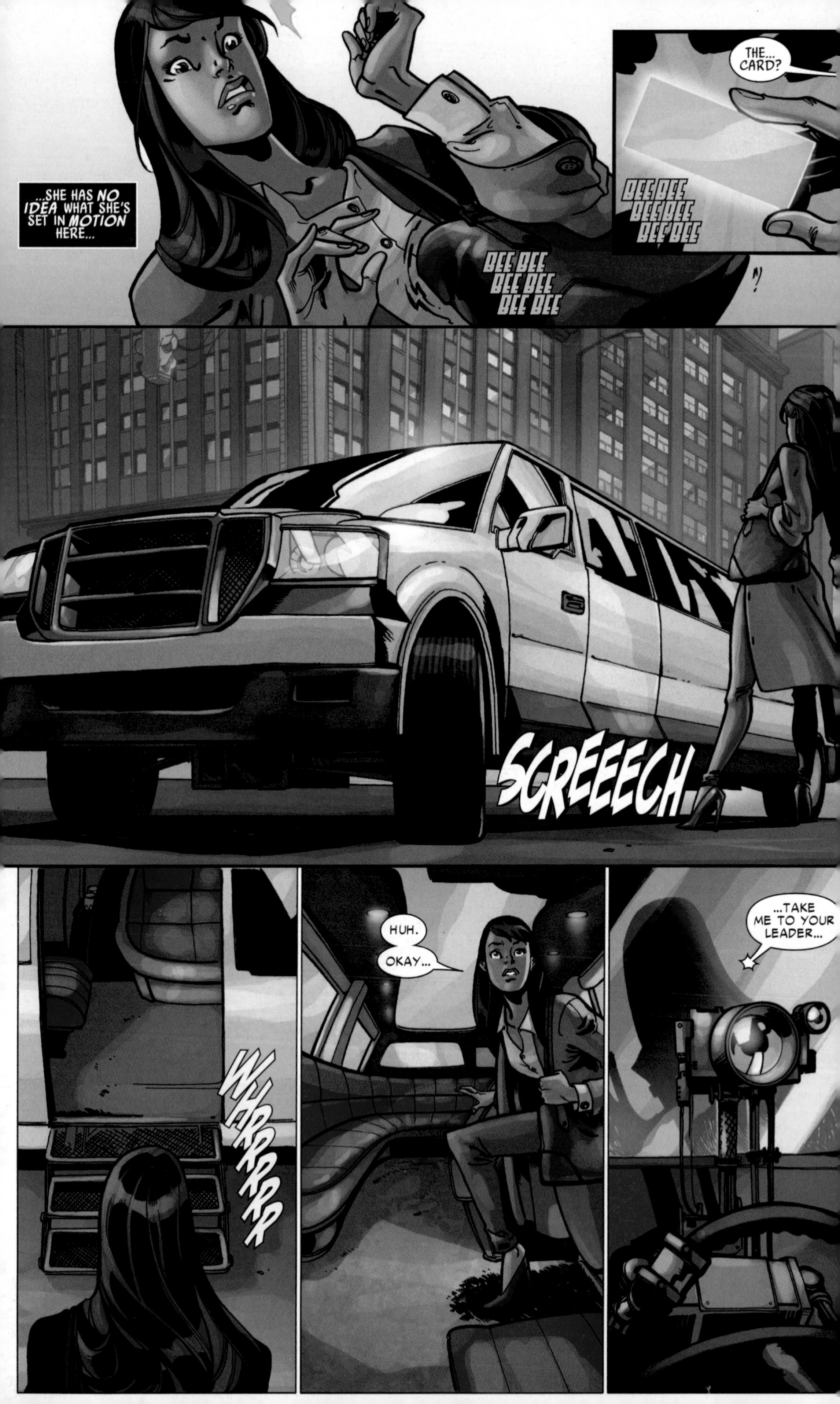
...SHE HAS NO IDEA WHAT SHE'S SET IN MOTION HERE...
BEE BEE BEE BEE BEE BEE
THE... CARD?
BEE BEE BEE BEE BEE BEE
SCREEECH
WHRRRRR
HUH.
OKAY...
...TAKE ME TO YOUR LEADER...

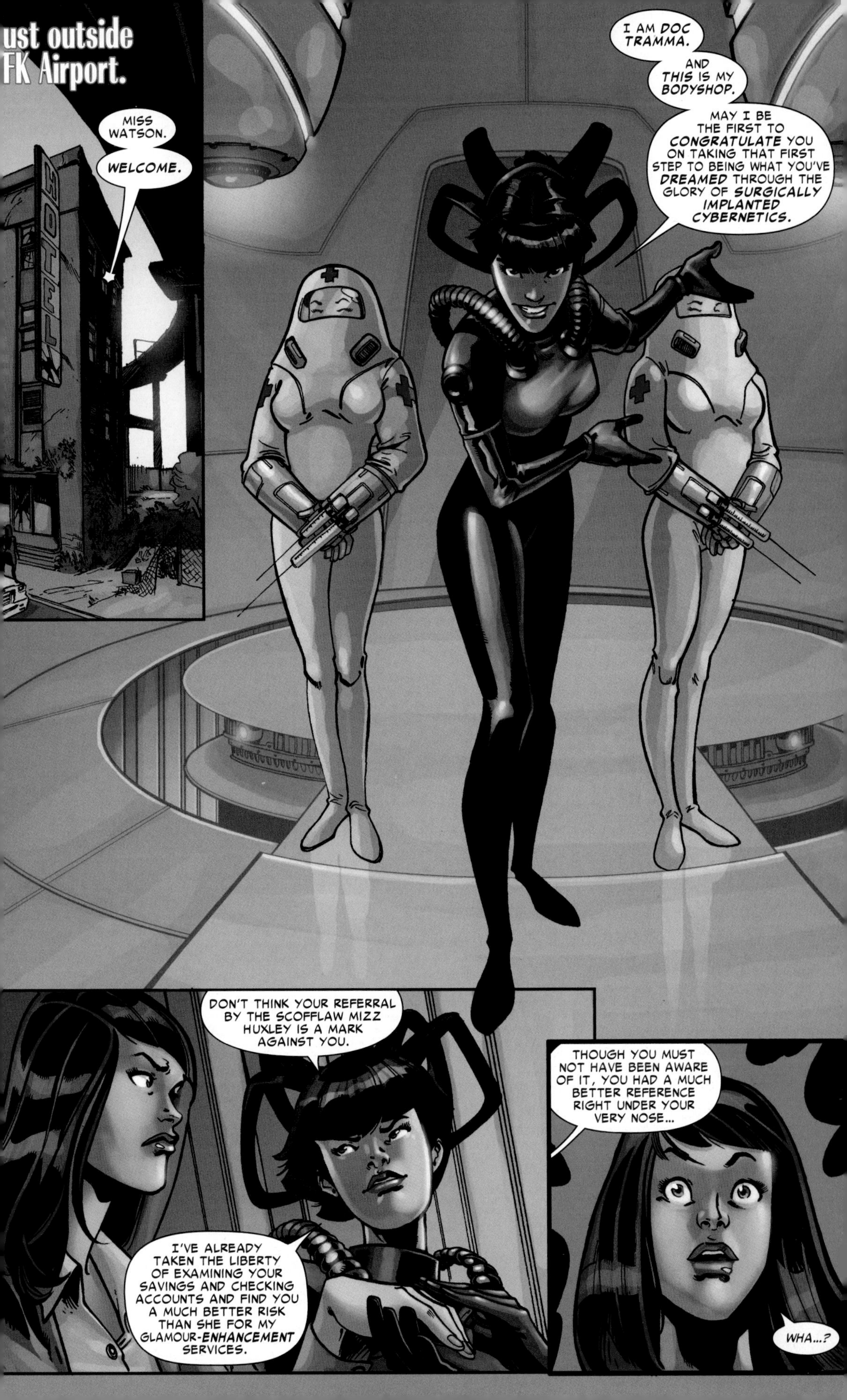
ust outside
FK Airport.
MISS WATSON.
WELCOME.
I AM DOC TRAMMA.
AND THIS IS MY BODYSHOP.
MAY I BE THE FIRST TO CONGRATULATE YOU ON TAKING THAT FIRST STEP TO BEING WHAT YOU'VE DREAMED THROUGH THE GLORY OF SURGICALLY IMPLANTED CYBERNETICS.
DON'T THINK YOUR REFERRAL BY THE SCOFFLAW MIZZ HUXLEY IS A MARK AGAINST YOU.
I'VE ALREADY TAKEN THE LIBERTY OF EXAMINING YOUR SAVINGS AND CHECKING ACCOUNTS AND FIND YOU A MUCH BETTER RISK THAN SHE FOR MY GLAMOUR-ENHANCEMENT SERVICES.
THOUGH YOU MUST NOT HAVE BEEN AWARE OF IT, YOU HAD A MUCH BETTER REFERENCE RIGHT UNDER YOUR VERY NOSE...
WHA...?

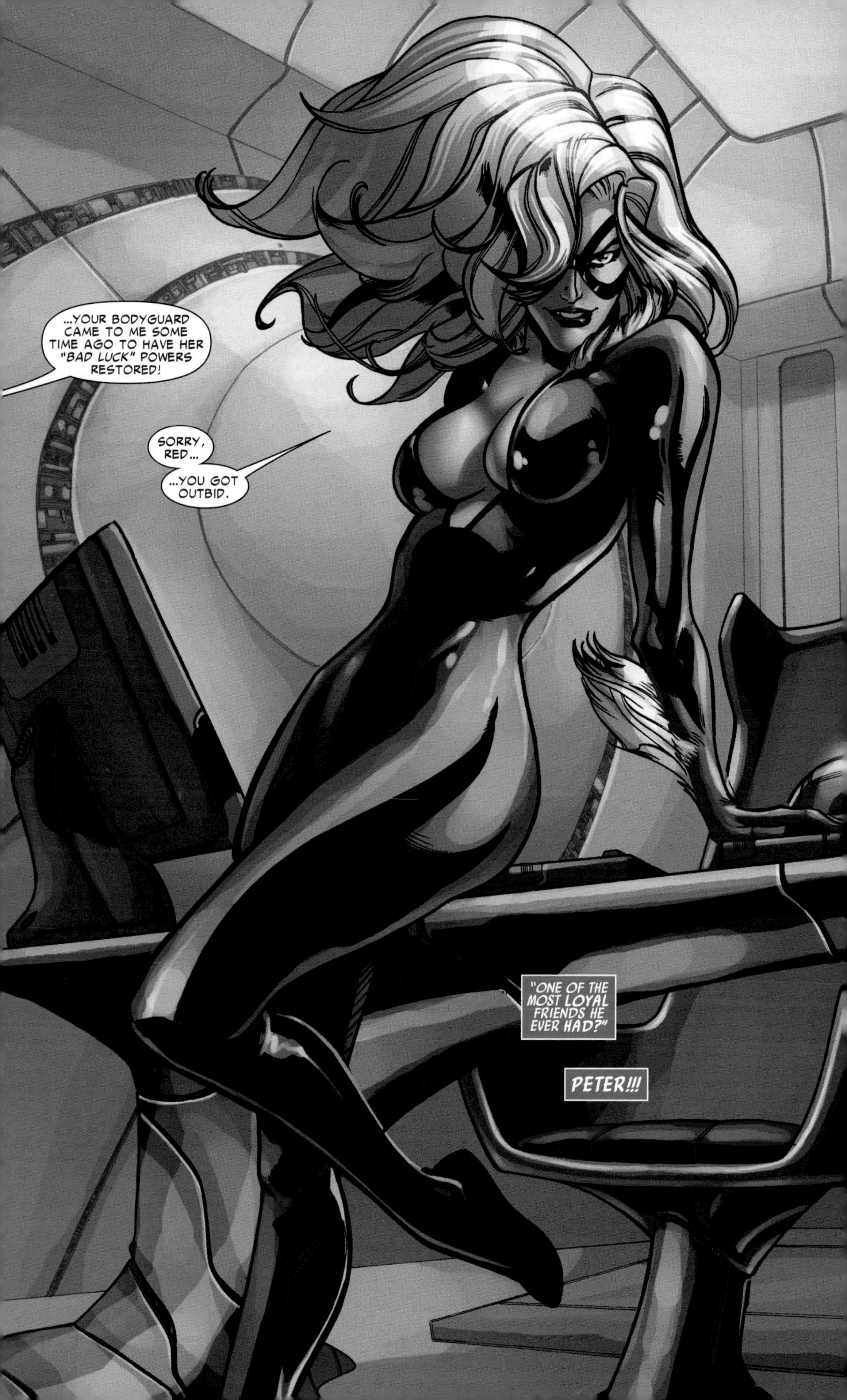
...YOUR BODYGUARD CAME TO ME SOME TIME AGO TO HAVE HER "BAD LUCK" POWERS RESTORED!
SORRY, RED...
...YOU GOT OUTBID.
"ONE OF THE MOST LOYAL FRIENDS HE EVER HAD?"
PETER!!!

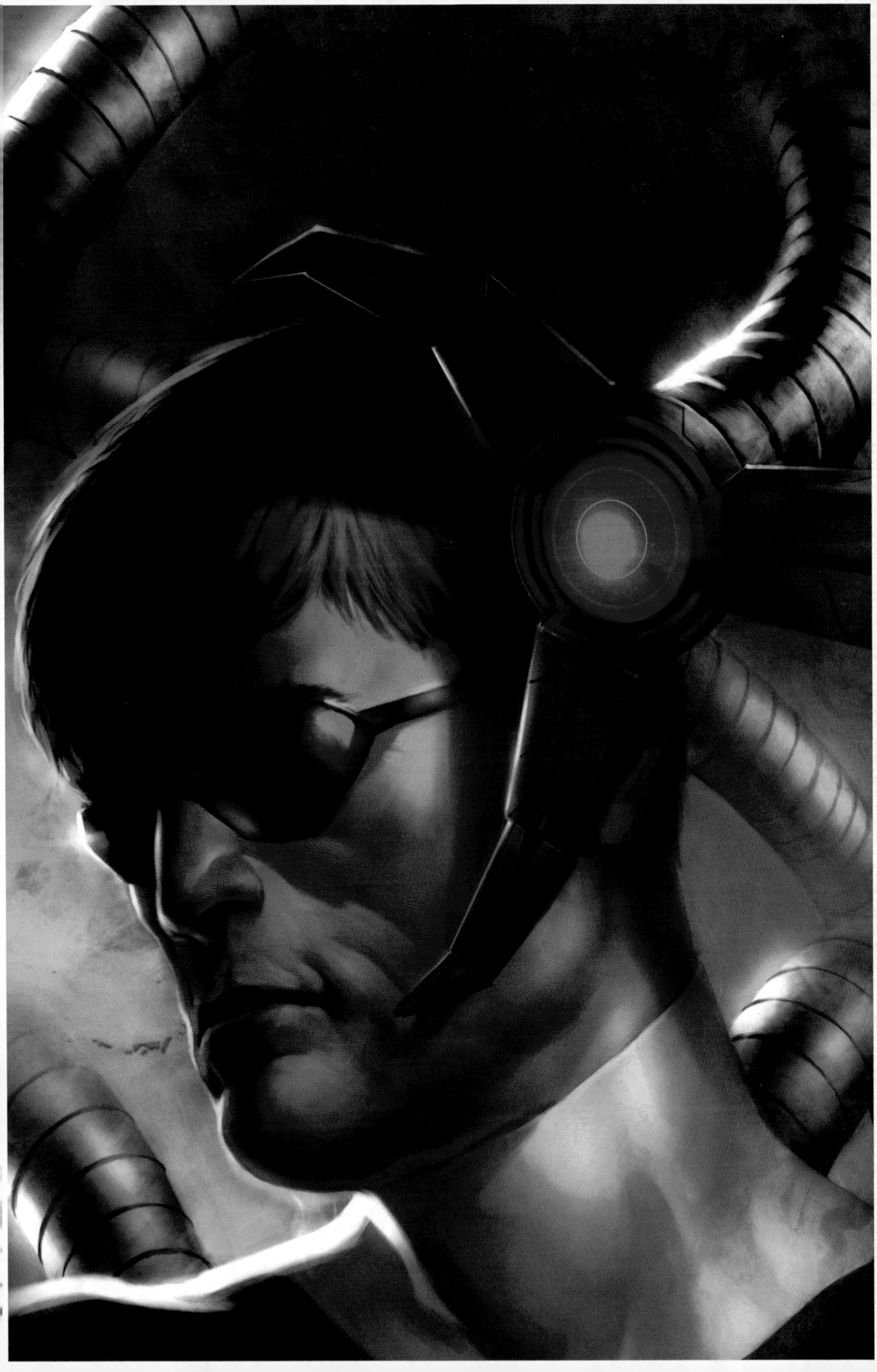

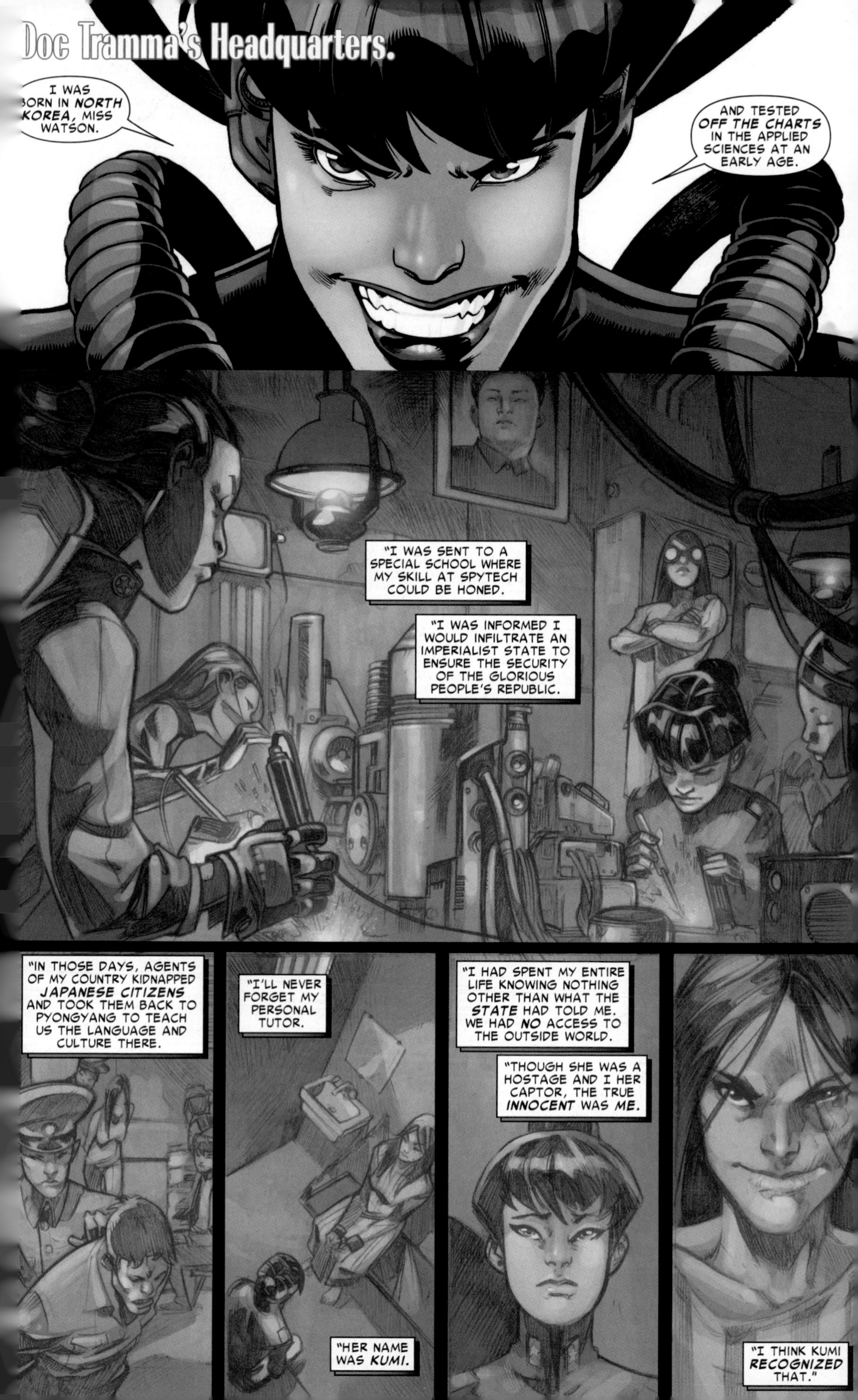
Doc Tramma's Headquarters.
I WAS BORN IN NORTH KOREA, MISS WATSON.
AND TESTED OFF THE CHARTS IN THE APPLIED SCIENCES AT AN EARLY AGE.
"I WAS SENT TO A SPECIAL SCHOOL WHERE MY SKILL AT SPYTECH COULD BE HONED.
"I WAS INFORMED I WOULD INFILTRATE AN IMPERIALIST STATE TO ENSURE THE SECURITY OF THE GLORIOUS PEOPLE'S REPUBLIC.
"IN THOSE DAYS, AGENTS OF MY COUNTRY KIDNAPPED JAPANESE CITIZENS AND TOOK THEM BACK TO PYONGYANG TO TEACH US THE LANGUAGE AND CULTURE THERE.
"I'LL NEVER FORGET MY PERSONAL TUTOR.
"HER NAME WAS KUMI.
"I HAD SPENT MY ENTIRE LIFE KNOWING NOTHING OTHER THAN WHAT THE STATE HAD TOLD ME. WE HAD NO ACCESS TO THE OUTSIDE WORLD.
"THOUGH SHE WAS A HOSTAGE AND I HER CAPTOR, THE TRUE INNOCENT WAS ME.
"I THINK KUMI RECOGNIZED THAT."

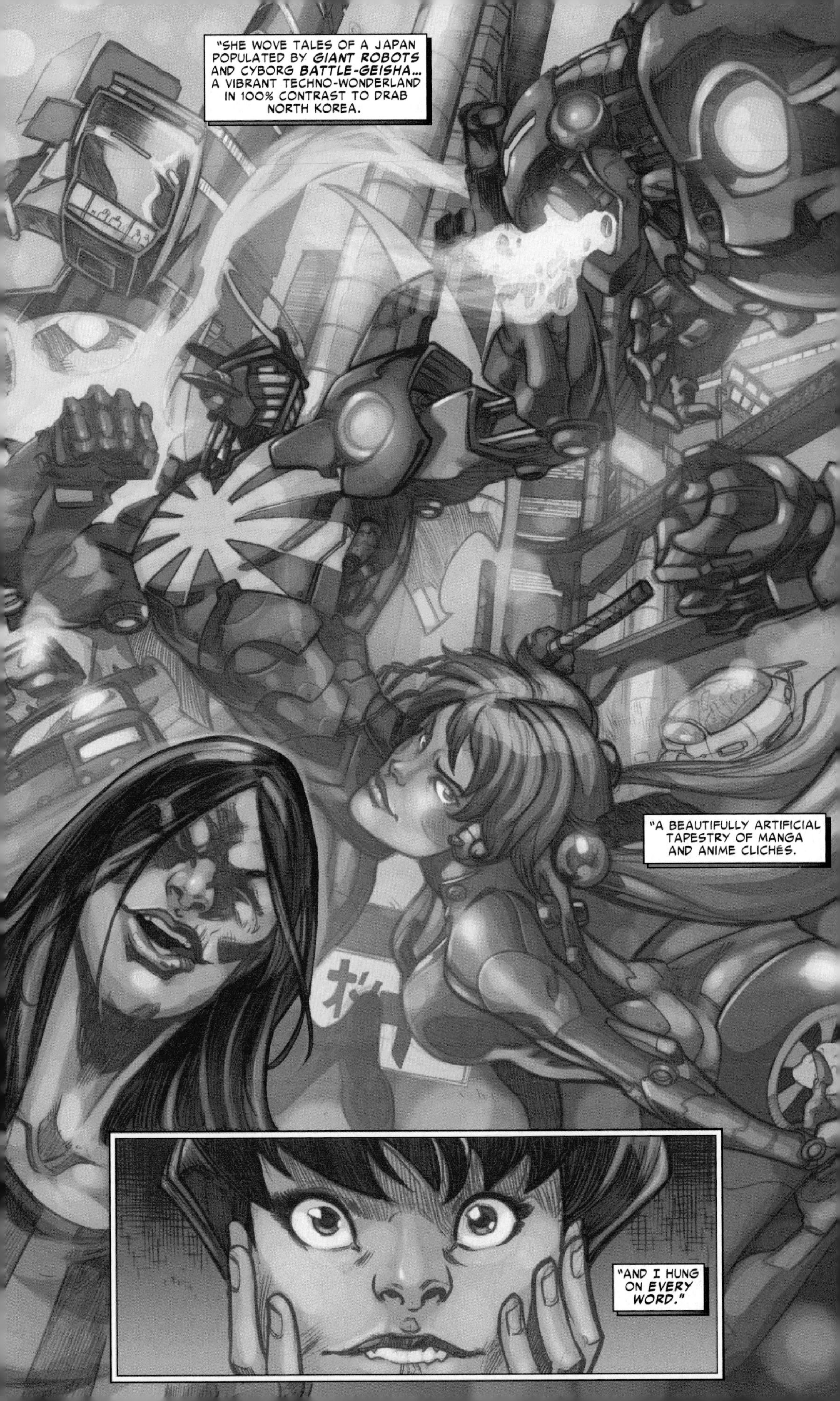
"SHE WOVE TALES OF A JAPAN POPULATED BY GIANT ROBOTS AND CYBORG BATTLE-GEISHA... A VIBRANT TECHNO-WONDERLAND IN 100% CONTRAST TO DRAB NORTH KOREA.
"A BEAUTIFULLY ARTIFICIAL TAPESTRY OF MANGA AND ANIME CLICHÉS.
"AND I HUNG ON EVERY WORD."

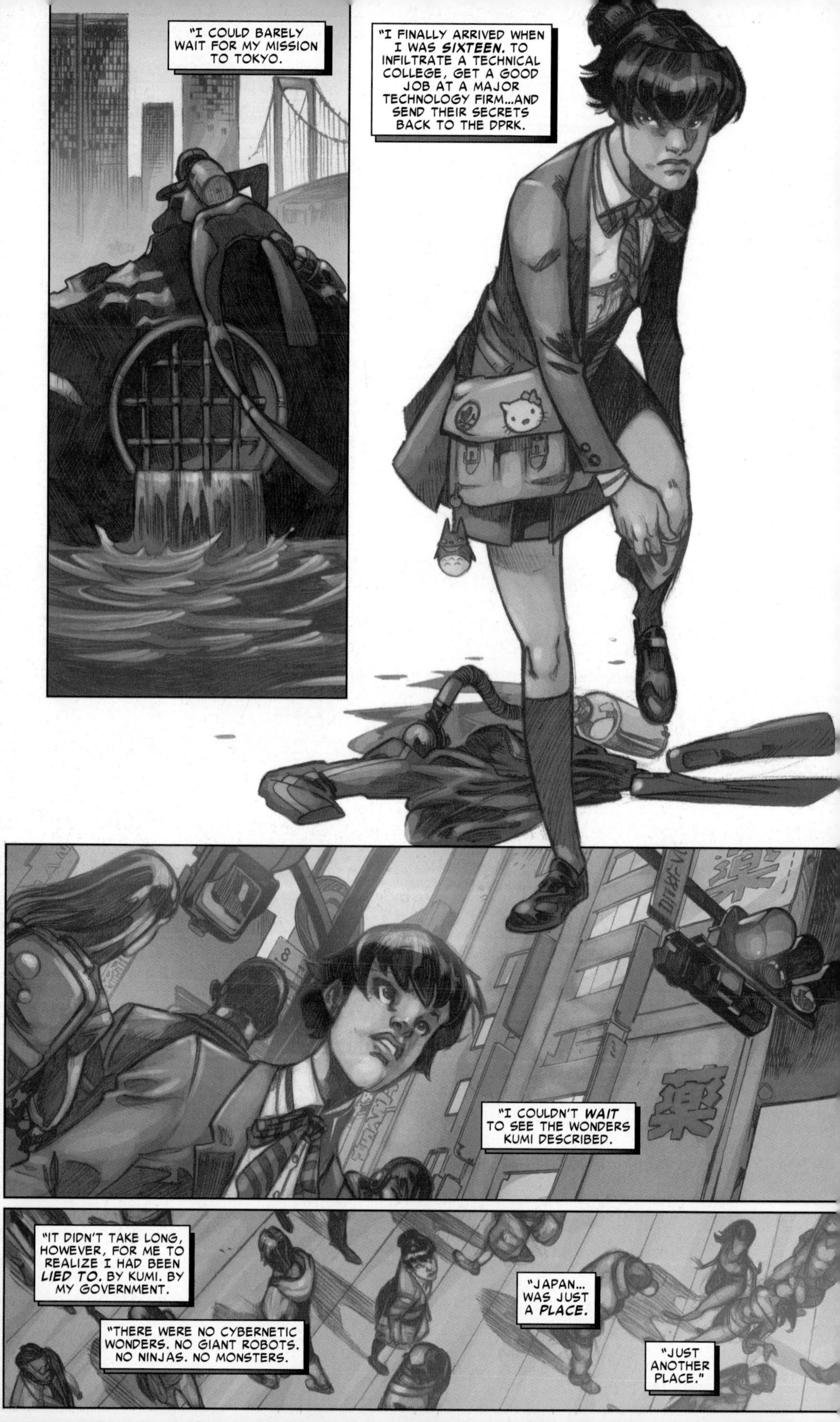
"I COULD BARELY WAIT FOR MY MISSION TO TOKYO.
"I FINALLY ARRIVED WHEN I WAS *SIXTEEN.* TO INFILTRATE A TECHNICAL COLLEGE, GET A GOOD JOB AT A MAJOR TECHNOLOGY FIRM...AND SEND THEIR SECRETS BACK TO THE DPRK.
"I COULDN'T *WAIT* TO SEE THE WONDERS KUMI DESCRIBED.
"IT DIDN'T TAKE LONG, HOWEVER, FOR ME TO REALIZE I HAD BEEN *LIED TO.* BY KUMI. BY MY GOVERNMENT.
"THERE WERE NO CYBERNETIC WONDERS. NO GIANT ROBOTS. NO NINJAS. NO MONSTERS.
"JAPAN... WAS JUST A *PLACE.*
"JUST ANOTHER PLACE."

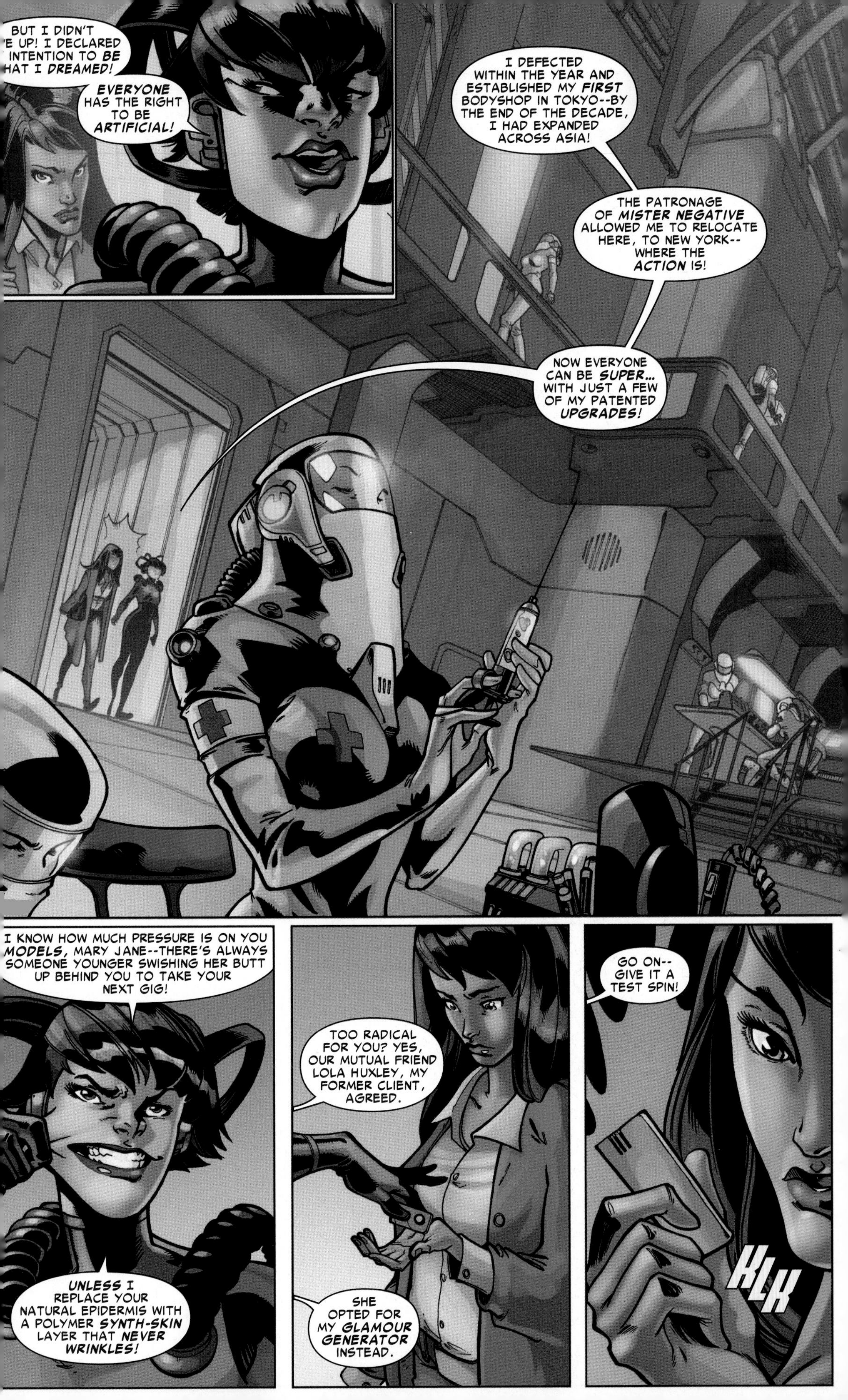
BUT I DIDN'T 'E UP! I DECLARED INTENTION TO BE HAT I DREAMED!
EVERYONE HAS THE RIGHT TO BE ARTIFICIAL!
I DEFECTED WITHIN THE YEAR AND ESTABLISHED MY FIRST BODYSHOP IN TOKYO--BY THE END OF THE DECADE, I HAD EXPANDED ACROSS ASIA!
THE PATRONAGE OF MISTER NEGATIVE ALLOWED ME TO RELOCATE HERE, TO NEW YORK-- WHERE THE ACTION IS!
NOW EVERYONE CAN BE SUPER... WITH JUST A FEW OF MY PATENTED UPGRADES!
I KNOW HOW MUCH PRESSURE IS ON YOU MODELS, MARY JANE--THERE'S ALWAYS SOMEONE YOUNGER SWISHING HER BUTT UP BEHIND YOU TO TAKE YOUR NEXT GIG!
UNLESS I REPLACE YOUR NATURAL EPIDERMIS WITH A POLYMER SYNTH-SKIN LAYER THAT NEVER WRINKLES!
TOO RADICAL FOR YOU? YES, OUR MUTUAL FRIEND LOLA HUXLEY, MY FORMER CLIENT, AGREED.
SHE OPTED FOR MY GLAMOUR GENERATOR INSTEAD.
GO ON-- GIVE IT A TEST SPIN!
KLK

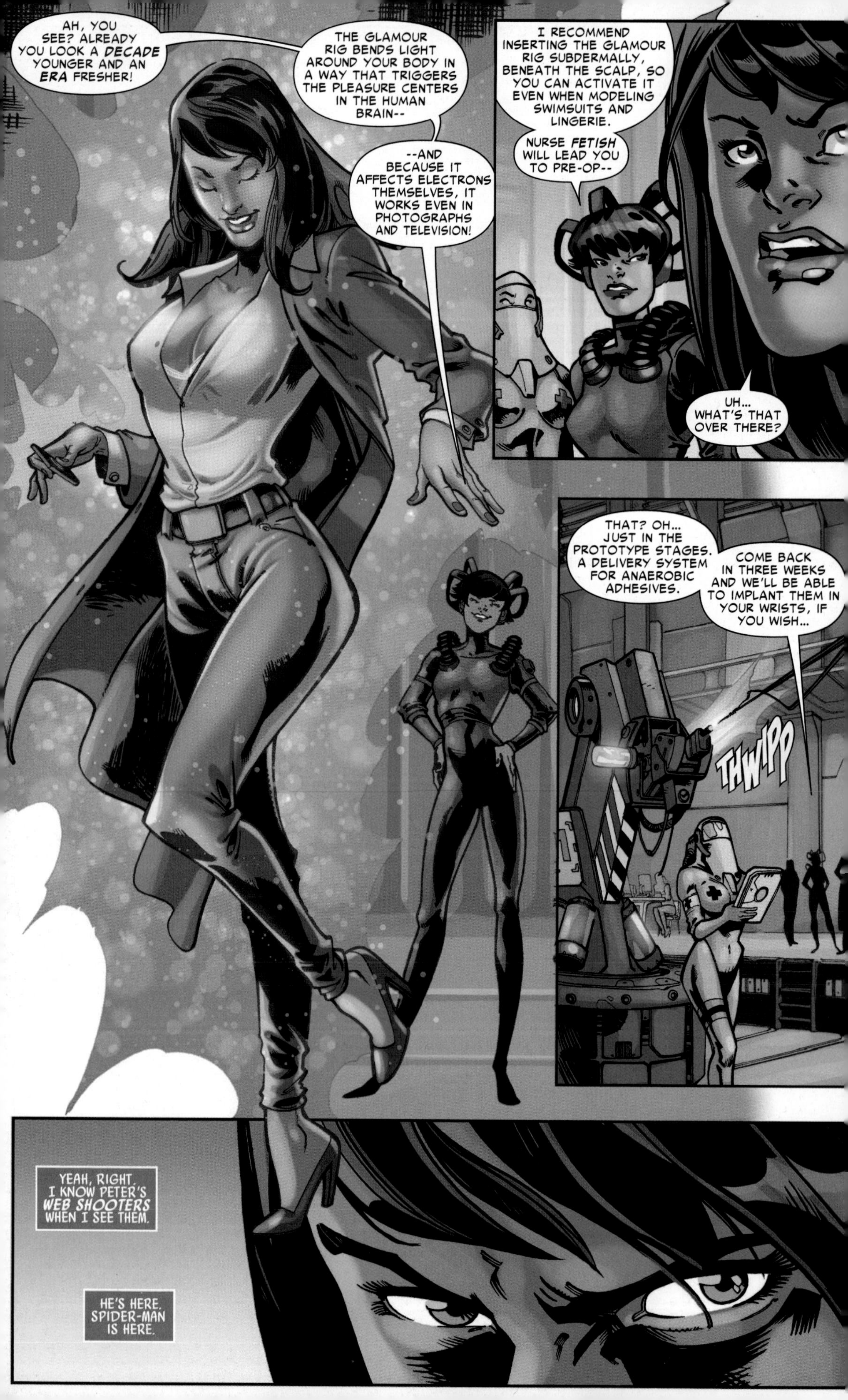

AH, YOU SEE? ALREADY YOU LOOK A *DECADE* YOUNGER AND AN *ERA* FRESHER!
THE GLAMOUR RIG BENDS LIGHT AROUND YOUR BODY IN A WAY THAT TRIGGERS THE PLEASURE CENTERS IN THE HUMAN BRAIN--
--AND BECAUSE IT AFFECTS ELECTRONS THEMSELVES, IT WORKS EVEN IN PHOTOGRAPHS AND TELEVISION!
I RECOMMEND INSERTING THE GLAMOUR RIG SUBDERMALLY, BENEATH THE SCALP, SO YOU CAN ACTIVATE IT EVEN WHEN MODELING SWIMSUITS AND LINGERIE.
NURSE *FETISH* WILL LEAD YOU TO PRE-OP--
UH... WHAT'S THAT OVER THERE?
THAT? OH... JUST IN THE PROTOTYPE STAGES. A DELIVERY SYSTEM FOR ANAEROBIC ADHESIVES.
COME BACK IN THREE WEEKS AND WE'LL BE ABLE TO IMPLANT THEM IN YOUR WRISTS, IF YOU WISH...
THWIPP
YEAH, RIGHT. I KNOW PETER'S *WEB SHOOTERS* WHEN I SEE THEM.
HE'S HERE. SPIDER-MAN IS HERE.

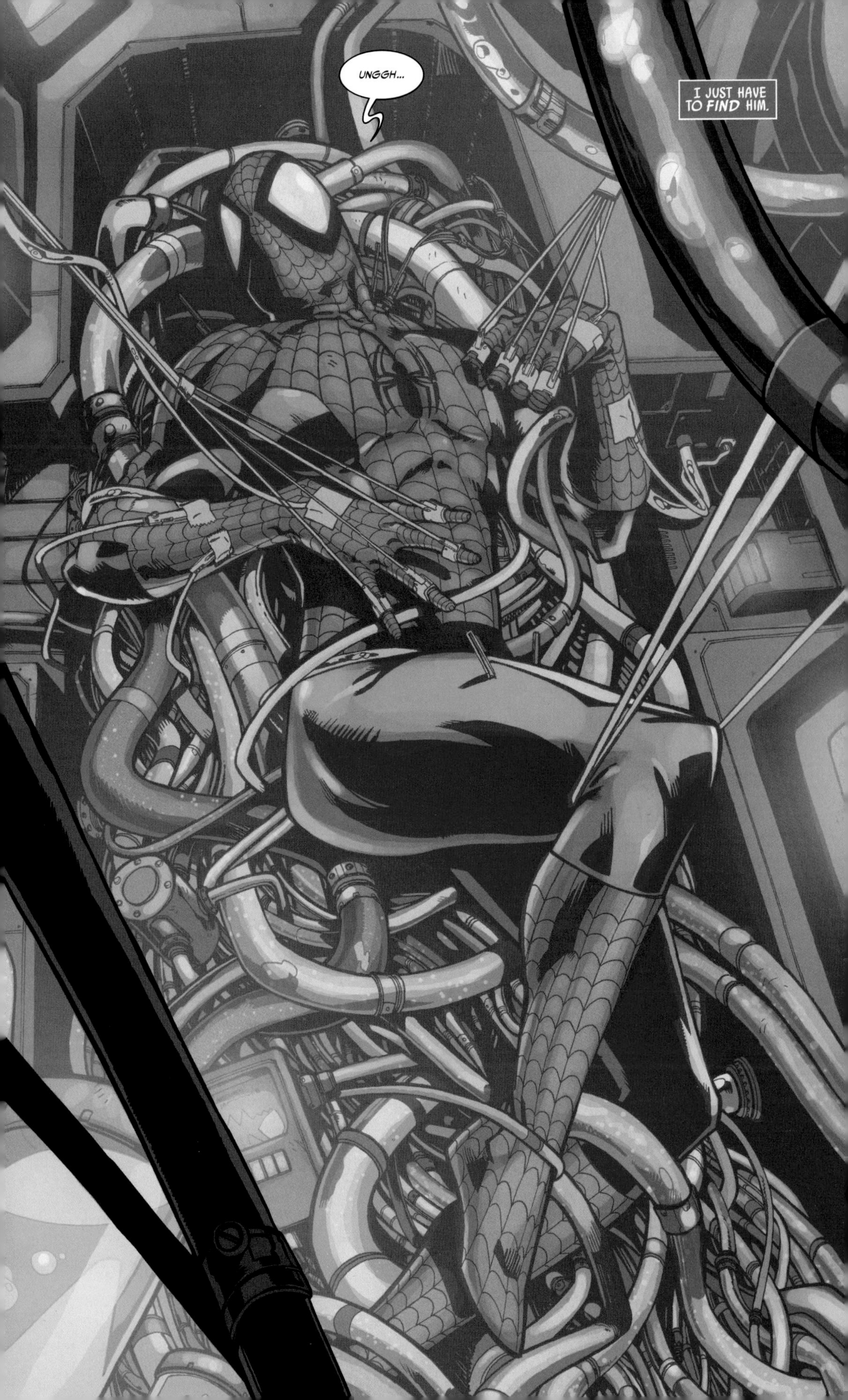
UNGGH...
I JUST HAVE TO FIND HIM.

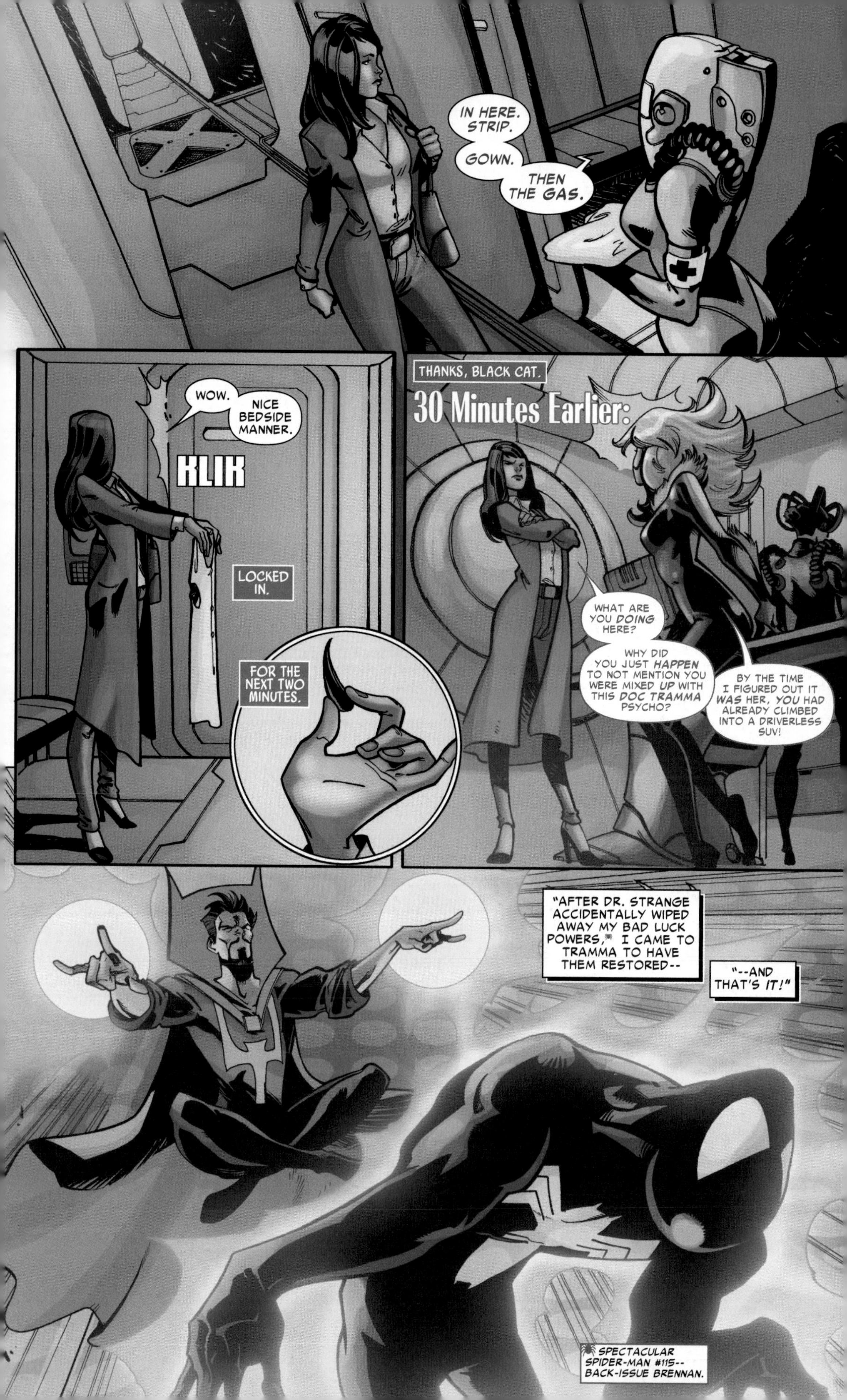

IN HERE. STRIP.
GOWN.
THEN THE GAS.
WOW.
NICE BEDSIDE MANNER.
KLIK
LOCKED IN.
FOR THE NEXT TWO MINUTES.
THANKS, BLACK CAT.
30 Minutes Earlier:
WHAT ARE YOU DOING HERE?
WHY DID YOU JUST HAPPEN TO NOT MENTION YOU WERE MIXED UP WITH THIS DOC TRAMMA PSYCHO?
BY THE TIME I FIGURED OUT IT WAS HER, YOU HAD ALREADY CLIMBED INTO A DRIVERLESS SUV!
"AFTER DR. STRANGE ACCIDENTALLY WIPED AWAY MY BAD LUCK POWERS,* I CAME TO TRAMMA TO HAVE THEM RESTORED--
"--AND THAT'S IT!"
*SPECTACULAR SPIDER-MAN #115--BACK-ISSUE BRENNAN.

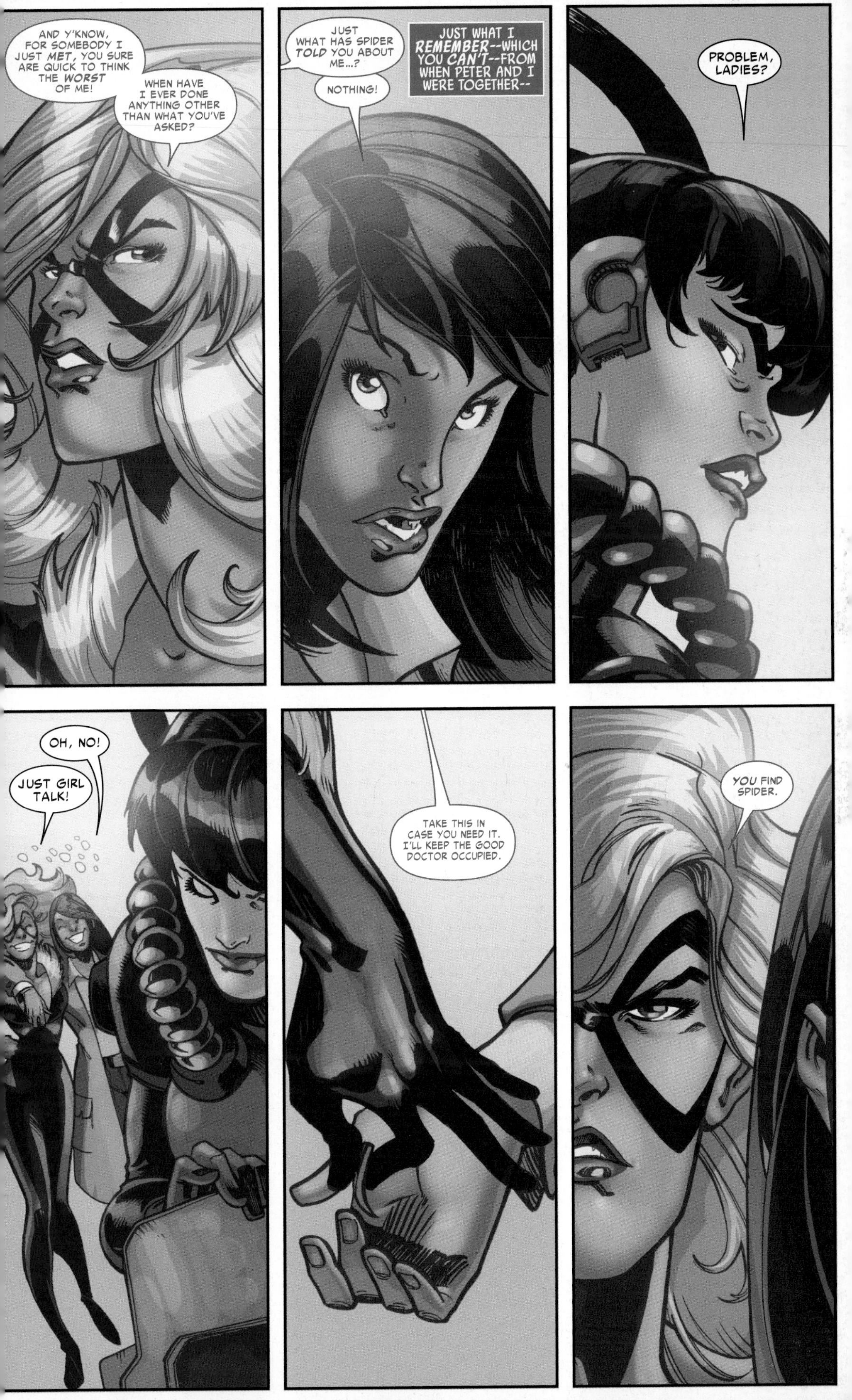
AND Y'KNOW, FOR SOMEBODY I JUST MET, YOU SURE ARE QUICK TO THINK THE WORST OF ME!
WHEN HAVE I EVER DONE ANYTHING OTHER THAN WHAT YOU'VE ASKED?
JUST WHAT HAS SPIDER TOLD YOU ABOUT ME...?
NOTHING!
JUST WHAT I REMEMBER--WHICH YOU CAN'T--FROM WHEN PETER AND I WERE TOGETHER--
PROBLEM, LADIES?
OH, NO!
JUST GIRL TALK!
TAKE THIS IN CASE YOU NEED IT. I'LL KEEP THE GOOD DOCTOR OCCUPIED.
YOU FIND SPIDER.

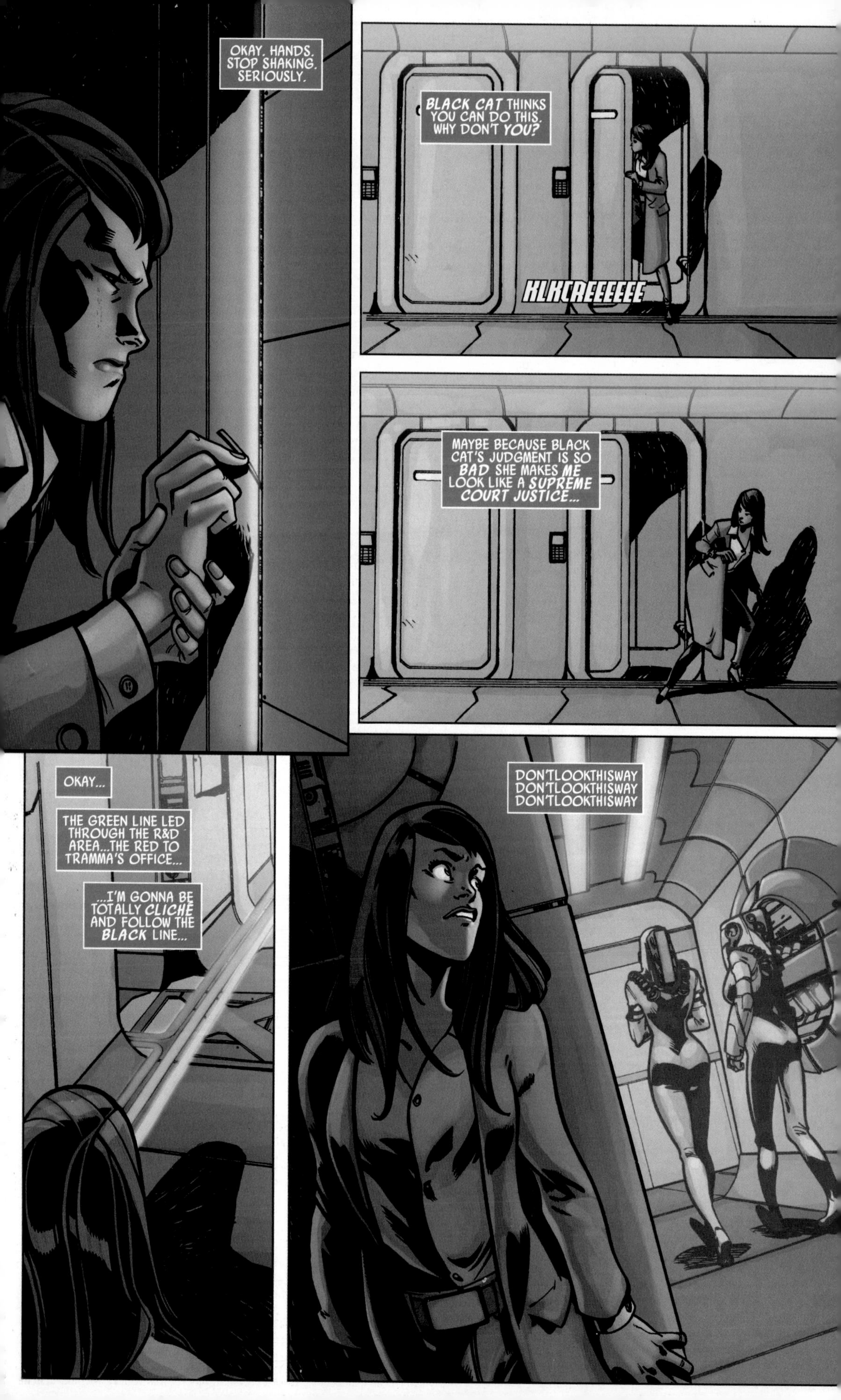
OKAY. HANDS. STOP SHAKING. SERIOUSLY.
BLACK CAT THINKS YOU CAN DO THIS. WHY DON'T YOU?
KLKCREEEEEE
MAYBE BECAUSE BLACK CAT'S JUDGMENT IS SO BAD SHE MAKES ME LOOK LIKE A SUPREME COURT JUSTICE...
OKAY...
THE GREEN LINE LED THROUGH THE R&D AREA...THE RED TO TRAMMA'S OFFICE...
...I'M GONNA BE TOTALLY CLICHÉ AND FOLLOW THE BLACK LINE...
DON'TLOOKTHISWAY DON'TLOOKTHISWAY DON'TLOOKTHISWAY

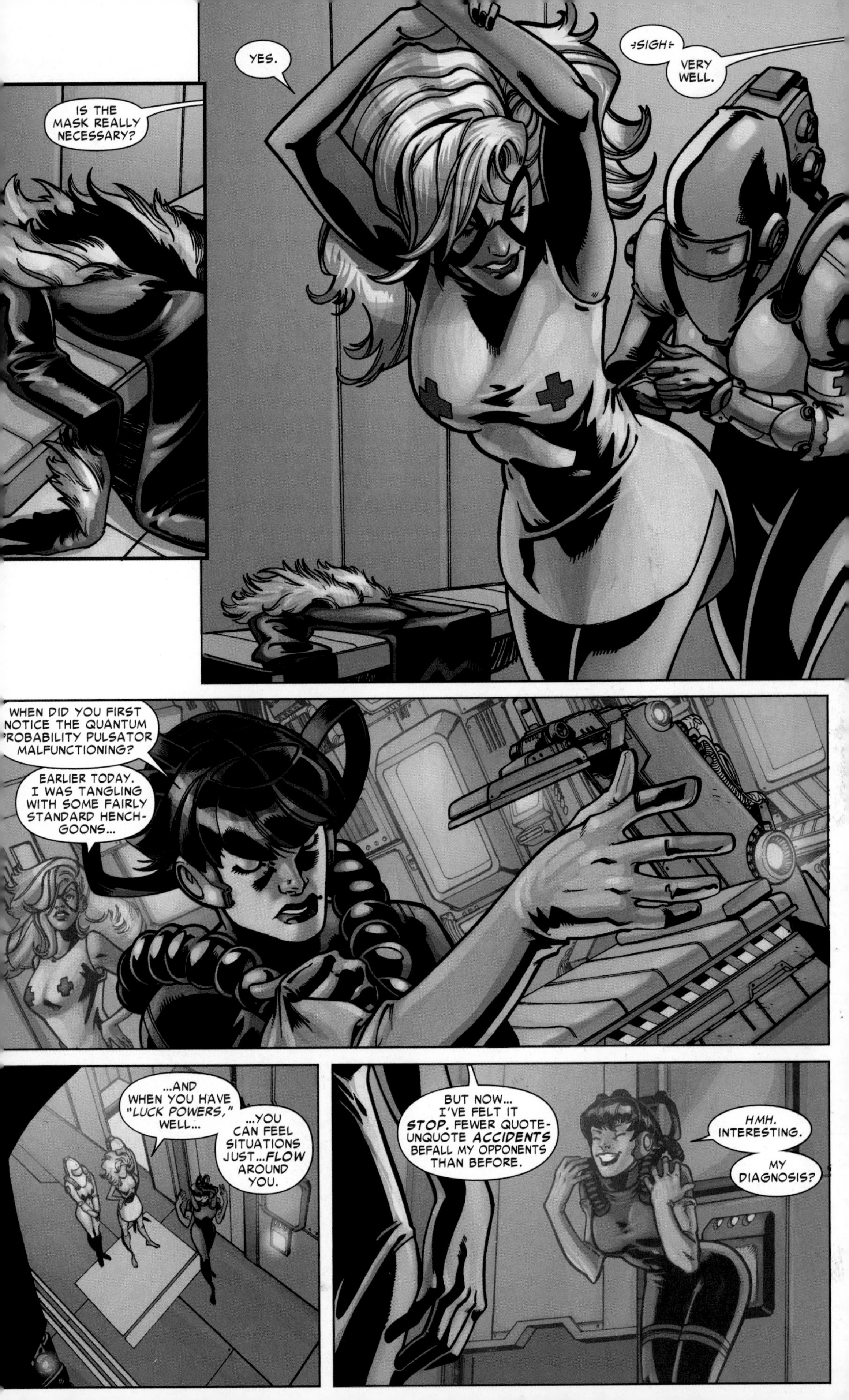
IS THE MASK REALLY NECESSARY?
YES.
-SIGH- VERY WELL.
WHEN DID YOU FIRST NOTICE THE QUANTUM PROBABILITY PULSATOR MALFUNCTIONING?
EARLIER TODAY. I WAS TANGLING WITH SOME FAIRLY STANDARD HENCH-GOONS...
...AND WHEN YOU HAVE "LUCK POWERS," WELL...
...YOU CAN FEEL SITUATIONS JUST...FLOW AROUND YOU.
BUT NOW... I'VE FELT IT STOP. FEWER QUOTE-UNQUOTE ACCIDENTS BEFALL MY OPPONENTS THAN BEFORE.
HMH. INTERESTING.
MY DIAGNOSIS?

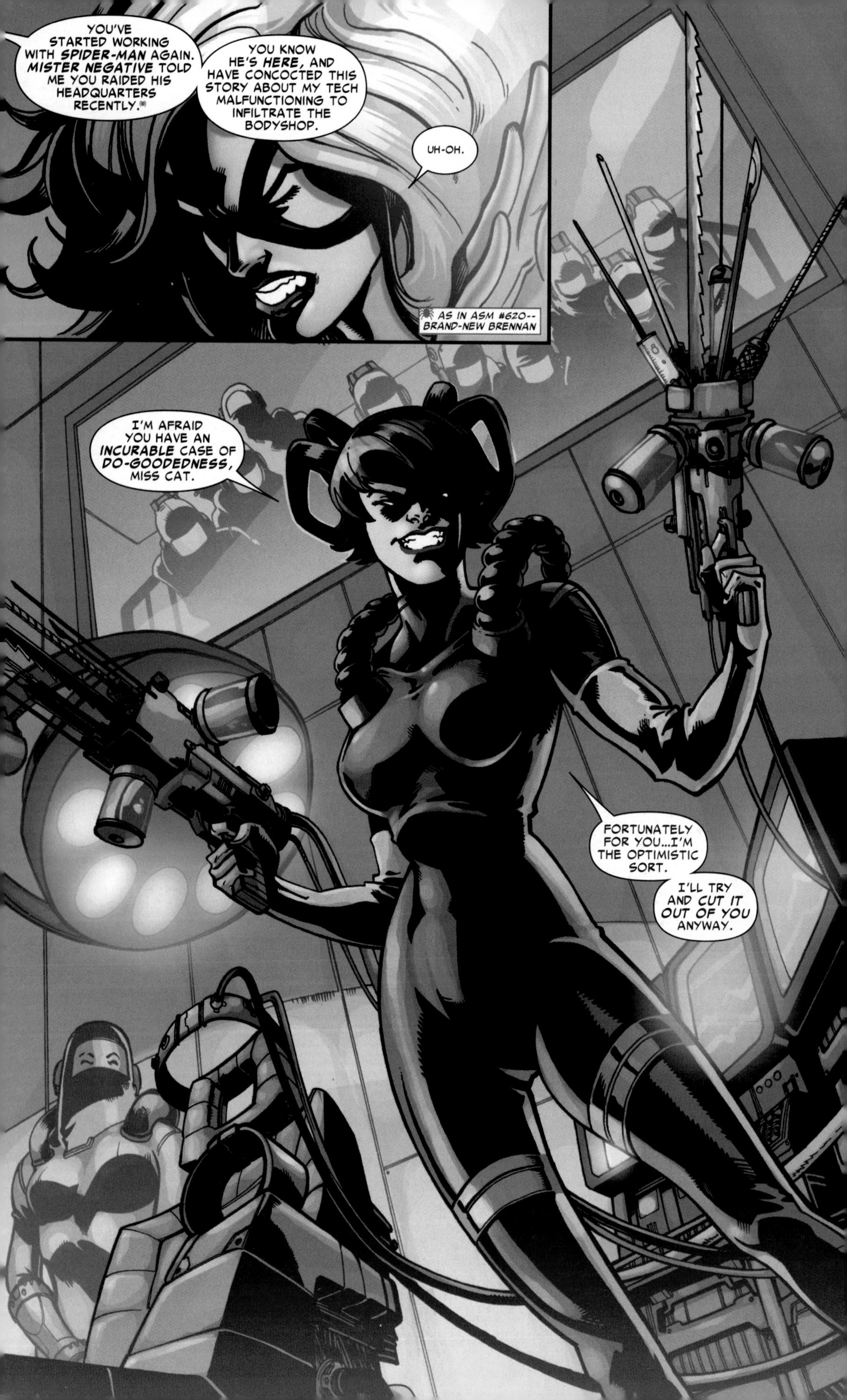
YOU'VE STARTED WORKING WITH SPIDER-MAN AGAIN. MISTER NEGATIVE TOLD ME YOU RAIDED HIS HEADQUARTERS RECENTLY.*
YOU KNOW HE'S HERE, AND HAVE CONCOCTED THIS STORY ABOUT MY TECH MALFUNCTIONING TO INFILTRATE THE BODYSHOP.
UH-OH.
*AS IN ASM #620-- BRAND-NEW BRENNAN
I'M AFRAID YOU HAVE AN INCURABLE CASE OF DO-GOODEDNESS, MISS CAT.
FORTUNATELY FOR YOU...I'M THE OPTIMISTIC SORT.
I'LL TRY AND CUT IT OUT OF YOU ANYWAY.

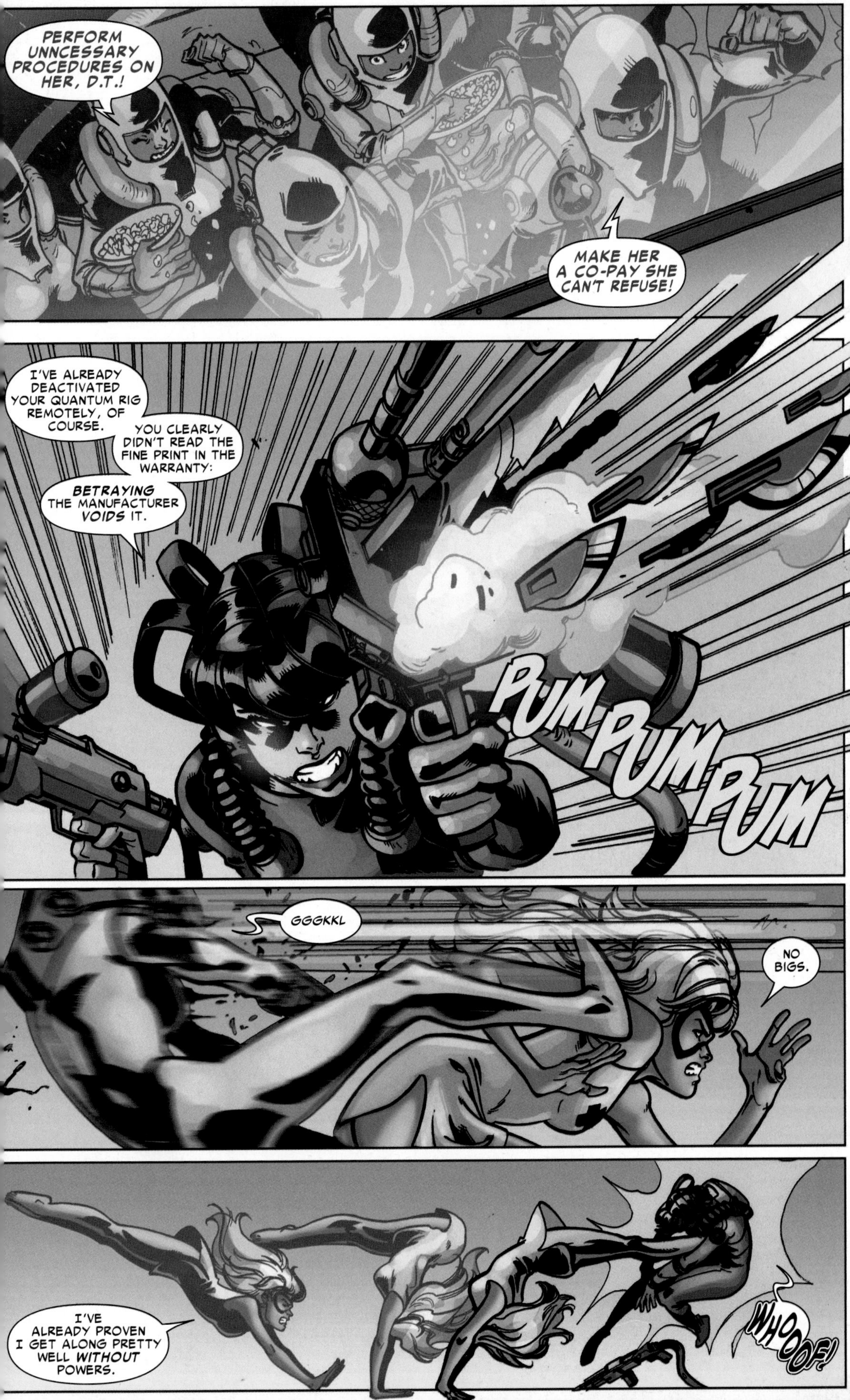
PERFORM UNNCESSARY PROCEDURES ON HER, D.T.!
MAKE HER A CO-PAY SHE CAN'T REFUSE!
I'VE ALREADY DEACTIVATED YOUR QUANTUM RIG REMOTELY, OF COURSE.
YOU CLEARLY DIDN'T READ THE FINE PRINT IN THE WARRANTY:
BETRAYING THE MANUFACTURER VOIDS IT.
PUM PUM PUM
GGGKKL
NO BIGS.
I'VE ALREADY PROVEN I GET ALONG PRETTY WELL WITHOUT POWERS.
WHOOOF!

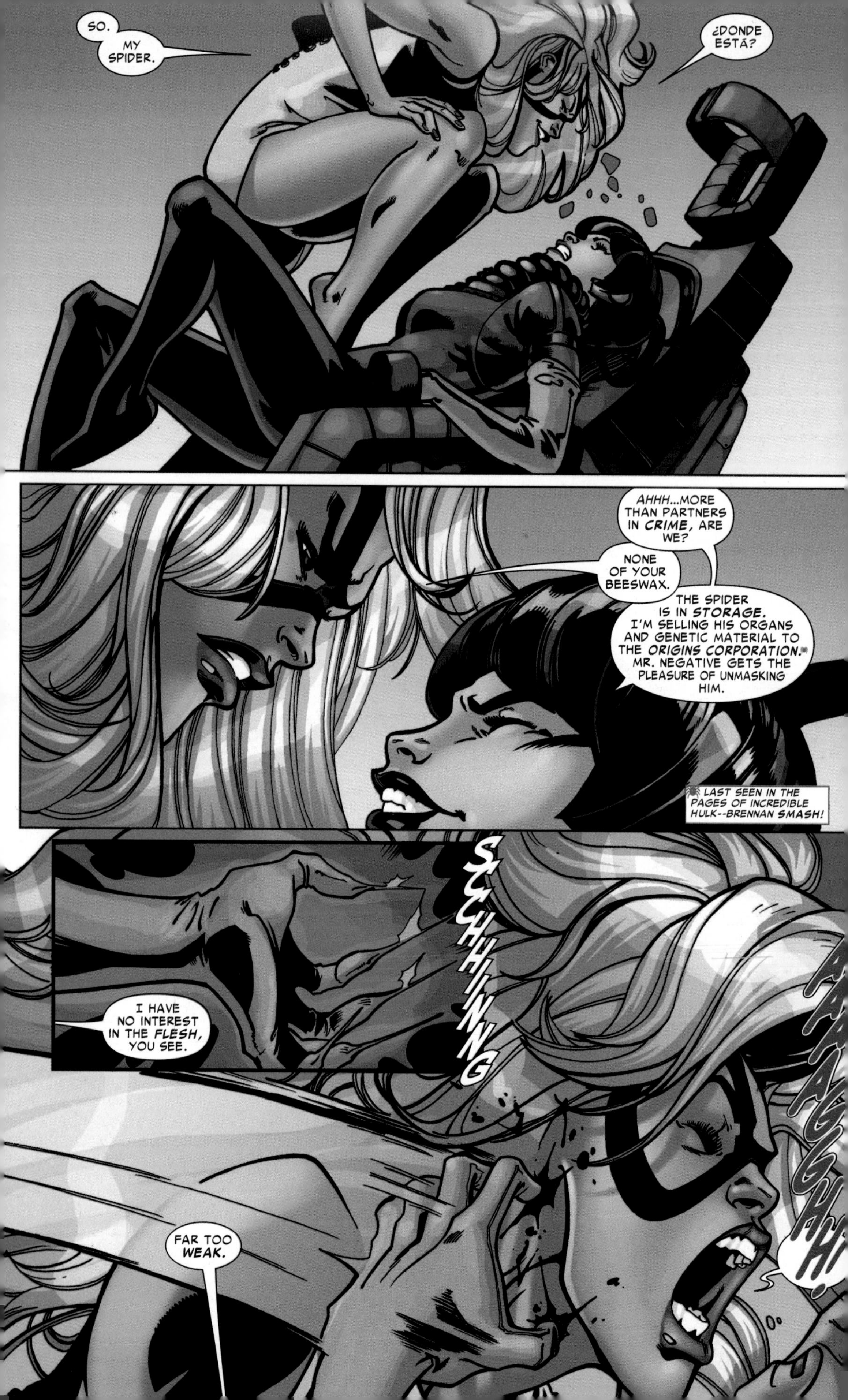
SO. MY SPIDER.
¿DONDE ESTÁ?
AHHH...MORE THAN PARTNERS IN CRIME, ARE WE?
NONE OF YOUR BEESWAX.
THE SPIDER IS IN STORAGE. I'M SELLING HIS ORGANS AND GENETIC MATERIAL TO THE ORIGINS CORPORATION. MR. NEGATIVE GETS THE PLEASURE OF UNMASKING HIM.
LAST SEEN IN THE PAGES OF INCREDIBLE HULK--BRENNAN SMASH!
SCCHHINNNG
I HAVE NO INTEREST IN THE FLESH, YOU SEE.
FAR TOO WEAK.

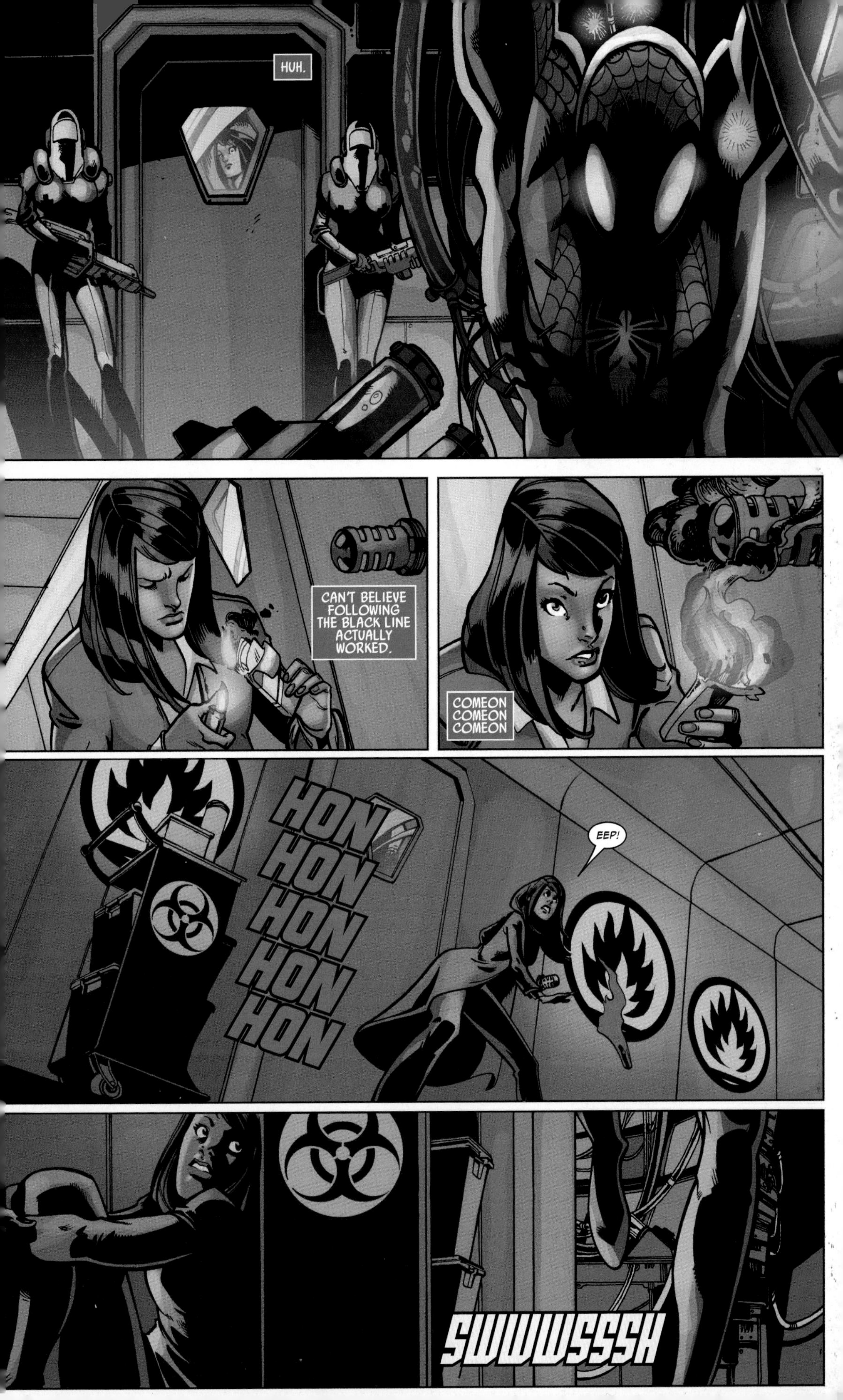
HUH.
CAN'T BELIEVE FOLLOWING THE BLACK LINE ACTUALLY WORKED.
COMEON COMEON COMEON
HON HON HON HON HON HON
EEP!
SWWWSSSH

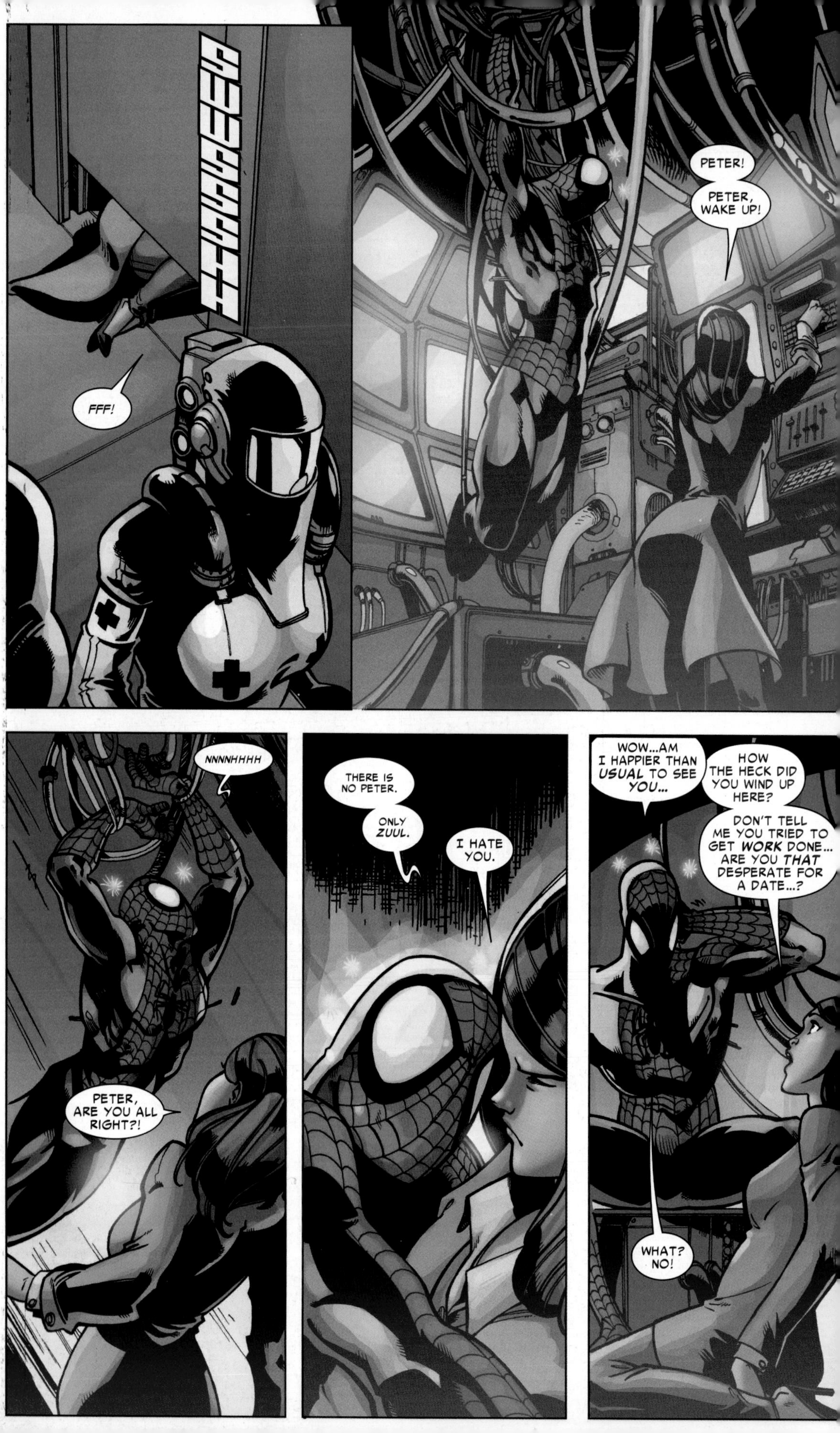
SWSSSSHHH
FFF!
PETER!
PETER, WAKE UP!
NNNNHHHH
PETER, ARE YOU ALL RIGHT?!
THERE IS NO PETER.
ONLY ZUUL.
I HATE YOU.
WOW...AM I HAPPIER THAN USUAL TO SEE YOU...
HOW THE HECK DID YOU WIND UP HERE?
DON'T TELL ME YOU TRIED TO GET WORK DONE... ARE YOU THAT DESPERATE FOR A DATE...?
WHAT? NO!

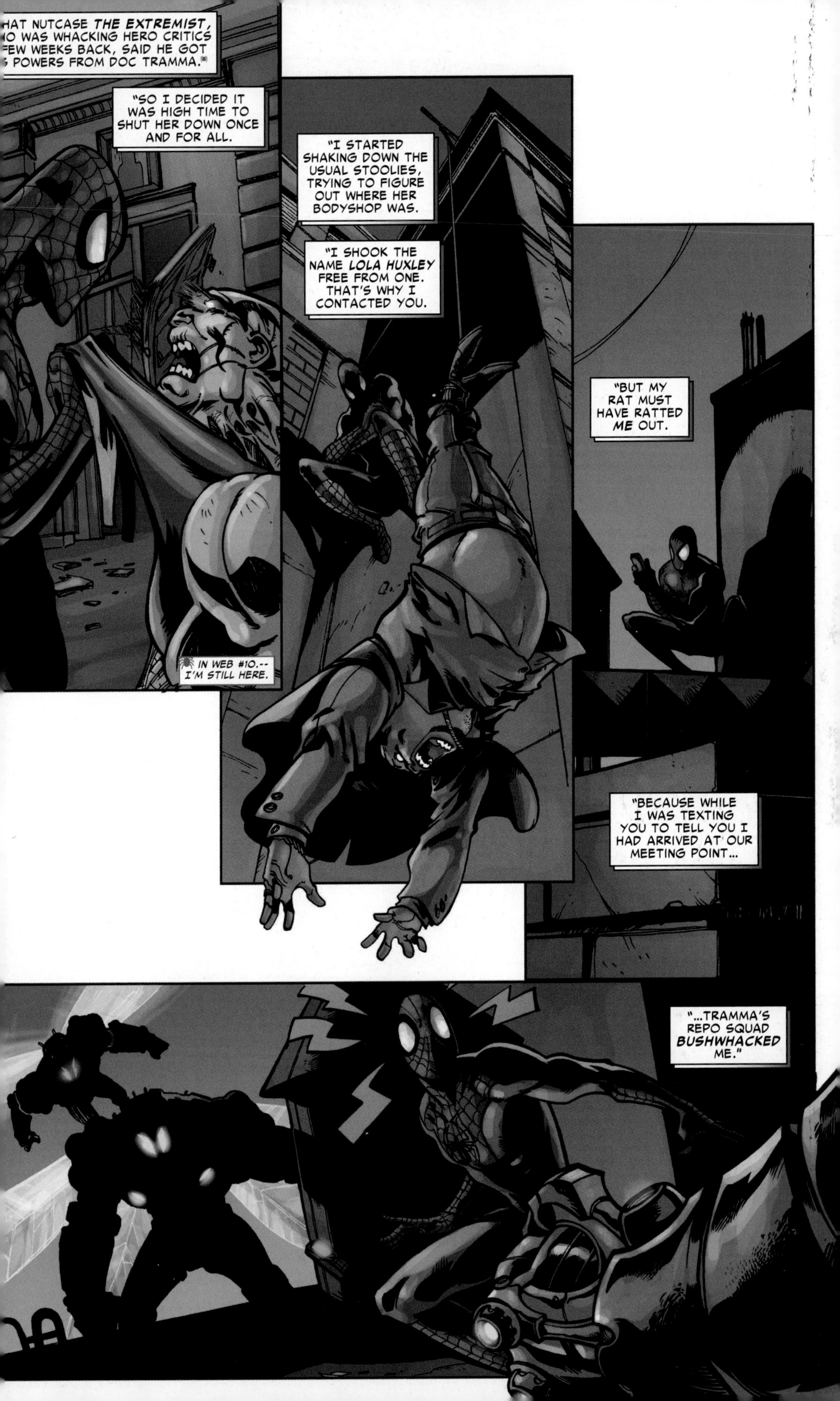
HAT NUTCASE THE EXTREMIST, HO WAS WHACKING HERO CRITICS FEW WEEKS BACK, SAID HE GOT POWERS FROM DOC TRAMMA.*
"SO I DECIDED IT WAS HIGH TIME TO SHUT HER DOWN ONCE AND FOR ALL.
*IN WEB #10.-- I'M STILL HERE.
"I STARTED SHAKING DOWN THE USUAL STOOLIES, TRYING TO FIGURE OUT WHERE HER BODYSHOP WAS.
"I SHOOK THE NAME LOLA HUXLEY FREE FROM ONE. THAT'S WHY I CONTACTED YOU.
"BUT MY RAT MUST HAVE RATTED ME OUT.
"BECAUSE WHILE I WAS TEXTING YOU TO TELL YOU I HAD ARRIVED AT OUR MEETING POINT...
"...TRAMMA'S REPO SQUAD BUSHWHACKED ME."

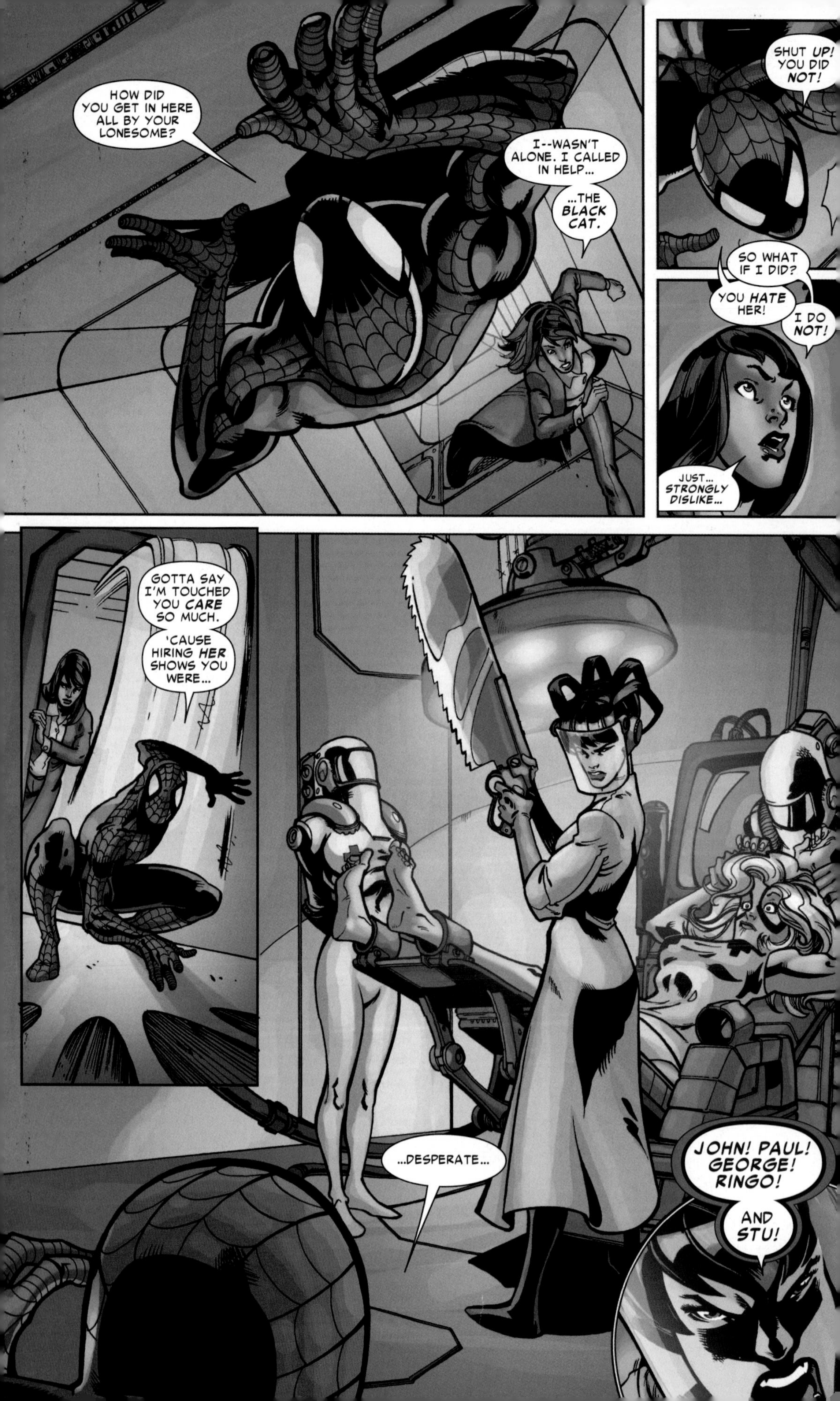
HOW DID YOU GET IN HERE ALL BY YOUR LONESOME?
I--WASN'T ALONE. I CALLED IN HELP...
...THE BLACK CAT.
SHUT UP! YOU DID NOT!
SO WHAT IF I DID?
YOU HATE HER!
I DO NOT!
JUST... STRONGLY DISLIKE...
GOTTA SAY I'M TOUCHED YOU CARE SO MUCH.
'CAUSE HIRING HER SHOWS YOU WERE...
...DESPERATE...
JOHN! PAUL! GEORGE! RINGO!
AND STU!

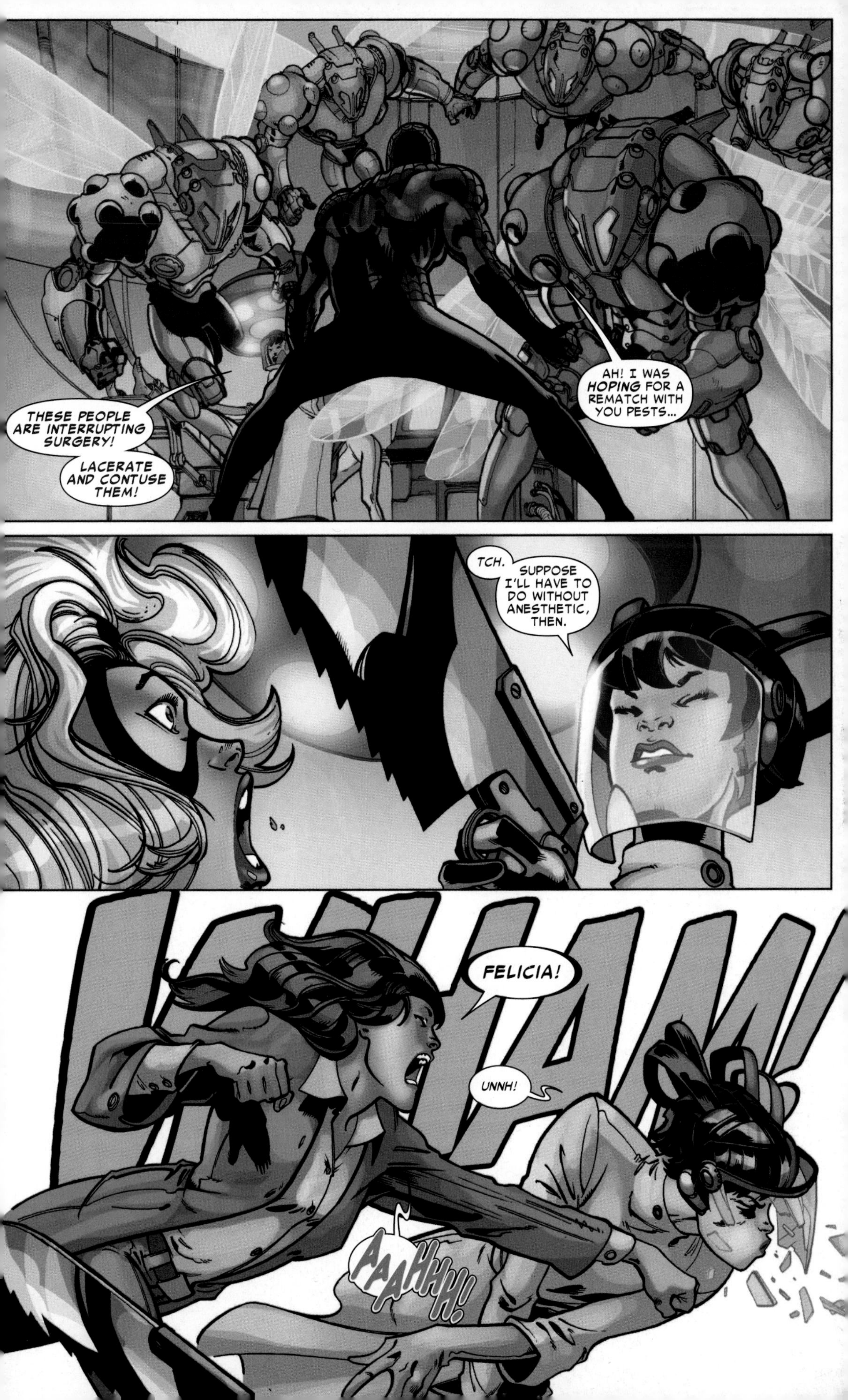
THESE PEOPLE ARE INTERRUPTING SURGERY!
LACERATE AND CONTUSE THEM!
AH! I WAS HOPING FOR A REMATCH WITH YOU PESTS...
TCH.
SUPPOSE I'LL HAVE TO DO WITHOUT ANESTHETIC, THEN.
FELICIA!
UNNH!
AAAHHH!

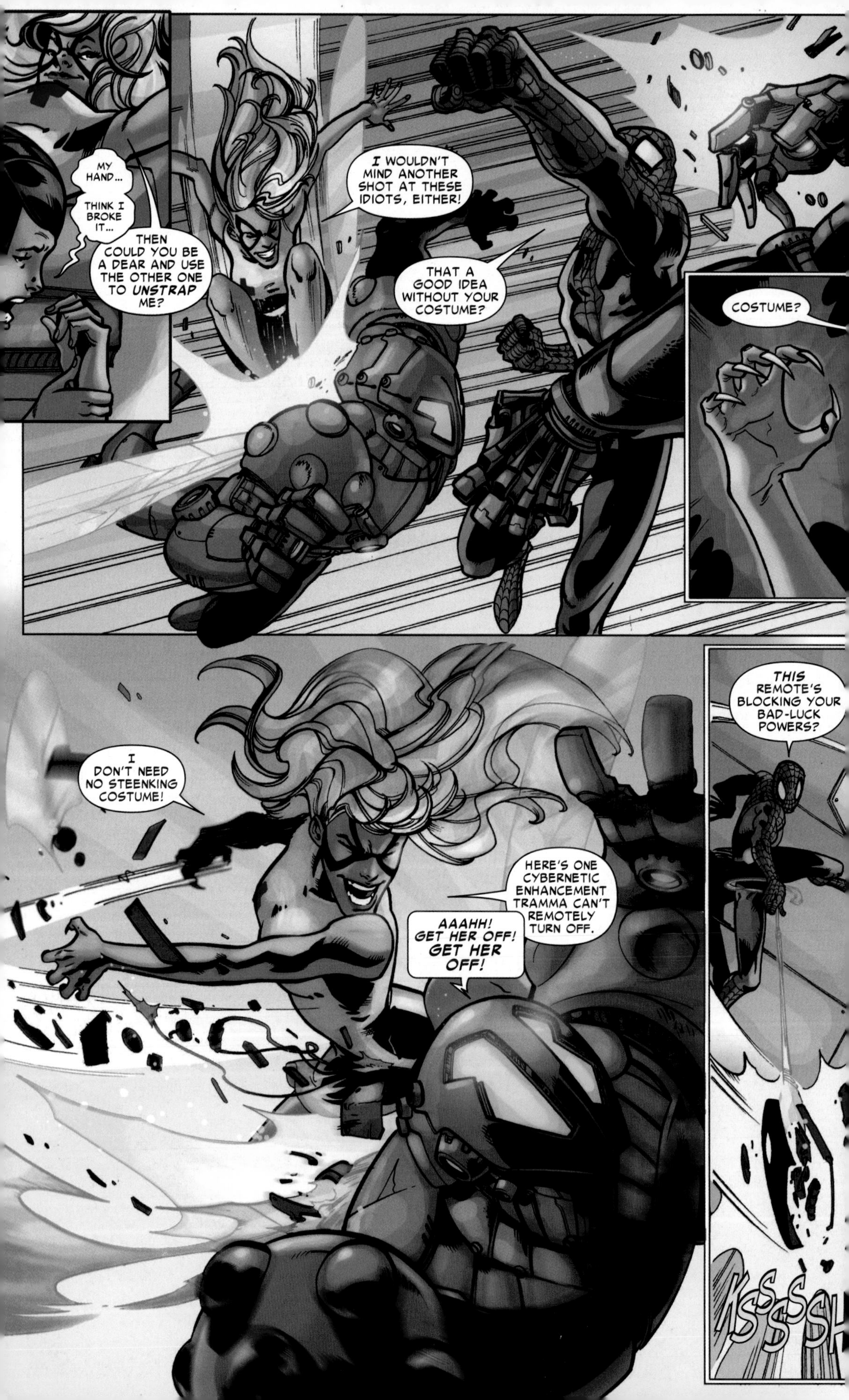
MY HAND...
THINK I BROKE IT...
THEN COULD YOU BE A DEAR AND USE THE OTHER ONE TO *UNSTRAP* ME?
I WOULDN'T MIND ANOTHER SHOT AT THESE IDIOTS, EITHER!
THAT A GOOD IDEA WITHOUT YOUR COSTUME?
COSTUME?
I DON'T NEED NO STEENKING COSTUME!
HERE'S ONE CYBERNETIC ENHANCEMENT TRAMMA CAN'T REMOTELY TURN OFF.
AAAHH! GET HER OFF! **GET HER OFF!**
THIS REMOTE'S BLOCKING YOUR BAD-LUCK POWERS?
KSSSSH

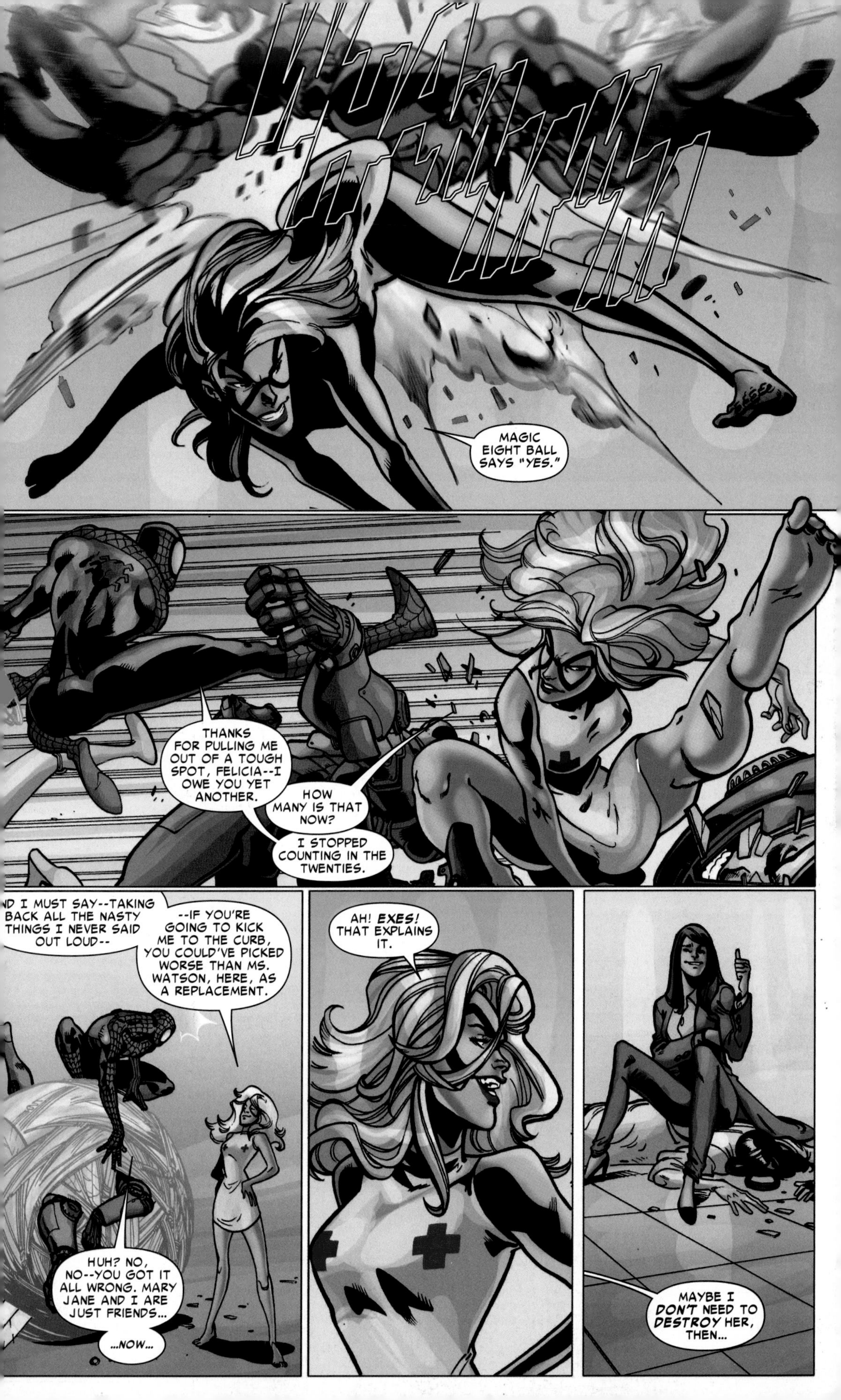
MAGIC EIGHT BALL SAYS "YES."
THANKS FOR PULLING ME OUT OF A TOUGH SPOT, FELICIA--I OWE YOU YET ANOTHER.
HOW MANY IS THAT NOW?
I STOPPED COUNTING IN THE TWENTIES.
ND I MUST SAY--TAKING BACK ALL THE NASTY THINGS I NEVER SAID OUT LOUD--
--IF YOU'RE GOING TO KICK ME TO THE CURB, YOU COULD'VE PICKED WORSE THAN MS. WATSON, HERE, AS A REPLACEMENT.
HUH? NO, NO--YOU GOT IT ALL WRONG. MARY JANE AND I ARE JUST FRIENDS...
...NOW...
AH! EXES! THAT EXPLAINS IT.
MAYBE I DON'T NEED TO DESTROY HER, THEN...

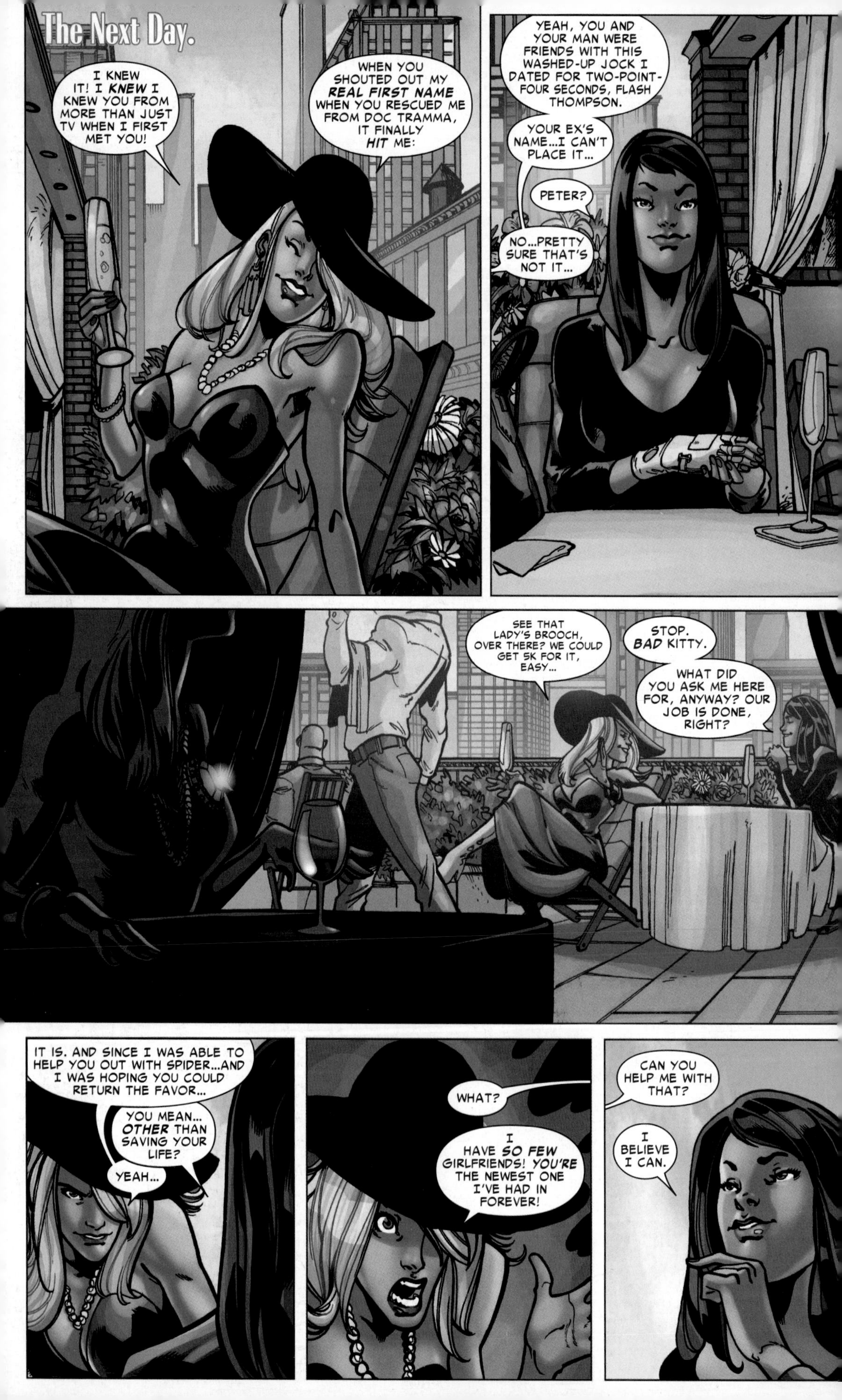

The Next Day.
I KNEW IT! I KNEW I KNEW YOU FROM MORE THAN JUST TV WHEN I FIRST MET YOU!
WHEN YOU SHOUTED OUT MY REAL FIRST NAME WHEN YOU RESCUED ME FROM DOC TRAMMA, IT FINALLY HIT ME:
YEAH, YOU AND YOUR MAN WERE FRIENDS WITH THIS WASHED-UP JOCK I DATED FOR TWO-POINT-FOUR SECONDS, FLASH THOMPSON.
YOUR EX'S NAME...I CAN'T PLACE IT...
PETER?
NO...PRETTY SURE THAT'S NOT IT...
SEE THAT LADY'S BROOCH, OVER THERE? WE COULD GET 5K FOR IT, EASY...
STOP. BAD KITTY.
WHAT DID YOU ASK ME HERE FOR, ANYWAY? OUR JOB IS DONE, RIGHT?
IT IS. AND SINCE I WAS ABLE TO HELP YOU OUT WITH SPIDER...AND I WAS HOPING YOU COULD RETURN THE FAVOR...
YOU MEAN... OTHER THAN SAVING YOUR LIFE?
YEAH...
WHAT?
I HAVE SO FEW GIRLFRIENDS! YOU'RE THE NEWEST ONE I'VE HAD IN FOREVER!
CAN YOU HELP ME WITH THAT?
I BELIEVE I CAN.

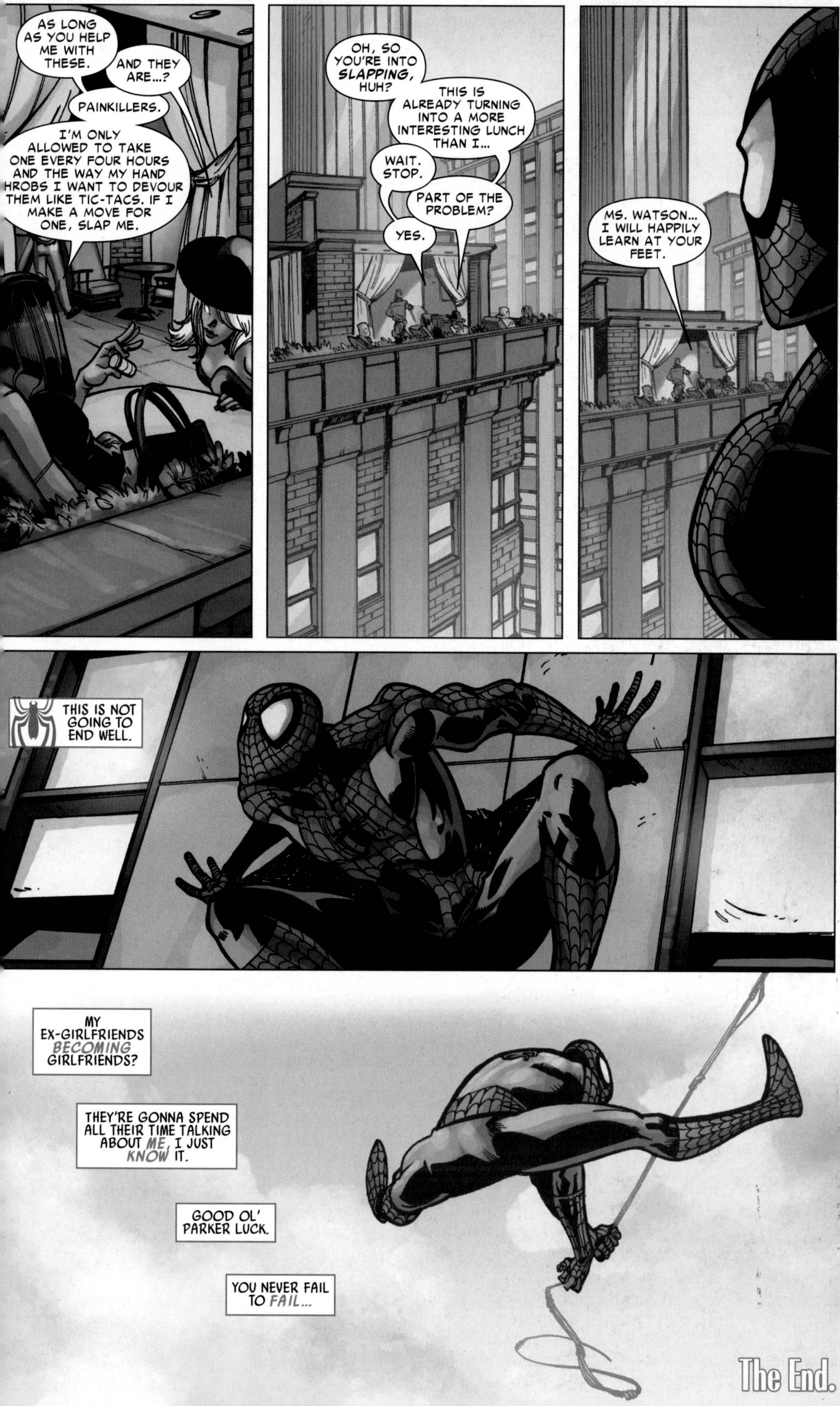

AS LONG AS YOU HELP ME WITH THESE.
AND THEY ARE...?
PAINKILLERS.
I'M ONLY ALLOWED TO TAKE ONE EVERY FOUR HOURS AND THE WAY MY HAND HROBS I WANT TO DEVOUR THEM LIKE TIC-TACS. IF I MAKE A MOVE FOR ONE, SLAP ME.
OH, SO YOU'RE INTO SLAPPING, HUH?
THIS IS ALREADY TURNING INTO A MORE INTERESTING LUNCH THAN I...
WAIT. STOP.
PART OF THE PROBLEM?
YES.
MS. WATSON... I WILL HAPPILY LEARN AT YOUR FEET.
THIS IS NOT GOING TO END WELL.
MY EX-GIRLFRIENDS BECOMING GIRLFRIENDS?
THEY'RE GONNA SPEND ALL THEIR TIME TALKING ABOUT ME, I JUST KNOW IT.
GOOD OL' PARKER LUCK.
YOU NEVER FAIL TO FAIL...
The End.

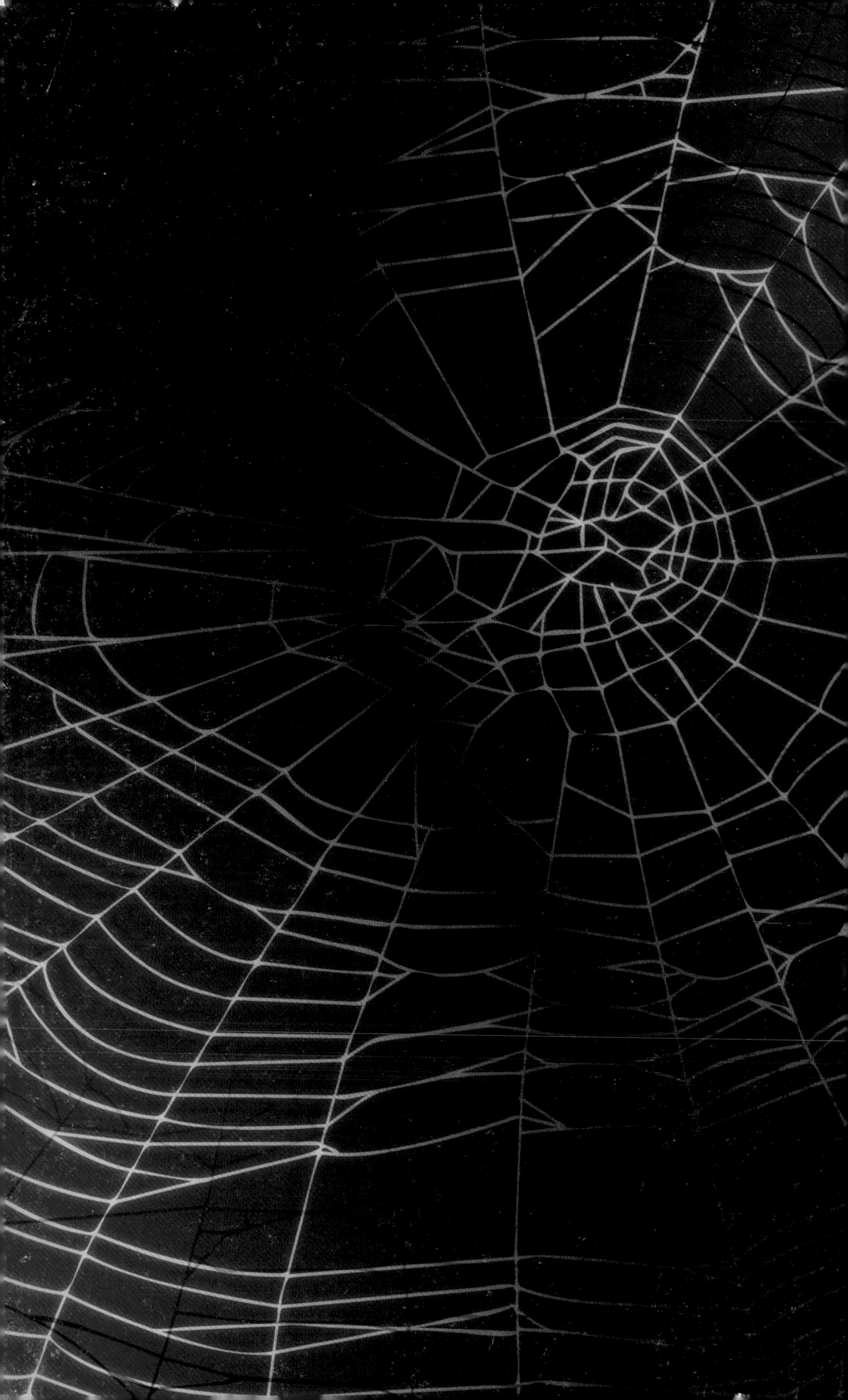